DUNFERMLINE ABBEY

BY

The Rev. J. M. WEBSTER, B.D.

AUTHOR OF "HISTORY OF CARNOCK (FIFE)"

REGALITY SEAL OF DUNFERMLINE

THE CARNEGIE DUNFERMLINE TRUST
ABBOT STREET
DUNFERMLINE

Published in 1948

MADE IN GREAT BRITAIN
—
PRINTED BY McCORQUODALE & CO. LTD.,
MAXWELL STREET, GLASGOW, C.1.

CONTENTS

LIST OF ILLUSTRATIONS

ACKNOWLEDGMENTS

Dr. Chalmers and Dr. Henderson did yeoman service in their day in collecting information about Dunfermline Abbey, but a good deal of material has become available since that time.

Mr. Dollar, the present incumbent of the charge, was quite alive to the desirability of something being done to amplify what has been already written, but he had no Assistant at the time the idea was first mooted, and, in any case, the ordinary duties pertaining to such a charge made it well-nigh impossible for him to undertake the work. He has, however, been in close touch throughout with what was being done and I am glad of the opportunity of publicly acknowledging my deep indebtedness to him.

I have had many other able and willing collaborators to one and all of whom I offer my sincere and very hearty thanks:—to the officials of the Historical Department, Records Office, Edinburgh, including Dr. Donaldson, who is no longer there; to Mr. H. M. Paton, Museum of Antiquities, Edinburgh, for invaluable help in checking dates; to Miss Roger of the Public Library, Dunfermline, where most of the work of research was done, and her Assistants, for unfailing courtesy and kindness—particularly to Miss Barr who compiled the Index; to Mr. R. Culbertson, M.A., Classical Master, and Mr. N. F. Donald, M.A., English Master, Dunfermline High School; to the Rev. J. B. P. Bulloch, B.D., Tranent, and to my fellow-Presbyter, the Rev. D. M. G. Stalker, B.D., Aberdour, who revised the proofs; to Mr. Andrew Shearer, O.B.E., who contributed all excerpts from the Burgh Records of later date than 1584; to Mr. James Shearer, R.S.A., not only for extracting from the Heritors' Records the long-drawn-out story of the provision of a New Church, but for the most generous encouragement and help throughout; to his son, Mr. James Shearer, Junr., who was responsible for the illustrations; and last, and not least, to the members of the Carnegie Dunfermline Trust, who, in addition to making publication financially possible, converted a remote possibility into a speedy reality.

J. M. WEBSTER.

Dunfermline
JUNE, 1948

FOREWORD

BY

J. D. MACKIE, C.B.E., M.C., M.A.,
PROFESSOR OF SCOTTISH HISTORY AT THE UNIVERSITY OF GLASGOW

It is nearly nine hundred years since Queen Margaret and her husband built the little church whose foundations may still be seen beneath the floor of the existing nave, and there can be little doubt that long before the days of Margaret a religious house of the Celtic church had been established on the hill above the winding stream. For centuries the house of God has been the centre of a community, and it is its personal and human history which Mr. Webster now presents to the world. In approaching his theme from this angle the author is wise. Little can be added to the full account of the actual buildings given in the Report of the Royal Commission on Ancient and Historical Monuments, and in more than one authority the organisation and religious life of abbeys in general can be adequately studied. Mr. Webster has put the men who lived and worked in the Abbey of Dunfermline in the centre of his picture; telling their lives, he tells us much not only of the development of the Abbey, but of the history of the town.

How small the town was, is hard to realise. The pitiful account of the great fire of 1624, in relating that two hundred and twenty tenements and two hundred and eighty-seven families had been burnt out, asserts that " the wholl body of the toune " had been destroyed. The narrative need not be taken too literally; its object was to excite charity, and no doubt there were suburbs, like Pittencrieff, which were not reckoned as being within the town, but as the " poore toune " had only seven hundred communicants and three hundred and twenty bairns of six years and under, it was, if not limited to two hundred and twenty houses, certainly very small. As late as 1791-2 there were in the town and suburbs, including Pittencrieff, only 5,192 souls.

So small a community must have been dominated by the church, and even in the days of my father's youth, when the

7

city boasted " Free " kirks and " U.P." kirks besides those of the " Establishment " and besides kirks of other denominations, the Abbey, still magnificent despite a not very happy restoration, was still the great landmark of the town. In those days the monastic buildings had not been excavated, the chimneys appeared as passages in the earth through which bold adventurers could climb, and the little patch of green which adjoined the Pends was devoted in summer to the game of cricket. On one occasion a ball was hit into a passing cart and, as it could not be counted " lost," many runs were made. Several of my father's contemporaries recollected this historic stroke ; most of them—indeed all of them except Colonel Andrew Shearer—thought they had made it themselves.

Until the development of Rosyth—and it is interesting to know that in 1710 Daniel Defoe recommended the establishment of a naval station there—the community of Dunfermline changed very little with the passage of the years, and the names of many families well-known in Dunfermline in 1900 are to be found in the lists of those who held parcels of land from the Abbey in the sixteenth century.

The story of a community so close-knit is readily approached through the stories of abbots, monks and ministers and Mr. Webster who, in pursuit of material, has examined the charters and other original documents, has shed a welcome light upon the everyday life of our forebears. Amid much that is valuable, the information given as to the fall of the Roman Church is conspicuous. The author is not concerned with assertions and counter-assertions about generalities ; he tells us what actually happened to the abbot and monks of the Roman church and to the ministers who struggled to establish the reformed faith in Dunfermline. To a community so small and so dependent upon the Abbey, the collapse of the Roman Church must have been of tremendous import ; and yet, on the evidence produced by Mr. Webster, the cataclysm was less overwhelming than might have been supposed. For some time before 1560, Dunfermline had been held *in commendam* usually by the Archbishop of St. Andrews. The commendator, like other commendators of the time, had alienated, or tried to alienate, the lands. From an absentee abbot to a protestant commendator was no long step, and the appearance of a lay commendator was almost a foregone conclusion. As for the monks (page 77), some of them had prepared for the evil day by intromitting the church lands; some entered the reformed kirk and others received pensions of £50 a year, plus 20s. for coal, with their chambers and yards, from the commendator (page 97). John Knox and his friends had hoped that the kirk whose creed and discipline they defined would inherit all the wealth of the Roman Catholic Church in Scotland, but these ideas were found to be "devote imaginationis" after the battle was won. The lands and revenues of the old kirk, some of which had already passed into the hands of laymen, remained in the hands of their owners who were, however, compelled to surrender one third of their annual income to be divided between the Crown and the ministers. Said Knox in his anger, "I see Twa partis freely gevin to the Devill, and the Thrid maun be devided betwix God and the Devill." "My Lordis of the Twa parte," as Huntly called them, fared not too ill; it was the struggling ministers of the reformed kirk who were in difficulties. These difficulties were severe. Since the abbot's house presumably went with the secularised abbey to the commendator Robert Pitcairn, there was no manse available for the minister. Only in 1627 was his right to a manse and glebe established, and even then the right could not be realised for many years. It seems probable that at one time a house was used as a manse; but about 1800 the general impression was that there never had been a manse, and the present manse was obtained only in 1816. The second charge, which was created in 1643, had neither manse nor glebe. It was not only a house that Ferguson lacked. He lacked money too and though, thanks perhaps to his connections and his marriage, he had some cash in hand when he died in 1598, much was still owed to him in respect of his stipend. Two of his daughters married ministers and it is interesting to notice how, through the intermarriages of ministerial families, there began to emerge what must have been a solid bloc (pages 108 and 118). It is easy to understand both the strength of the Presbyterian ministry in Scotland and also its tendency towards heredity and an aristocratic conservatism.

The services rendered by the Church to the community appear from the pages of this book. Not least were the services to education, and Mr. Webster is to be congratulated upon his proof that in the days before the Reformation there was in the " Ratonraw " (Queen Anne Street) a Scola Grammaticalis. This school, like some other medieval schools, may have been under the supervision of the Abbey, but obviously it stood outside the precincts, and must be distinguished from the Abbey school (page 169). No doubt its function was to teach young boys, some of whom would become novices, but it seems probable that teaching was given to boys who did not intend to become clerics. If the medieval monastery did far less for education than has sometimes been asserted, it perhaps did more than its critics have been disposed to allow. On this point, as on all others, Mr. Webster shows himself wise and moderate. He has given his references fully and clearly. Not only has he set before us what may be called the personal history of Dunfermline Abbey, but he has provided his readers with a key which will unlock new treasures for them.

The city of Dunfermline to-day is very different from the " auld grey toun " of loom shops that was still present to the eyes of my father long after the reality had disappeared ; it is far more different from the eighteenth century burgh wherein merchant-guild and trade-incorporations contended ; and more different still from the little medieval town which clustered round the abbey. Dunfermline of to-day boasts amenities our ancestors could never have contemplated, and with the growth of new ideals for the future some of the interest in the past has gone. Yet, though the face of the city has changed, the old tradition lingers. Dunfermline is still proud of its history, and it is a matter of congratulation that the Carnegie Dunfermline Trust, so potent an agency for progress, should have sponsored a book upon the Abbey, and that there should have been found within the city one who was able and willing to undertake and to achieve a task of great difficulty. To Mr. Webster and to the Carnegie Dunfermline Trust all lovers of Dunfermline owe a debt of gratitude.

J. D. MACKIE.

9 *The University,*
   *Glasgow, W.*2

ABBOTS OF DUNFERMLINE

The story of a monastery is largely determined by the men who were in charge of it. No doubt this is more or less true of almost any institution, but there were features of the monastic life that make it particularly applicable. It is not merely that the powers entrusted to an abbot were ample and far-reaching; the fact that obedience was of the very essence of the life made the employment of these powers unusually easy. No matter how he came to be elected, the moment he was installed in office, he was in absolute control. His will was supreme; his decisions final. He might be animated by the purest of motives, or the most sordid considerations of self-interest, but he had always to be reckoned with.

Nor was his rule confined to the precincts of his monastery.

The lands under the control of the Abbot of Dunfermline extended from Urquhart in Moray almost to the English border, and over all who dwelt upon these lands, whether church-vassal or mere serf, he had powers which, if not always clearly defined, were yet unquestionably real. He had official residences in Dunfermline, Perth, Stirling, Kirkcaldy, Haddington, Musselburgh (Inveresk Lodge) and Edinburgh (John Knox's House), and it may well be in other places, too—to say nothing of a so-called "summer residence" in Pinkie. Four burghs acknowledged him as overlord (Dunfermline, Kirkcaldy, South Queensferry, and Musselburgh), and three distinct Courts of Regality dispensed justice in his name—one in Fife, one for the Abbey lands south of the Forth, and one for the Priory of Urquhart. Undoubtedly a person to be reckoned with!

As for national affairs, even a cursory glance at the list of men who held office in Dunfermline makes it clear that there was scarce one of them who did not play some part, and not a few of them a leading one, on the very highest levels.

To attempt to tell the story of the Abbey without reckoning with the abbots would be little short of sheer futility.

That much of it will prove tedious reading goes almost without saying. Authoritative sources for these early days are few and far between, and the information they contain is not only meagre, but prosaic to a degree. The material for light reading simply isn't there. And then there is the question of dates, which, from the historical point of view, is of the first importance.

So few of the old charters and other documents are dated. Almost the only way to get at the period to which they belong is by the dates in office of the abbots or other ecclesiastics who either issued or witnessed them; and close scrutiny and comparison of conflicting dates is apt to cramp the style of even a ready writer. Whoever attempts to write a story of the kind very soon finds himself confronted with an awkward choice.

What is to be the chief aim he is to set before himself ? Is it to give, as far as his ability and ascertained fact will permit, a full and well-authenticated account of his subject ? Or is it to write a story that will commend itself to the interest of the general reader ?

Either would be a perfectly commendable ambition, but it is far from easy to combine the two, and sooner or later he has to make up his mind as to which is to be the primary consideration.

If the scales tilt in favour of historical accuracy, then he must reckon with the fact that for part, at least, of the journey he will almost certainly lose touch with the general reader; and nowhere, so far as the writer of these notes is concerned, does that possibility bulk so large as in the attempt to tell the story of the abbots.

But while knowledge of the abbots is of the very core and essence of the story, external circumstances sometimes lend not a little colour to it.

Before the monastery came into being, there was a royal residence in Dunfermline, and from first to last its connection with Royalty was one of the monastery's outstanding features. The original place of sepulture for Scottish Kings was, no doubt, Iona, but from the time of Malcolm III, Dunfermline became, in the words of Boece, " the common cemetery of the kings of Scotland," and so large is the list of royal and distinguished personages buried there that the description of Dunfermline as the Westminster Abbey of Scotland seems not unjustified.

With the exception of St. Margaret's Shrine, no memorials of royal personages remain, but there is reason to believe that the majority of them were buried in ground now occupied by the north transept of the parish church—though Walcot (p. 245) says that " At Dunfermline, six kings lay in front of the high altar, with three queens and at least three royal princes hard by."

The fact, too, that it occupied so central a position in the country led to the monastery being freely used for purposes outside the range of its normal life.

Matthew of Westminster complains of its having been used about 1296 for meetings of the Scottish Parliament. If it was not so used then, it certainly was later :—

" 27 Jan., 1335—Sir Andrew Moray assembled a parliament at Dunfermline, and was acknowledged by that assembly as Regent." (Hailes' Annals ii. 362).

Parliament met again in Dunfermline in 1585 (page 114).

Because of its central position, the Church itself did not hesitate to make free use of the monastery for purposes that were outwith the scope of its original purpose—the election of bishops, for example—though even in a matter of this sort proximity to the Court was often a largely determining factor.

In 1195 Reinaldus (Reginald), a monk of Melrose, was at Dunfermline elected Bishop of Rosemarkie (Ross) (Melr. 50), concerning which Lawrie in his Annals (299) so approvingly comments :—" O mira Dei dispositio de qua processit talis electio." (O wonderful disposition of God, from which proceeded such an election !)

In 1441 we are confronted with a still more unusual case— that of James Bruce (brewhous), formerly rector of Kilmany, who was not only elected in Dunfermline Bishop of Dunkeld, but actually consecrated there. (Dowden, Bps. 73.) Perhaps the fact that the bishop in question was the son of a younger son of Sir Robert Bruce of Clackmannan may have had something to do with the choice of place. He died in Edinburgh in 1447, chancellor of the kingdom, and was buried at Dunfermline in St. Mary's Chapel.

At the other end of the scale, we have the grim experience of the monastery being used as a prison.

Because of the differences between king and pope arising out

13

of the erection of St. Andrews into an archbishopric, Patrick Graham, grandson of King Robert III, first Archbishop of St. Andrews, fell into disfavour, was deposed and condemned to perpetual confinement in a monastery, " or other place," under four guards. His first place of imprisonment was Inchcolm, but, through fear of rescue by the English Fleet, he was transferred to Dunfermline, and afterwards to Lochleven Castle, where he died at the age of 45 and was buried in the island of St. Serf—a man against whom no crime of any sort had been proved, and second to none of his day in respect of either character or learning.

" His unhappy fate, his sentence and punishment as a heretic and blasphemer, reveal a tragedy without one scene of courtesy or charity, and without one touch of chivalry, save the mass which James IV founded for the repose of his kinsman's soul." (H. & H. i. 69).

" The weight of the charge against him lay in his being a heretic and schismatic, and it is therefore not improbable that he had become a convert to the reforming principles of the Lollards, then spreading—a supposition in conformity with which most of the allegations against him may well be explained, while it may not have been thought expedient to betray too broadly the direction in which so great a dignitary of the church had apostatised. This would also suffice to account for the fact that he stood so entirely destitute of sympathy from any influential quarter, even from his kinsman the king, while Scheves, who was free from all suspicion of reforming tendencies, rose higher into favour than ever." (Accounts of the Lord High Treasurer, i. liii.)

But such uses were merely incidental. The normal life of the monastic community centred in the abbot, and it is pre-eminently by the life and rule of the abbot that the well-being, or otherwise, of the monastery was determined.

Geoffry I (Galfrid, Gaufrid, Gosfridus).
1124—1154

There is a difference of opinion about the beginning of the monastery. According to some, it began as a priory and did not reach the dignity of an abbey till Geoffry was consecrated in 1128, and, in support of this contention, they adduce the case of Peter, described as Prior of Dunfermline, who was sent back to Canterbury on a special mission. As against this, it is urged that the reference to a prior is no proof that there was no abbot, and that the delay in Geoffry's consecration was simply due to the fact that there was a prolonged vacancy of four years in the bishopric of St. Andrews. He was consecrated by Robert, Bishop of St. Andrews.

Geoffry was formerly prior of Christ's Church, Canterbury, and was brought to Dunfermline as its first abbot by David I.

He is described as a man of singular piety, but little else is known of him. He died in 1154—the longest reign of any abbot of Dunfermline.

From the Chartulary we learn that there was an agreement made between G(eoffry), Abbot of Dunfermline, and Robert, Bishop of St. Andrews, in the presence of King David, his son, Henry, and their barons, in the Castle of Edinburgh, from which it appears that, on the same day that Alexander I dedicated the chapel in Stirling Castle, he granted the tithes of his lordships in the *sock* of Stirling to it. So that, quite clearly, tithes were no novelty prior to 1124, when Alexander died. (*Reg.* 4.)

Incidentally, the first historical notice of gold occurring in this country is the grant by David I to the Abbey of Dunfermline, just before the death of Geoffry, of a tithe of all the gold which should accrue to him from Fife and Fothryf. (*Reg.* 16.)

When Geoffry arrived from Canterbury with his monks, they would find a church (Queen Margaret's) ready for their use, but very little, one imagines, in the way of adequate accommodation for themselves, and one of the first things to be done would be to make some temporary provision.

But, as the interests of the monastery extended with every addition to its grants, it soon became evident that provision would require to be made for the occasional residence of the abbot outside Dunfermline altogether, and consequently we find King David, as already indicated, granting a *mansura* (manse or residence) for the abbot in Perth, Stirling and Edinburgh.

The deed, like so many others, is undated, but it was granted by King David (1124-1153) and witnessed by Robert, bishop-elect of St. Andrews. Like Geoffry himself, Robert had to wait some time for consecration because of a dispute as to who was to consecrate him, and there is some difference of opinion as to the exact dates of election and consecration, but the following quotation from Bishop Dowden's *Bishops of Scotland* (pp. 4 and 5) may be accepted as the nearest approximation that can be got :—

" We shall not be far wrong if we place Robert's election in January 1123-24.

" There does not seem to be any good reason for doubting that the consecration took place in 1126, or possibly 1127."

We conclude, therefore, that the deed (*Reg.* 26) was issued and signed some time between these dates.

The somewhat unexpected feature of this gift is that it not only provided official residences for the abbot when duty called him to some distance from the monastery; it at the same time provided him with a *mansura, libera et quieta* (free and quiet) in Dunfermline itself.

The Registrum (Chartulary) is disappointingly reticent about the history of the monastery, but the impression definitely left upon one's mind by the terms of this deed is that, hitherto, the abbot and his monks had lived together; now he was to have a place of his own, quiet and free from interruption.

The point is interesting because of its possible bearing on the story of the well-known Abbot House.

The first authentic reference to this house is when, following the Reformation, Robert Pitcairn became Commendator of the Abbey. As it stands, it is a composite structure, suggesting various dates, but the vaulted cellars may conceivably belong to a period as early as the close of the thirteenth century, or the beginning of the fourteenth, and, while far from suggesting that this was the actual house gifted by King David, it definitely strikes one as a possibility that the original *mansura* may have stood on or near the same site. The ground to the south of the main monastic buildings was largely taken up with stables and other outhouses, and the remainder of it was afterwards the site of St. Lawrence's Croft and yard—an unlikely site for the Abbot's House.

The ground to the north, on the other hand, while apart from the other monastic buildings, was still within the precincts, and was much more likely to meet the requirements of a house " free and quiet."

16

Processional Door.   South Aisle to Cloister Court.

Geoffry II. 1154—1178

A nephew of his predecessor, his name is unhappily associated with what is known as the *Treaty of Falaise* (1174).

In an incursion into England, William, King of Scots, was surprised and captured with a handful of his followers and carried for safety to Falaise in Normandy, where he eventually purchased his liberty by agreeing to become the liegeman of the English king.

The passage from Rymer's *Foedera* is of such interest and importance as to make it worth reproducing :—

" The King of Scotland, David his brother, his barons and other liegemen, agreed that the Scottish Church should yield to the English Church such subjection in time to come as it ought of right and was wont to pay in the days of the kings of England, Henry's predecessors.

" Moreover, Richard, Bishop of St. Andrews, and Richard, Bishop of Dunkeld, Geoffry, Abbot of Dunfermline, and Herbert, Prior of Coldingham, agreed that the English Church should have that right over the Scottish which in justice it ought to have. They also became bound that they themselves would not gainsay the right of the English Church."

Before condemning out of hand the representatives of the Scottish Church for the part they played, it is well to remember that the two bishops were royal chaplains who would doubtless find it difficult to oppose the will of the king, and that the Abbot of Dunfermline, like his uncle, was an Englishman by birth. Above all, it must be kept in mind that the social boundary in those days was nearer to the Humber or the Trent than to the Tweed.

It was a difficult situation and it may be going too far to accuse them of having played false to their country.

In any case, the reaction of the Scottish people was plain and unmistakable. They repudiated the claim as utterly without foundation.

Since the landing of the Allied Armies in Normandy in 1944, Falaise has acquired very different associations.

It was an experience that was not likely to be forgotten— particularly by the king himself.

" A natural feeling of anxiety oppressed the mind of William

17

as he recalled the events of his early manhood, and remembered the consequences of his former war with England.

" His kingdom was still unsettled, his health was beginning to fail, whilst his heir was still a mere child, and Scotland had hardly yet recovered from the disastrous state of anarchy into which she had been plunged by the capture of her king at Alnwick.

" Impressed with gloomy forebodings, the king determined upon passing the night by the shrine of his sainted ancestress at Dunfermline; where, his reluctance to engage in hostilities assuming the form of a warning dream, he dismissed his army on the following morning, assuring them that he had been forbidden by a heavenly vision to attempt the invasion of England." (*Robertson, E. William, Scotland under her Early Kings,* p. 416.)

In 1163 every monk was prohibited from forsaking the abbey, after his professions, without the abbot's permission, unless he entered into a stricter order. (*Reg.* 237.)

Geoffry II died in 1178. (*Melr.* 42.)

Archibald Douglas. 1178—1198

In nearly every case this abbot is referred to by his Christian name only, but that his surname was Douglas is vouched for by Lawrie's Early Scottish Charters (324).

He was one of the prelates to whom Pope Urban III entrusted authority to suspend Hugh, Bishop of St. Andrews. The bishop was suspended, and afterwards excommunicated. (*Lawrie, Annals,* 259.)

A precept was issued in Abbot Archibald's favour by William the Lion requiring the Burgh of Haddington to pay him three merks annually, one half at the Feast of St. Martin, the other at that of Pentecost, for lighting the church at Dunfermline. (*Reg.* 153-8.)

The monks of Dunfermline had a long connection with Haddington—though the latter's natural connection was with Holyrood. The abbot, as already noted, had a *mansura* there, confirmed by succeeding kings and popes. At the Reformation the bailies of Haddington paid 40s. to the Abbey. (*Lawrie, E.S.C.,* 415.)

Douglas died in 1198, and was succeeded (*Melr.* 50) by

18

Robert de Berwick.   1198—1201

Of him nothing is known beyond the fact that, after a very short reign, he was deposed for some irregularity by the Cardinal Legate, John de Salerno, at a general court held at Perth in 1202. (*Ibid.* 51.)

Patrick.   1201—1223

According to the Charters of Inchcolm, Patrick became abbot in 1201 (117). He had previously been sub-prior of Durham and Dean and Prior of Canterbury. It was during his tenure of office that Bishop Malvoisin of St. Andrews deprived the Abbey of its right of presentation to the churches of Hailes and Kinglassie because, on the occasion of a visit to Dunfermline, the abbot and monks had failed to provide him with sufficient wine for his evening collation. The defence was that the wine had been consumed by the bishop's own attendants. (*Hailes' Annals I*, p. 330.)

During Patrick's time a dispute arose between the abbot and canons of Cambuskenneth and the abbot and monks of Dunfermline concerning tithes belonging to the church of Eccles (St. Ninians).

Pope Innocent III referred the matter, with advice, to the bishop of St. Andrews and the abbot of Arbroath, giving them authority to decide the question.

A week later, 28th March, 1207, the Pope renewed their charter of protection and privilege to Patrick, abbot of Dunfermline, and the monks of Dunfermline, adding to their possessions the church of Moulin and the church of Strathardle and appending this clause : "We also forbid that any person ecclesiastical or secular presume to molest you with undue or uncustomary procurations or exactions." (*Reg.* 245.)

On 5th April that same year he wrote to the abbot and convent of Cambuskenneth declaring that his grant of a privilege to the abbot and convent of Dunfermline was no new concession, but the preservation of an earlier privilege conferred by Pope Lucius.

William.   1223—1238

Dr. Chalmers (*Hist.* i. 183) says that there were two abbots about this time of the same Christian name, surnames unknown, and that the first died within a few months of his election.

The *Registrum* is of the opinion that there was only one, and says that he received from St. Andrews a grant of the church of Hailes, in Lothian, for the support of the poor and strangers, thus reversing part, at least, of the penalty imposed upon his predecessor.

About the year 1231 the abbot and monks signified to the Pope that there had formerly been thirty monks, and in future there were to be fifty; but the revenues of the monastery being insufficient for the expense of receiving strangers, visitors and the poor, they had been obliged to contract debts. Therefore they besought the patronage of vacant churches, "that the abbey might not suffer from inability to support divine worship and discharge the duties of hospitality."

Abbot William figures in a disputed case of thirlage in the parish of Aberdour—a fruitful source of trouble all up and down the country. The lands of Couston belonged to Robert of Rosyth and were thirled to the Mill of Aberdour. That is to say, those who farmed the lands of Couston had to get all their grinding done at this mill, and no other, and settle with the miller for his dues.

Trouble ensued and in 1233 William, Abbot of Dunfermline, Henry, Prior of Culenros (Culross), Peter de Ramsay, who afterwards became Bishop of Aberdeen, John de Haya, Sheriff of Fife, and Archibald de Douglas were appointed adjudicators. It seems to us heavy artillery to bring to bear upon so small a matter, but it is not easy for us to see the trouble with the eyes of our forefathers.

" And these grave and potent seigniors, having heard both sides, settle the controversy in this fashion:—Robert of Rosyth and his heirs are to pay eight shillings yearly to the brethren of the Monastery, as the mill-dues of the lands of Couston; and after doing this, they are to be left free to grind their corn where they please, and even to build a mill for themselves on their own ground, if they feel inclined to do so, and be free from all further exactions as regards the Mill of Aberdour." (*Ross, Aberdour and Inchcolme, p.* 86.)

" Half the rents of the mills of Aberdour had been granted to Inchcolm by William de Mortimer, *c.* 1180.

" It is not necessary to suppose, with Ross (*Aberdour and Inchcolme, p.* 85) that the mill had since passed into the possession

20

of the monastery. The failure of any of the parishioners to bring their grain to the parish mill would, in any case, affect the monastery's income from multures. The compromise effected ensured that in the case of Robert de Rossive, the commutation of the multures of Couston for an annual sum of eight shillings would secure the monastery's interests, while he gained the valuable right of having a mill of his own; and in the case of Roger de Balmakmole (Balmule), while the monastery's revenue from the mill of Aberdour was safeguarded, he was set free from feudal services, e.g., supplying millstones to the mill.'' (*Inchcolm*, 121, 122.)

Both Ralph and John, abbots of a later date, had each in his day to play the same part as William had to do in 1233.

One of the mills belonging to the monastery at Dunfermline must surely have been unique—the one at Rossend, Burntisland. It is reputed to have been ingeniously driven by the incoming and retreating tides. (*Wilkie*, *The Benedictine Monasteries of Northern Fife*, p. 21n.)

Geoffry III. 1238—1240

William died in 1238 and was succeeded by Gaufrid, prior of the same house (Dunfermline), who died in 1240. (*Melr.* 86-7).

Robert de Keldeleth. 1240—1252

According to some authorities, Keldeleth is probably a variation of Kinloch. According to others, it more probably stands for Kinleith (Currie) on the Water of Leith.

Robert was the first Mitred Abbot of Dunfermline, receiving from Innocent IV in 1244 the privilege of exercising within the Abbey the function of a bishop, with the right to assume the badges of that office, mitre, ring, etc. (*Reg.* 180.)

According to Michael Barrett, quoting Theiner (*Vetera Monumenta*, p. 50), he proved somewhat over zealous in the exercise of his new powers. In 1248 Innocent IV forbade him to give the pontifical benediction in presence of any bishop who was unwilling for him to do so, and admonished him not to confer minor orders, as he had twice done already, on any clerics except his own subjects.

Among other rights possessed by the abbot of Dunfermline was that of attending Parliament. It is generally assumed, too,

that the monastery had the right of sanctuary, but Bishop
Dowden (*Medieval Church, p.* 151) does not find the evidence
conclusive that "its right of affording asylum was other than
that possessed by other churches having the right of sepulture."
In 1245 the monks of Dunfermline were allowed to wear caps
because of the cold, but not during Elevation or Gospel. Permission to do so, which could be given only by the Pope, was
regarded as a distinction and an honour—apart from consideration of climate—and was sought after as a mark of favour.
(*Lindores*, lxxxiv.)

"Between 1240 and 1252, the Pope had ordered Abbot
Robert to give a benefice in the diocese of St. Andrews to
Andrew, a canon of Florence. Robert gave him the church of
Potin; but the Bishop of St. Andrews gave the same church
to another priest.

"Andrew sued, and was awarded a pension of 20 marks a
year to be paid by the bishop until the bishop should give him
another benefice worth 30 marks of silver. The bishop refused
to provide this benefice. The Pope ordered Abbot Robert to
do so.

"Robert had retired to the Cistercian order; therefore the
Pope ordered a papal writer, master Innocent, living in England,
to take up the case and see that, at the death of the bishop,
the benefice was given to Andrew instead of the pension."
(*Anderson, Early Sources of Scot. Hist.*, ii. 518.)

"On 30 August, 1250, Pope Innocent IV wrote to the
bishops of St. Andrews and Dunkeld, and to (Robert) the
abbot of Dunfermline, a papal chaplain, bidding them assist
Richard Giffard, the King of Scotland's cousin, and Giffard's
cousins, Thomas Paynel, Alan de Lasceles, and Adam Penkethan,
on their way to Palestine, out of funds raised for the crusade."
(*Ibid.* ii. 563.)

From the same source we get particulars about Queen
Margaret's canonisation.

In letters written on 27th July, 1245, and 13th August,
1246, Pope Innocent IV caused inquiry to be made regarding
the sanctity of Queen Margaret (*Reg.* 281, 285). Sanction to
enrol her in the catalogue of saints was implied in his letter of
16th September, 1249. (*Ibid.* 290.) In his letter of 21st
September, she was called *sancta*; and yearly relaxation of

22

40 days was granted to penitents who visited the greater church of Dunfermline on her day. (*Reg.* 291.)

It was during this abbot's incumbency that the so-called "Translation of St. Margaret" took place. Hitherto the possibilities of worship must have been somewhat circumscribed by building operations, but by 1250 these were so far completed that the whole church was now available for use. With a view, no doubt, to adding solemnity to the first service to be held in the new buildings, it was arranged to transport the body of St. Margaret from its place in the nave to the new shrine prepared for it " in the choir beyond the High Altar."

Andrew Winton, Prior of Lochleven, writing at a somewhat later date, embodies in the following lines the traditional belief of what then took place :—

> " That yeir with veneratioun
> Was maid the translatioun
> Of Sainct Margret the haly quene ;
> A fair mirakil thair wes sein . . .
> With all thair power and thair slicht
> Her bodie to rais they had na micht
> Na lift her anis out of that place
> Quhair scho that tyme lyand was. . . .
> Quhile (till) first they tuk up the bodie
> Of her lord, that lay thairby,
> And bair it ben until the queir,
> Lichtlie sune in fair maneir
> Her cors they tuik up, and bair ben,
> And thaim interrit togidder then.
> Swa trowit all they that gadderit thair
> Quhat honour til her lord scho bair."

" The shirt of St. Margaret, queen of Malcolm III, was long a cherished relic at Dunfermline. It was carried to Mary of Gueldres at the time of the birth of James III. This appears from the Account of the Bailies of Inverkeithing rendered in Exchequer 19 July, 1451, for the year then ended. . . .

" A similar payment is entered by the Treasurer for sending it to Queen Margaret at the time of the birth of James V." (*Accounts of the Lord High Treasurer*, i. lxxiii.)

" And for the pasage-money of two stones for the tomb of Queen Margaret under construction at Dunfermline, and for carriage from London in 1368. x.li. (£10)" (*Exch. Rolls.* ii. 300).

In the closing scenes of the Culdee Church Abbot Robert had his part to play—and not a very pleasant one.

The particular question at issue was the management of the affairs of St. Mary's Church, St. Andrews.

" In these affairs the prior and convent of that city claimed to be supreme. This claim the Culdees refused to allow, and asserted in turn that their own prior, Mr. Adam Malkirwistun, was provost of St. Mary's and they themselves the canons. The dispute was ultimately referred to the Pope who made a remit to two independent authorities. . . . The outcome of the investigations of these delegates was a finding against the contention of the Culdees and their immediate suspension from the exercise of their functions. . . .

" The pronouncing of final sentence was remitted to Robert, Abbot of Dunfermline, one of the Papal Chaplains and Chancellor of Scotland, and Robert, Treasurer of Dunkeld Cathedral, who were also appointed to enquire at the same time whether these Culdees and their vicars had celebrated divine ordinances in disregard of the sentence of suspension. November 7, 1250, was the day chosen for this dual purpose, and the Church of Inverkeithing the place of meeting. The Abbot and Treasurer duly appeared, but the Culdees did not present themselves. The judges acted with clemency.

" In accordance with their instructions, they enquired into the attitude of the Culdees towards their sentence of suspension. But their full commission they delayed carrying out and appointed the Culdees to meet with them in the Church of the Blackfriars at Perth on the Sabbath after the feast of St. Andrew when both matters would be dealt with. The Culdees were also reminded that their refusal to appear at Inverkeithing amounted to contumacy, and that the judges had full power of pronouncing sentence." (*Stephen, Hist. of Inverkeithing,* 346— quoting *Balfour's Coll. of Ancient Charters, MS.,* 16.)

It is not suggested that this is the last reference we have to the Culdees, but it is generally accepted that, from about this time, they practically ceased to exist as an organised body of believers.

In 1251 Robert, becoming suspect of participation in a plot concerning the succession to the throne, resigned his office as

Chancellor of Scotland and withdrew to his monastery, but receiving there somewhat scant respect after his disgrace at court, he resigned his abbotship as well in 1252, and, for a time, little is heard of him.

In 1254 the Calendar of Papal Letters (i., 198) refers to him as having been transferred to the Cistercian Order, and later, the Chronicle of Melrose, describing him as a monk of New-battle, which was a Cistercian house, records his election as Abbot of Melrose in 1268 (144); so that it is quite a possibility that he may have been at Newbattle the whole period between his abbatial offices.

John. 1252—1256

John was formerly Prior of Dunfermline and is described as " a man of wonderful mildness."

In 1256 certain Scottish monasteries were put under interdict by papal authority because Gamelin, Bishop of St. Andrews, had pledged them for the expenses of his consecration and his pleas at Rome.

" In that year, John, Abbot of Dunfermline, on his way to Rome to reconcile his own monastery, died at Pontigny beyond the sea." (*Scotichronicon* ii. 90.)

On the other hand, Lawrie, in his *Early Scottish Charters* (232) tells us that John, Abbot of Dunfermline, died in 1251. Differences as to date are not uncommon in dealing with these early records, which is not surprising when one remembers that the charters, from which so much of the information is derived, are, as already noted, so often undated. But sometimes the difficulty lies deeper. In the Chartulary of Lindores, for instance, we find it stated that Gilbert was Abbot of Dunfermline in 1254 (65) and that N. was abbot on 25th January, 1281 (274).

It is not merely that we know from various reliable sources that other men held the abbacy on these particular dates, but nowhere else is there any indication that a man of the Christian name of Gilbert or one whose Christian name began with an " N " ever held the office of Abbot of Dunfermline. And yet the Chartulary of Lindores is a contemporary record, and, generally speaking, quite reliable. It may be, of course, that the scribe has inadvertently used the word " Dunfermline " when he really meant some other monastery.

Matthew. 1256—1267

Monks in the early days had the right to elect their abbots, and though Matthew, one of their own number, had never held higher office amongst them than that of Cellarer, he was yet chosen by them, and if little concerning him is recorded, there is no reason to suppose that he did not fill the office well.

Any monk of legitimate birth might become abbot of his order, and even the bar of illegitimacy operated only if it arose from adultery or incest. (*Reg.* 108.)

Simon. 1267—1275

Simon appears as a witness in the Kelso Register, 1st June, 1267, so that Matthew cannot have held office, as Dr. Chalmers seems to think, till 1270.

Along with the Earl of Mar, he was sent as ambassador to England for the recovery of the King's Earldom of Huntingdon.

" In the reign of Alexander III, Colban, Earl of Fife, did homage to Simon, Abbot of Dunfermline, and John Thyanus, the abbot's chamberlain, got a well-furred cloke for the homage." (*Dalyell's Antiq.*, p. 22.)

Simon was deposed by Baiamund (Bagimont), the papal legate, " for obstinacy and crossness to the poor." (*Fordun* ii. 123.)

Radulphus (Ralph) de Grenlaw. 1275—

He had been sub-Prior of Dunfermline and is described as " mild, cautious, and well trained in monastic discipline."

The history of The Ferry Passage is dealt with in detail in Dr. Stephen's *Story of Inverkeithing and Rosyth*, from which the following extracts have been taken to show its connection with the monastery of Dunfermline :—

" The earliest direct reference . . . does not occur till the reign of David I who in 1129 or 1130 granted to the Monastery of Dunfermline ' the Passage and Ship of Inverkeithing as I have it in my Lordship.' This grant subsequently received confirmation from various kings and Popes. In some of those cases the expression used is ' half of the Passage.' That indicates that the monastery did not at first possess the complete holding.

" But in or about 1321 Robert I granted to the Abbey of Dunfermline ' half of the Passage of the Queen which the late Roger de Moubray possessed.' . . .

" The effect of the papal confirmations was to put the Abbey's possession of the ferry under the protection of the Church . . .

" In 1275 Abbot Radulphus granted eight oars in the new boat of the Passage to seven persons, one of whom was a woman, and their heirs. One of the individuals had two oars, the others one each; and the *reddendo* was 8d. yearly for each one, in addition to service use and wont, and the payment of the old rent to the tenant of the Passage. This feudal holding, of which there is no subsequent record, indicates what is explicitly stated in a later narrative, that the abbot supplied the boats. It also reveals that, instead of working the ferry directly himself, he let it on lease.

" At the Reformation the Passage became part of the Lordship of Dunfermline which, excepted from the general annexation of Church property to the Crown, was bestowed by James VI on November 23, 1589, on his queen, Anne of Denmark, as a wedding-gift. . . .

" It will be noted that of the working of the Passage the Dunfermline Regality Court was the controlling body. But by Act of Parliament of December 23, 1669, a new element of management was introduced. It was ordained that the Passage, in common with similar undertakings, be carried on under the supervision of the Justices of the Peace, and Sheriffs and their Deputies were empowered to prepare lists of ferries, and to survey and repair the same; and the Justices were to see how far the repairs were carried out."

In 1290 the Pope granted Relaxation of one year and forty days of enjoined penance to penitents who visit the Church of St. Margaret, Dunfermline, on her Feast. (*C.P.R.* i. 520.)

Registrum (291), as already noted, speaks of yearly relaxation of 40 days.

Ralph must have been in office during the first two visits of King Edward I to Dunfermline, and swore fealty to him on both occasions—the first time at Dunfermline, " along with many others, some of them above the Great Altar, and others in the Chapter House of the monastery "—the second time at Berwick, Parliament having been summoned to meet there.

There seems to have been a general round-up of " officials " in the neighbourhood of Dunfermline at the time.

" William, Vicar of the Church of Carnock, swore fealty to Edward I, 28 August, 1296." (*Prynne's Records of the Tower of London*, ii. 663.)

The form of oath, as used at Berwick, is on record :—

" Whereas . . . we have sworn upon the holy Gospels. And for ourselves, and for each of us severally, we have done homage to our lord, the king aforesaid, in these words :—

' I become your liege man of life and of members and of earthly honour against all persons who can live and die.'

" And the same king, our lord, received them in this form :—

' We receive this for the lands whereof you are at present seized, saving our right and the right of others, and excepting the lands which John Balliol, formerly King of Scotland, gave you since we surrendered to him the realm of Scotland, and also excepting those lands which we have seized before you have come to our peace.' " (*Historical Documents, Scotland, 1286-1306*, ii. 67.)

Probably the bulk of those who took the oath did so with the mental reservation that it was only binding so long as it could be enforced.

Just when Ralph's tenure of office ceased and that of his successor began is uncertain, but the probability is that he was still in office on the occasion of the third visit too, when Edward, on his departure, ordered the monastery to be set on fire.

It was bound to have been a heart-breaking experience, not only for the abbot in charge, but for all associated with it even in the humblest capacity. Little more than fifty years before the great church had been completed and opened for worship in the presence of the king, and the greatest assembly of nota-bilities, both civil and ecclesiastic, that ever gathered within its walls. Some of the monastic buildings may even have been of later date.

To stand by helplessly and see this glorious structure, of which they were all, naturally, so intensely proud, committed by their country's enemies to the flames was almost more than flesh and blood could stand. For the English version of what happened, see page 211.

Whether it was Ralph or his successor who had to set about the task of reconstruction is uncertain, but the probability is that the bulk of the work fell on his successor.

On the occasion of this visit, Edward I and his son (first Prince of Wales) each gave a jewel to the shrine of St. Margaret, a house was built at the king's command outside the great door of the Abbey and 40 men were engaged in making an entrenchment round the town. (*B.R.* xxiii n.)

In the Indenture of State Papers of Scotland carried away by Edward at this time there is a reference to a Calendar of Charters of the Kings of Scotland which Dene Thomas, monk of Dunfermline, had in his keeping for the purpose of transcription. The date of the Indenture is 1292.

This is one of the few references to be met with to monks being engaged on such work at such an early date.

Professor Coulton seems to think that work of the kind was mostly done by " professional scribes," who moved from one monastery to another as their services were required. If it was done by a local monk, it meant " special merit " for the monastery.

The Indenture makes it quite clear that the scribe in this case was a " monk of Dunfermline," and that the work he was engaged on was not the usual one of copying service books for the use of the monastery but transcribing state documents for preservation.

In the year 1300, William de Lamberton, Bishop of St. Andrews, in premising the great perfection of discipline, the commendatory life and charity of the monks, to render them still more fervent, gives them the vicarage of a church. (*Dalyell* 16.)

" 1304—The abbot and convent of Dunfermline shew the King and Council that they are seised by gift of King David of a town called Kirkcaldy, which they hold as a free burgh, but have no market there.

" Wherefore they pray the King that as the said town is one of the most ancient burghs of Scotland, and is ten leagues or more from any market town, he would grant them a weekly market there on Thursday, and a yearly ' fayr ' in the octaves of Easter, to last for three days." (*Cal. of Doc. relating to Scot.* ii. 432.)

Hugh.   1309 and 1315

The beginning and end of his reign are uncertain, but in 1309 he appeared as a leading witness in an Inquisition ordered by mandate of Clement V to the Bishop of St. Andrews and John of Solerium, clerk to the Pope, concerning the Order of Templars. These Knights of the Temple were a military order founded in 1119 to protect pilgrims going to the Holy Sepulchre. In Europe their houses were used as strongholds for the royal treasure and the order became wealthy through being the great international financiers and bankers of the time—with the usual result : wealth meant relaxation of discipline and decay.

At the trial, 1309, many witnesses stated that they (the Templars) neglected the poor, showing hospitality only towards the rich.

In the course of his evidence, Hugh, " by divine permission Abbot of Dunfermline," testified that " he had an unfavourable suspicion against them."

In September, that same year, he, and the Abbot of Westminster, with certain priors, were appointed " protectors of the privileges of the Cistercian Order." (C.P.R. ii. 58.)

There is a reference to Abbot Hugh in the early part of 1315. (Antiq. of Abdn. and Banff, ii. 313.)

This may have been 1314-15.

Robert de Crail. 1314-15—1332

Witnessed a deed at Scotlandwell, as Abbot of Dunfermline, in the eighth year of Robert the Bruce. (Inchaffray, 114-5.)

In January, 1316, Duncan, Earl of Fife, did homage to him for the lands of Cluny, near Kinglassie, and in 1332 he issued a charter relative to the great customs of the four burghs attached to Dunfermline Abbey. (B.R. xi.) (Reg. 349.)

The first reference to St. Catherine's Chapel occurs in a charter by this abbot. It stood, with the almshouses associated with it, to the north of the entrance to the Glen, opposite the Abbey.

" Chalmers' History (i. 159, ii. 53) says that this chapel was on the south side of the Nethertown, at the east corner of Grange Road. But this is clearly wrong, and any ruined chapel standing there ca. 1800 must have represented still another. According to Henderson's Annals, this was St. Mary's Chapel." (B.R. xxvii.)

" No conjecture can be offered as to the significance of the heavily buttressed wall of a structure of fourteenth or fifteenth century date which still stands in Pittencrieff Glen to the north-west of the church." (*Roy. Comm., Fife,* 114.)

This is somewhat difficult to understand in view of the fact that the boundaries of St. Catherine's Yard, with the pigeon house built thereon, are defined as follows :—" between the tower or fortalice burn on the west, and the mansion or chapel of St. Catherine on the east, and the garden of William Durie on the north, and the common road on the south." (*Dr. Henderson quoting MS. Reg. of Chart., Edin.*)

Before Bridge Street was built, the road to the west passed through Pittencrieff Glen.

" For the part of *JOHN DE OWTHTERGAWN* (Auchter-gaven, i.e., Bankfoot, in Perthshire), monk of Dunfermline, it is represented that he has wisely exercised the office of Almoner of the said monastery for some twenty years, has made houses and other reparations, and at great cost and expense is having rebuilt the chapel of St. Catherine, Virgin, which was destroyed and demolished, and has rendered an account of all the rents and fruits every year, or at the will of the abbot. May the Pope therefore give mandate by his letters that John may not be removed from that office by any authority until he has been able to carry out his plan for the rebuilding of the said chapel."

The papal finding is :—Let him not be removed without cause. December, 1420. (*Scott. Suppl.* iii. 238.)

The Chapel of St. Catherine was built prior to 1327. (*Reg.* 253-4.)

In the year 1320, during the incumbency of Robert, a question arose between the Abbey and the " men " (bondmen) of Tweeddale belonging to it which throws an interesting light on the status of these unfortunate people. The story is recorded in the *Registrum* (354) and we are indebted to Dalyell's *Monastic Antiquities* (40-48) for the following notes concerning it.

" From various passages it is evident that, if the lower orders of peasantry were not actual slaves, they were but one degree removed from bondage. A man and his whole posterity could be gifted by one to another like so many beasts of burden.

" There is a charter with the specific title *de Servis*; and this contains a donation by the King of Gillandream Macsuthen and his children in *perpetuam elemosinam* to the monks about the years 1171-1178.

" David gives Ragewin, Gillepatrick and Ulchill for ever to the church of the Holy Trinity of Dunfermline ' as my own men.'

" The master, it appears, was entitled to any acquisition the slave or bondman might make and to the property he enjoyed.

" David grants that the abbot and monks shall have all men and all that belongs to them that were on the lands on that day when they were offered up and given to the church of the Holy Trinity. It is certain that such persons could not change their residence, that they were bound to remain on the lands. . . .

" With regard to the obligations of the monastery toward its own bondmen, there is some elucidation in the verdict of a jury as early as the year 1320. This jury, which consisted of eight persons, sat in the chapel of Logyn (Logie) on a question between the abbey and the men of Tweeddale belonging to it.

" The latter, in the first place, demand that the abbot shall appoint a bailie of their own race, who shall repledge them to the court of the monastery; to which it is answered by the jury that such a bailie should be given to them, not only from feudal right, but from use and wont.

" Secondly they require that, if any of their race be verging on want, or disabled by old age, they be maintained by the monastery; to which the jury reply, on their oath, that the monastery is not bound to do so from strict law, but from regard, as they are men belonging to it.

" Thirdly, if one of their race shall slay a man, or commit any other crime, for which he may be reduced to seek the immunity of the Church, and shall retire to the monastery of Dunfermline for safety, that so long as he remains there, he shall be defended from the property of the abbey; to which the jury answer, that, as the monastery would do so to a stranger, much more must it be done to their own man.

" Fourthly, they demand that, if any one of their race commits homicide, and pays a composition for it, abbot and monks shall contribute twelve marks to discharge the composition; the jury declare ' that they never heard of such a thing in all their lives.'

" One of the abbots, A.—probably Alexander—towards the earlier part of the fourteenth century, by a written deed,

32

Abbot de Bothwell's Porch (Marriage and Christening Porch)

testifies that ' Marcorun and Edmund and Michael, the son and heir of Edmund, as also the brothers and sisters of Edmund . . . and their whole progeny, are our freemen and at peace with us and the church. That they have our liberty to dwell where they please (as freely and quietly as their predecessors and their descendants, whom King David gave to our church with Crebarin), delivering to us an ox two years old, or four shillings yearly.'

" These are the chief passages of the chartulary illustrating the condition of a class of people whose unjust debasement has long been abrogated in Scotland."

" We learn something of the price of the serf from the efforts which were made by the Church for his manumission. . . .

" In 1247, Patrick de Prendergest, burgess of Berwick, bought the freedom of Renaldus, a slave, with his whole family following for twenty merks sterling.

" This is a remarkable transaction; for Patrick, the burgess, had formerly been a slave, or at least a native, and obtained his liberty through the house of Coldingham; but what is more curious, Reynald, who was thus emancipated for a sum of money, is styled in the charter *prepositus*, meaning, no doubt, alderman or bailie of the town of Berwick; and that accounts for the greatness of his price; for about the same time the Abbey of Coldingham purchased the freedom of Joseph, the son of Elwald, and all his posterity, for the price of three merks; and Eustace of Newbigging sold to the Prior of Coldingham the freedom of William of Newbigging, and Brunhild his wife, and Walter and Mabil their children, and all their issue, for the sum of fifteen shillings. These are instances of purchased emancipation." (*Scotland in the Middle Ages*, Cosmo Innes, 142, 143.)

The chief event of the closing years of King Robert the Bruce's reign was the establishment of peace with England. The terms agreed upon included the renunciation by Edward of his claim of feudal superiority, the acknowledgment of Robert as King of Scotland, and the payment by Scotland of a sum of £20,000—the Abbot of Dunfermline, Robert de Crail, being designed as depositary of the money for the contribution. Over and above the £20,000, the sum of 4,000 marks had to be paid to the Pope for the recall of the excommunication which, on the instigation of Edward, had been imposed upon the King and people of Scotland. One of the stipulations attached to the treaty was that David, eldest son and heir of the Bruce, aged about 4, was to marry Joanna, the sister of Edward, and, without delay, the marriage of the children was solemnised.

King Robert himself died on the 9th of June, 1329, less than eleven months after the marriage of his son, and from the Exchequer Rolls we get a detailed account of his death and funeral.

" His growing weakness is indicated by the recurrence of entries regarding physicians and apothecaries, though four large payments, succeeding each other in 1329, to John the apothecary, amounting in all to £37 6s. 8d., may be partly connected with the embalming of the body and the removing of the heart after death.

" The accounts enable us to follow his remains from Cardross, by way of Dunipace and Cambuskenneth, to their resting-place in front of the high altar of the abbey church of Dunfermline.

" A marble monument made in Paris was erected over the grave, and the entries regarding it show that it had been commissioned in the king's lifetime.

" In the Chamberlain's account ending in August, 1329, one Richard Barber was paid £13 6s. 8d., ' de anno precedenti pro dictis tumbis,' and there is a payment of £66 13s. 4d. to Thomas of Charteris, who seems to have had the principal charge connected with it.

" The workman of the tomb was paid £12 10s. for its freight and his expenses in bringing it from Paris *via* Bruges to Dunfermline, and the mason got £38 2s., in which sum a gratuity from the Regent was included.

" The tomb was surrounded with an iron railing, and large purchases of gold-leaf were made for its decoration, partly at Newcastle and York. A chapel of Baltic timber (*bordis de Estland*) was erected over the grave on the day of the funeral; and John of Lithgow, the painter, employed in gilding and decorating it, rendered an account for his wages and expenses, in addition to which he had a gift of £3 6s. 8d.

" £66 13s. 4d. was paid to the abbot, and 562 stones 5 lbs. of wax were bought for candles, which were prepared by the abbot's servants.

34

" We have charges for vestments for the altar and the gilding of a hearse and horses for the litter. The purchases further included large quantities of lawn, of crape (*nigri cindonis*), black persic, and cloth for robes for the Steward and his people, and furs for the Knights. Offerings were made on the day of the funeral of £66 13s. 4d. to the Abbot of Dunfermline—a sum agreed upon beforehand—and £20 to the rector of Cardross.

" As might be expected, there are various payments made, sometimes in money, sometimes in grain, ' pro anima regis defuncti.'

" £14 had previously been in use to be paid out of the fermes of Ayr to three chaplains in the church of that town; and in the accounts after this date the sum is said to be paid them to say masses for the soul of King Robert.

" Bruce's Queen and second wife, Elizabeth, daughter of Richard de Burgh, Earl of Ulster, had predeceased him in November, 1327. Her body was embalmed at Cullen, where she died, and buried at Dunfermline." (*Exch.* i. cxxi.)

" Elizabeth had been more than twenty years married before the birth of her son David. . . . There were two daughters, and only two. . . . Both were doubtless older than David, though neither can have been born before 1316. . . .

" David was born 5 March, 1323-24.

" Among the events of 1325 Fordun gives the birth of David as having taken place ' on Monday, 5 March, in the first week of Lent, in the monastery of Dunfermline after complines ' ; but the 5th of March was neither Monday nor in the first week of Lent in 1325-26, though it was so in 1323-24." (*Exch.* i. cxxvi. and note.)

There is nothing improbable in his having been born in the monastery. If anything remained by this time of King Malcolm's Tower, it would have been quite unsuitable as a royal residence. The monastic buildings had not yet been altered or extended for use as a palace, and there was no other place in Dunfermline where the king could live but the guest-chambers of the monastery.

" Though David became king on his father's death, in the year 1329, about a year and a half passed before he was crowned ; and something took place at his coronation which had never taken place before.

"David was the first King of Scots to be anointed.

"Now, in those days a king was not thought to be a real king unless he had been anointed, and the English used to say that the kings of Scots were not kings at all, as none of them had been anointed like their own kings.

"But Bruce, who seems to have thought of everything, had thought of this also, and he asked the Pope that his son might be anointed when he became king.

"The Pope agreed to Bruce's request, and he sent the holy oil to Scotland, though the Scots had to pay 12,000 gold florins for it." (*Hume Brown, Hist. of Scotland for Schools*, p. 181.)

A deed by the abbot and monks, which is dated on Sunday, in the year 1330, mentions that John de Kinros, perpetual vicar of Inverkeithing, had represented to them that this place was so much exhausted by exactions and contributions, apostolical as well as royal, that sufficient funds were wanting to repair the choir; and the monastery agreed to pay half the expense of doing so on this occasion. (*Reg. 372*).

"In the fifth year of Edward (1331) there came into England a man called Edward de Baliol, pretending to have right to the Crown of Scotland, and drew unto him many who had great possessions in Scotland, either by themselves or by their wives.

"These all came to the king and asked leave to enter Scotland, going through his land.

"The king would give them no leave because David, King of Scots, had wedded his sister.

"Then got they ships and took the sea about the feast of St. Laurens (10 Aug.) and landed fast by the Abbey of Downfermelyn, where they found great resistance of Scots; but a few of our archers occupied the Scots till our armed men were landed." (*Capgrave's Chronicle of England*, p. 201.)

Alexander de Berwick.   1332—1351

"Alexander de Berewick, Abbot of Dunfermline, had gone to Rome to beg from the Pope a general indulgence. On his way home through Lombardy he was seized by the plague, and, with his entire retinue, perished at Stephano, in 1353." (*Macphail's Pluscarden*, 102.)

The fact may be correct, but the date is wrong. Alexander was certainly defunct by 22nd June, 1351, if the records in

36

Theiner's *Monumenta* (p. 297) and *C.P.R.* (iii. 423) are to be believed.

Besides, the Pope who dealt with the matter was dead by 1352.

One of the surprises that accompany the study of these early days is the frequency with which the threat of excommunication is brought into operation for the flimsiest of reasons. We read, for instance, that in 1314, during the reign of Robert I, the vicar of Inverkeithing had been found liable for eight merks to the monastery of Dunfermline, for non-payment of which it was declared that he should be excommunicated. But in the time of Abbot Alexander we have the interesting account of how once the sentence of excommunication was recalled. The story is based on the *Registrum* (381) and is told by Dalyell as follows :—

" In the year of God 1342, on Wednesday before the Feast of Bartholomew the Apostle, Alexander, by the grace of God Abbot of Dunfermline, went down to the south side of the Queensferry, at request of James de Dundas, concerning an amicable termination of a dispute that had arisen between him and the abbot on account of his molesting the abbot's men and boats landing at two rocks within the flowing of the tide, as they were wont to do.

" However, James de Dundas had alleged these rocks to be his property ; though the abbot, his predecessors, and the monastery had quietly and peaceably enjoyed the right of landing there beyond the memory of man ; and on this had a charter from King David, their founder and first patron, as also the confirmations of various kings, his successors, and several Popes, as the abbot then exhibited, in presence of the subscribers . . . and many others, inhabitants of the Ferry.

" James de Dundas had, on account of his molestation, incurred the general sentence of excommunication contained in the confirmation of the Popes, which he had during some time obdurately resisted, until, on the day before-mentioned, he humbly supplicated the abbot, sitting along with some of his council on these rocks, as being in possession of them, that he would absolve him from the sentence of excommunication, and he should abstain from molesting the men and boats in future. The abbot, yielding to this humble supplication, absolved him

37

from the sentence of excommunication, as far as lay in his power, on finding security to abstain from the like molestation; but, were it ever repeated, he should immediately again incur the same censure."

Although the monastery had by this time been nearly 200 years in existence, we still read of considerable additions in the way of grants. Randolph, Earl of Moray, for instance, Bruce's famous lieutenant, makes over to the monks of Dunfermline the lands of Culhelach (Cullelo), in the barony of Aberdour, to secure prayers for his uncle, King Robert the Bruce, his predecessors and successors; and at the same time presents gifts to the chapel of St. Mary, the Virgin, within the Conventual Church. (*Reg.* 357.)

A little later, he gives the lands of Bandrum, Kineddar and Drumcapie, in the parish of Saline, for a similar service to himself. (*Reg.* 358.)

Both deeds are undated, but were probably issued about 1320.

References to money being lent by the monastery are comparatively rare, though it is well known that the practice existed.

Under date 13th September, 1347, however, there is an entry rather pathetic in its suggestiveness. The gist of it is that Christian Beseth (Bisset), relict of Sir John Beseth, and daughter of the deceased Sir David de Hunyoth, Laird of Klerkinton-Hunyoth, had a son, Walter Beseth, who was a prisoner in England, and in order to raise money for his ransom she disposed of an annual-rent of £3 9s. sterling which she had upon the lands of Luscar-Unyoth. In consideration of her " extreme necessity," Abbot Alexander de Berwick purchased the annual-rent for the sum of £40 sterling, and thus apparently enabled her to redeem her son. (*Reg.* 382.)

The sums involved do not seem large, but it has to be remembered the £1 sterling represented £12 Scots.

Another entry records certain disbursements on the ground, apparently, of services rendered.

" The abbot, on account of fidelity and good offices, grants to William de Yetam ' our clerk,' particular lands, as also honourable support for himself and one clerk or esquire, in his option; also three boys and three horses, and a stable for the boys and horses, and the same provision for them as for those of the abbot, along with a chamber for himself." (*Dalyell* 38.)

38

What does surprise one not a little is that, as late as 1479, we find the monastery borrowing money. In the early days when so many new buildings had to be erected, or the damage done by English invaders had to be made good, it is easy to understand that the financial resources of the monastery might easily have been at a very low ebb. But in 1479 there was nothing of that sort, and yet in that year the abbot acknowledges "tyl haue ressauit beforhands fra Mathou Forster a sowm of twa hundreth punds of usual mony of Scotland geuyn tyl us in our myster, and turnyt in the comon profit and nedeful utilitie of our place." (*Reg.* 481.)

John Black. 1351

The right of the inmates of a monastery to elect their abbot was one that was jealously guarded, and not without reason, for almost every infraction of the rule, whether by kings or ecclesiastics, was attended with unfortunate results.

The first case of the kind in Dunfermline happened at this time.

Alexander de Berwick having died furth of Scotland, the monks elected John Black, their cellarer, to be abbot, and this choice had the support, not only of the bishop of the diocese, but of the king as well. It happened, however, that a young monk of the abbey, John Stramiglaw, was at that time studying in Paris. Hearing of the abbot's death, and fearing, as he said, that the dignity would fall into the hands of a stranger, he hastened to Avignon and persuaded Pope Clement VI to appoint him to the vacant office—the appointment apparently being made on the strength of a general reservation to the Supreme Pontiff of all offices becoming vacant under such conditions.

When the Apostolical Legate appeared at Dunfermline, accompanied by Stramiglaw, Black resigned and handed over the insignia of office to the legate, who manifested his appreciation by providing Black with an honourable pension.

So runs the story as told by Fordun.

The writer who continues Fordun's narrative adds the note that Stramiglaw received that dignity from the liberality of the Apostolical See upon this condition, that the right of the monastery should remain thereafter as at first, and the right of confirmation to the Lord Bishop as clear, unimpaired and entire as of old, and (as it was) from the first foundation of the house, without any diminution of its right or prejudice or exaction whatsoever.

In the reign of James III Parliament passed an Act declaring any nomination made otherwise than by the monks to be invalid. But the king who sanctioned the law was the first to break it, being induced thereto, it is suggested, by a sufficiently attractive bribe—which is not unlikely. It opened the door to many evils. (*Paisley*, 136.)

Black was afterwards appointed Prior of Urquhart.

"On 27 November, 1351, the abbots of Dunfermline and Newbattle, acting as conservators of the rights of the Cluniac order, under a commission from Clement VI, sub-delegated to certain canons of Glasgow to deal with an accusation against Martin, Bishop of Argyll, that he had taken possession of the tithes and fruits of three churches in his diocese belonging to the monastery of Paisley.

"The process seems to have been a long one, for it is not till 30 May, 1362, that we find the sub-delegates suspending the bishop *a pontificalibus* for contumacy in not appearing before them, although he was at the time in the town of Glasgow. On 9 June, however, an amicable composition was made between the parties." (*Dowden*, *Bps.* 382-3.)

Rivalry between bishops and abbots, cathedrals and monastries, was, in the nature of the case, more or less inevitable. Their interests were so frequently diametrically opposed.

It was not merely that bishops, as a rule, were supporters of the king, while abbots were inclined to look naturally to the Pope. The unfortunate thing about it was that nearly every new grant to the monastery, whether in the way of lands or churches, proved to be to the diminution of the status and prestige of the bishop of the diocese. On his first appointment the abbot had to be consecrated by the bishop; otherwise there was little difference in their status; and two authorities of more or less equal standing in one area does not make as a rule for harmonious working.

Time and again we find the bishops claiming the right to elect the abbots within their diocese. Not that they were alone in this. Kings and Popes were equally ready to make the same claim. But the bishops being in closer proximity to the monks, who had the lawful right to elect, their action was all the more resented.

In this particular case, the trouble arose from an attempt on the part of the Bishop of Argyll to withdraw from the monastery of Paisley three churches in his diocese that rightfully belonged to it.

The abbot appealed to the Pope, who gave authority to the abbots of Dunfermline and Newbattle to settle the dispute.

Alexander de Berwick, as already noted, was dead before 22nd June, 1351, and this authority was issued 27th November, 1351. The situation at Dunfermline, as between Black and Stramiglaw, was too uncertain for either of them to take action, and so the settlement was delegated to certain canons of Glasgow who proved so high-handed in their attitude that they suspended the bishop for not appearing before them when visiting Glasgow. An amicable composition was eventually reached after eleven years, but it is one of many instances of a trouble that left its mark upon the history of the times.

John Stramiglaw. 1351—

John Black's election took place in 1351, but there is no record of the date of his renunciation and the installation of Stramiglaw, unless the reference in the Register of Paisley, 27th November, 1351 (140) is attributable to him, which is quite possible, and indeed likely, because Stramiglaw was appointed by the Pope in July, 1351.

" To John de Stramigloe, monk of Dunfermline, appointing him Abbot of Dunfermline, void by the death of Alexander on his return from Rome whither he had gone to obtain the remission of the Jubilee Year, and reserved to the Pope ; the election of John Blayk, monk of the same, having been made in ignorance of such reservation and therefore annulled." (*Avignon*, 10 *Kal. July*, 1351.) (*C.P.R.* iii. 423.)

" Mandate on Petition of Clergy of Scotland to compel the abbot (Stramiglaw) and convent of Dunfermline to exact no more tolls or passage dues from ecclesiastics than they do from nobles or their servants at the port called Queensferry." (*C.P.R. 7 Id. July*, 1364.)

How long he held office is not known.

His name occurs in a curious story told in the Papal Registers concerning the succession of abbots at Lindores.

On the death of Roger, a certain William appears to have secured provision from the Papal Authority at Avignon, but John Steil, a monk of Lindores, being elected by the other monks, took possession.

William, being deprived of Lindores, secured further provision (6 Non. March, 1383) of Dunfermline, said to be void by the resignation of John de Stramigloke. If Dunfermline is not available, he is to obtain appointment to some other monastery. Three months later (3 Kal. June, 1383) he is granted £20 upon the abbatial *mensa* (table) of Dunfermline till he obtains possession of the goods of Lindores or other monastery.

Next we are told that John Steil and his accomplices have taken a topaz, valued at £20, as well as books, vestments, copes, clothes and other goods, so that William and those who adhered to him had for two years been forced to beg among their friends.

William excommunicated John and his adherents, but, in spite of this, two of them, John de Strathmygloke and Donald de Echlyn, continued to celebrate divine offices. The papal mandatories (the Bishop of Brechin and the officials of St. Andrews and Dunkeld) are accordingly directed to see that the clothes are restored and provision for food and clothing made from the rents of Lindores until William shall obtain possession, the sentences of excommunication to be solemnly published, and the said John de Strathmygloke and Donald de Echlyn suspended from their orders until they come to the Apostolic See to be absolved.

It is a curious story, and it seems that in the end Steil triumphed.

It has, of course, to be remembered that there were rival Popes at the time, and that in the Registers we have only one side of the story. Besides, Clement III had expressly given the monks of Lindores the right to choose their own abbot. If Steil was, as appears, the choice of the majority, then the goods belonged of right to him, and Stramiglaw and Echlyn had committed no offence.

But nothing in the story gives the slightest clue as to why Stramiglaw left Dunfermline. Steil is said to have been formerly Prior of Coldingham, and as such would probably have been known to Stramiglaw, Coldingham having been attached to Dunfermline in 1378.

Following Stramiglaw, the succession is hopelessly confused and unreliable.

Dr. Chalmers (i. 178) in succession to John Black and John Stramiglaw, gives the names of other four Johns, numbered on his list XIX, XX, XXI, and XXII; but there is nothing to show that XIX was not Stramiglaw, that XX was not also XXI, or XXI also XXII.

The *Registrum* of Dunfermline simply ignores the three Johns numbered XIX, XX and XXI in Chalmers' list.

But there does seem to be something to be said for number XX—John of Balygirnach (Balgerno)—if only the fact that he had a distinctive surname; although there is nothing to indicate when he was appointed or for how long he held office.

On 18th June, 1389, a three-years' truce was concluded at Dunfermline—the king being in residence there—between France, England and Scotland. According to Bower, the envoys were cordially received and liberally treated, and after they had harangued long and eloquently on the blessings of peace, the king gracefully conceded all that they desired. In the Chamberlain's account for 1389 we have a payment of £19 11s. 10d. for the king's expenses at Dunfermline for wine, spices, and cloth. We also find £4 3s. 4d. given to a herald bringing a letter from the King of England, a horse worth £10 bestowed on one of the English knights, and four horses presented to the French envoys. (*Exch. Rolls.* iii, lxx.)

An allowance for wages to boys at the king's court at Dunfermline on the same occasion is also recorded, amounting to 13s. 4d. (*Ibid.* 701.)

Like David II, James I was born in the monastery of Dunfermline. The date of his birth, though for some time in doubt, is now accepted as 25th July, St. James' Day, 1394—which may be the explanation of why it is that the name, previously rare in Scotland, was given to the child and to six of his successors on the throne. Some 40 years later, he remembers his nurse and sends to her in Dunfermline a present of three barrels of beer. (*Exch.* ii. 627.)

His mother, Annabella Drummond, "faire, honorabil and pleasand," though dying at Perth, was buried in Dunfermline Abbey, where she is commemorated by a stained-glass window.

John de Torry. 1399—1409

Appears as a witness to a charter in 1399, and is noticed in the *Registrum* on 4th December, 1404, and 13th June, 1409.

In the last reference he is credited with having increased the allowances of his monks because of increases in the price of clothing.

William de St. Andrea. 1413—

A monk of Dunfermline, and had previously been Prior of Urquhart. Received provision to Dunfermline in 1416. As, however, he appears in the *Registrum* (280) in December, 1413, and in the Glasgow Register (310) on 17th March, 1415-16, it is possible that he may have been *postulate* before his definite appointment and provision in 1416.

The Preface to the *Registrum* (p. xv) says that he was abbot in 1414 and 1419, but that nothing is known of him but his name.

A good deal of information concerning him has become available since that time (1842).

By 1419 accusations were lodged against him in Rome and a rival arose in the person of Robert de Scotland.

" On the death of John, Robert de Scotland, claustral prior of Dunfermline, was elected, but (Schism then flourishing in the Church of God) failed to obtain confirmation.

" In the meantime, William de St. Andrea, a monk of Dunfermline, by unlawful allegation and bribery, obtained provision and took over the rule and administration. According to Robert, William was a public perjurer and concubinary, . . . is branded with apostacy, and, because of his exceeding faults and demerits had been excommunicated and, by a judicial sentence, deprived of a certain priory (Urquhart).

" Moreover, he had caused Robert to be taken to Bruges and there detained in irons in the prisons of laymen and to be inflicted with divers losses and injuries.

" Robert asks for inquiry, and, in the event of William being deprived, for his own appointment as abbot."

Granted. 20th March, 1419. (*Scott. Suppl. pp.* 25-6.)

In trying to assess the value of a record such as this, it is well to keep in mind the unbridled intemperance of language that was unfortunately characteristic of so many medieval controversies and to make allowance for it.

It should be remembered, too, that these supplications were

not drafted by the supplicant himself, but by a professional "drafter of the supplication" whose one object was to buttress his case as strongly as possible.

It is not suggested that serious charges against a man's moral character could be lodged without some appearance of justification, but, while the facts vouched for in the supplication were supposed to be true, it by no means followed that they represented the whole truth.

To-day a court of law would almost certainly look askance at a suggestion that, in the event of the accused being deprived of office, the accuser should succeed him; but in these early days nobody, apparently, was unduly perturbed by it.

There is no suggestion in this particular case of any sort of official recognition or encouragement of informers, but numerous cases of the kind are on record about this time in both Scotland and Ireland, though, curiously enough, no case is to be met with in England; and, wherever anything of that nature occurs, it indicates beyond question an utter lack of proper supervision and healthy discipline.

In the case of William of St. Andrews, it would appear that there was little or no substance in the charges made against him, for three months later, he asks for, and obtains, confirmation of his appointment.

"William de St. Andrew, having been provided and instituted as abbot by the Pope, and held the monastery for three years, asks for confirmation." Granted—22nd May, 1419. (*Scott. Suppl.* 53.)

The following year, 22nd May, 1420, in the course of a Supplication to the Pope, Richard de Bothwell, a monk of Dunfermline, charges William de Reston, Sacristan, with not only misusing goods of the sacristy, but conspiring against the abbot, William de St. Andrew, with a view to dislodging him from office, and asks for inquiry, and, in the event of his being found guilty, for provision to the office of Sacristan for himself. The Pope gives mandate to some good men "in partibus" to inform themselves diligently about the foregoing, and, if they find it, or any of it, to be true, or that de Reston has committed any other crime meriting deprivation, to remove and deprive him, and provide Richard by Apostolic authority to the said office. (*Scott. Suppl.* 199.)

In 1423 de Bothwell was appointed Sacristan, de Reston being by that time dead.

How long William de St. Andrew held office, or how his tenure of it terminated, we do not know. We only know that he was dead before 1442. (*C.P.R.* ix. 271.)

Andrew of Kirkcaldy. 1427—

For surname see Register of Cupar Abbey, p. 46.

" Promoted 10 September, 1427—16 cardinals being present—paid 132 florins 40 shgs. and 7 pence—receiving quittance 23 April, 1428. Offered 250 florins for his common service and the five customary little services." (*Apos. Cam.*, pp. 9, 10.)

As this is the first reference we have so far encountered to payments for promotion, it may be well to explain that the first sum, the smaller one, represents the expenses incurred in connection with the appointment, varying according to the number of cardinals present. The other is described as a voluntary offer, but there was nothing voluntary about it. It represents the estimated value of the first year's fruits of office, and, without guarantee of payment of this sum, the promotion would not be given effect to.

Nor did this apply only to abbots. Similar sums had to be paid for appointment as prior or sacristan, and, of course, on a much larger scale for appointment as bishop or archbishop.

With a view to his possible appointment as a cardinal, Andrew Forman (see p. 58) had to promise a payment of 5,000 ducats to the bankers for the Roman Court.

Scotland was a poor country in those days, and it needs little in the way of imagination to realise how terrible was the strain on its resources due to these constantly recurring claims by Rome.

The church of Perth, like many others, was attached to the monastery of Dunfermline and, during Andrew's incumbency, the question arose as to liability for repairs and maintenance.

The matter was eventually settled by compromise.

The provost, bailies and community of Perth became responsible for repairs and furnishings, recovering costs from burials in the choir, the abbot and convent reserving such burial rights as belonged to them.—15 *Kal. August*, 1442. (*C.P.R.* ix. 267.)

" Upon the voidance of the said monastery by the death of Abbot William, during whose life Martin V had specially reserved it in provision, the convent, perhaps in ignorance of such provision, elected Andrew abbot, then a monk thereof and in priest's orders, who, likewise ignorant, consented to the election, and afterwards, upon learning the said reservation, set forth the matter . . . before the Pope, who, holding it void, has made provision to the same Andrew.—*Florence*, 15 *Kal. August*, 1442." (*C.P.R.* ix. 271.)

Richard de Bothwell.   1445—1470
" By goddis tholing abbote of Dunfermelyn."

His coat of arms, both outside and inside the nave, is that of Bothwell of Hallbank.   There was a small estate of that name on the south side of Dunfermline, " bordering the burgh " (*Annals* 195) so that it is quite possible that he was a local man. Such names as Bothwell Works and Bothwell Street would seem to confirm this.

The first reference we have to him is on 30th November, 1418, when he was given indult (indulgence) to choose a confessor. (*Reg. Vat.* 329, fol. 130 v.)

He seems to have had a weakness for that sort of thing, and money to spend on it, for in 1434 we find that he received indult that " the Confessor of his choice may grant him, being penitent and having confessed, plenary indulgence once only, namely, at the hour of death." (*C.P.R.* viii. 513.)

On 26th June, 1458, one of his own monks, Malizeus de Erlande, received the same indulgence—*de plenaria remissione.* (*C.P.R.* xi. 362.)

In 1418, he was one of four candidates for the Priory of Urquhart, vacant by the translation of William of St. Andrew to Dunfermline.   Each of the four held a formal appointment, but it was a time of rival Popes, and Bothwell had apparently backed the wrong horse, the appointment eventually going to Andrew Raeburn, who had previously been Prior of Coldingham.

Bothwell was a monk of Dunfermline, and had at this time already spent three years as a student in Universities and the Papal Curia.

Whether he returned to his studies with a view to the degree of Bachelor of Canon Law, which we know that he held, or whether he returned to his duties at Dunfermline, we do not know.

But we do know that on 2 Non. January, 1423, he was appointed sacristan of Dunfermline (*C.P.R.* vii. 290), the office having become vacant through the death of William de Rostan, and, so far as we know, he continued in that office till, on 26th June, 1444, he was appointed Abbot of Paisley, with dispensation to hold simultaneously the sacristanship of Dunfermline. (*Apos. Cam.* 33.)

Seven months later he was appointed Abbot of Dunfermline, a somewhat unusual proceeding, and involving, doubtless, double payments, but it was his own monastery, and he was still sacrist of it.

" 18 January, 1445—Provided in secret consistory—office void by death of the late Andrew—18 cardinals present—paid 108 florins, 16 shgs. and 8 pence—offered 255 gold florins as papal services."

In June, 1445, he was elected a representative of the Three Scottish Estates. (*Cupar*, i. 44.)

In 1449 he was a member of a Parliamentary Committee appointed to revise, collate and authenticate previous Acts of Parliament.

He was also one of the Committee appointed to regulate and average the bullion and coinage of the kingdom.

The following year (1450) he carried out that extensive scheme of renovation at the west end of the nave which, it is hoped, in spite of the tendency to forget, will always be associated with his name.

In 1456 he was one of three chosen from the clergy and sworn to administer justice and adjudicate complaints in various " cleyne places " of the kingdom in a year of pestilence in Scotland.

And so it went on, a full and busy life, no doubt of it, and, so far as one can judge, very usefully employed.

In 1463 we find one man at least—Thos. Bully, Canon of the Cathedral Church of Glasgow—who was so moved by gratitude for all the good that Richard de Bothwell had done to him and others that he left all his goods to make provision for the

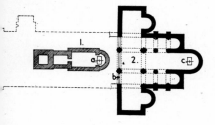

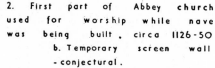

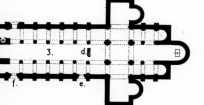

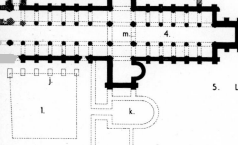

1. Queen Margaret's church added to original Culdee church circa 1072-74.

    a. Early high altar

2. First part of Abbey church used for worship while nave was being built, circa 1126-50

    b. Temporary screen wall - conjectural.

    c. High altar in 1150

3. Nave of Abbey church dedicated in 1150.

    d. Remains of rood screen

    e. East processional doorway.

    f. West processional doorway.

4. Conventual church and choir completed in 1250 including Saint Margaret's Shrine.

    g. North Porch built by Abbot de Bothwell in 1450.

    h. North series of buttresses -date stone 1625.

    j. South series of buttresses -date stone 1620.

5. Lady Chapel added in 14th. cent.

    k. Probable position of Chapter house.

    l. Position of Cloister court

    m. Pulpitum.

SCALE - -OF FEET

M. M. JOHNSTON. DEL.

abbot and his successors in office in their house at Stirling, and to ensure that when they do go there, they shall be absolved and free from all claim, demand or payment.

In 1450 King James II, in making provision out of the lands of Arlary for a chaplainry (unspecified) in the Church of Dunfermline for augmenting divine worship and service, assigns as one of the reasons for his gift the expenses " *quae ad nostrum honorem clare subiisse Ricardus Abbas probatur.*" (*Reg.* 430.)

On 26th November, 1468, about a year before he died, we find the abbot looking back upon it all and making provision for the day that had to come.

" The recent Petition of Richard, Abbot of the Benedictine monastery of Dunfermline, contained that he, who has been abbot there for 24 years and has becomingly furnished it with books and ornaments and other ecclesiastical jewels, and has . . . bequeathed, set apart and assigned, 20 merks of the current money of the realm of Scotland to the prior and convent for a low mass to be said daily in the monastery church for the souls of himself and his parents and benefactors, and high mass with music on the day of his death ; . . . to the sacrist four like merks a year for the upkeep of a wax candle of one pound weight at the high altar near the picture of St. Margaret, sometime Queen of Scotland, the founder of the monastery, to burn during the divine office." (*C.P.R.* xii. 297.)

For the provision made by him for the schoolmaster and scholars of the town school of Dunfermline see page 167, and for details of the changes made by him on the nave, page 231.

" John de Bothwell, a monk of Dunfermline, received dispensation, being illegitimate, the son of unmarried parents. 6 July, 1447." (*C.P.R.* x. 352.)

Probably a relative—had he been the abbot's son, the form would have been, " son of a priest, and an unmarried woman."

Henry Crichton.   1470-71—1482

Like his predecessor, Richard de Bothwell, Crichton had previously been Abbot of Paisley, and thereby hangs a tale.

When Abbot Thomas of Paisley died, the Cardinal of St. Mark's, Venice, received from the Pope out of the revenues of Paisley a pension for life of 300 gold florins annually.

Henry Grethon (Crichton), learning of this, after his appointment, disputed payment, having probably paid well himself for the appointment, and a long and acrimonious dispute followed (*C.P.R.* xi, 388 and xii, 238), ending in the deposition of Crichton. Some three years later he made his peace with the authorities at Rome, and was restored, 27th February, 1469.

Soon afterwards he was appointed to Dunfermline, but again he was involved in serious contention. The story, as told by Bishop Lesley, is worth repeating.

" The abbacye of Dunfermeling vacand, the convent cheisit ane of their awn monkis, callit Alexander Thomsoun; and the King promovit Henry Creychtoun, abbot of Paisley thairto, quha wes preferrit be the Paip, through the Kingis supplicationis, to the said abbacye. And siclik, Mr. Robert Schaw, persoun of Mynto, was promovit be the King to the abbacye of Paisley. And sua than first began sic maner of promotione of secularis to abbacies by the Kingis supplicationis; and the godly erectionis war frustrate and dekayde, becaus that the court of Rome admittit the princis supplicationis, the rather that they gat greyt profrit and sowmes of money thairby; quhairfore the bischoppis durst not conferme them that wes chosen be the convent; nor thay quha wer electit durst not persew thair awn ryght. And sua the abbays cam to secular abussis, the abbots and pryouris being promovit furth of the court, quha levit court lyk, secularlye voluptouslye. And than ceissit all religious and godlye myndi. and deidis; Quhairwith the secularis and temporal men, beand sklanderit with thair evill example, fell frae all devoisoun and godlyness to the warkis of wikednes, quhairof daylie mekil evill did increase."

According to the Stirling Burgh Records (255), Crichton was Abbot of Dunfermline on 8th January, 1470-71, but his formal provision did not take place till 23rd December, 1471, in the presence of 14 cardinals, he paying 250 florins for common services. (*Apos. Cam.*)

" On 10 December, 1479, Henry Creichton, Abbot of Dunfermline, founded *de novo* the office of chaplain in the Chapel of St. James the Apostle in the Northferry, and bestowed it on ' our beloved chaplain Sir David Story.' The salary of the chaplain was 10 merks Scots, along with a manse and garden situated near the Chapel.

" Other emoluments were two acres of the low-lying lands of the Ferryhill; all the offerings made at the altar of the Chapel, with the exception of the oblations of the Pyx and those of the lights, which were reserved for lighting the Chapel; and 20 francs Scots annually for upholding the ornaments and vestments of the altar.

" The chaplain was required to perform a daily mass for the souls named in the Charter of Infeudation and to reside continually in the manse. Should he undertake any other cure, or involve himself in any other office, or have his residence elsewhere, thus causing the Services to suffer neglect, the chaplainry was to pass to the abbot or to his successor at the time, and be declared vacant. To the Abbey was reserved the patronage of the chaplain." (*Stephen, Hist. of Invkg., p.* 264.)

Adam Cant. 1483—1490

His " provision " is dated 16th April, 1483.

His reign was not long and does not seem to have been particularly eventful.

" A.D. 1489—Item, to a gentleman of the Kingis stabil to pass to Dunfermeling to warne the Abot of Dunfermeling for the Kingis cuming." (*Exch. Rolls* i, 128.)

" On the 4th of January (1489), the king rode to the moor of Lauder to the hawking. Returning by way of Edinburgh to Linlithgow he crossed the Forth on the 15th. to Dunfermline, to be the guest of the Abbot." (*Ibid*. i, xcviii.)

The only other reference to him that can be traced is to the effect that in 1489, the first year of James IV's reign, insurrection broke out and the Lords of the south and of the west were called to the host at Dumbarton, which the rebels had seized. Certain bishops and the abbots of Arbroath, Dunfermline, Lindores, and Scone were also summoned. But Dumbarton soon fell and the levies returned home. (*Accounts of the Lord High Treasurer*, i. 110.)

The last notice concerning him is dated 20th June, 1490. (*Reg.* 373.)

George Crichton. 1490—1499-1500

The exact date of his appointment is unknown, but we know that he was in office on 15th November, 1490 (*Antiq. Abdn. and*

Banff, iii, 418) and that he was still in office on 3rd February, 1499-1500. (*Fraser's Eglinton Bk.*, ii, 58.)

It is also known that on the day he was translated to Holyrood James Stewart was translated from Holyrood to Dunfermline, which, to say the least of it, is rather suggestive of "arrangement"—James Stewart being a son of King James III. (*Brady*, i. 182.)

Crichton afterwards became Bishop of Dunkeld, and Knox asserts that John Hamilton, Archbishop of St. Andrews, was by many "esteamed sone to the old Bischope of Dunkelden, called Crychtoun."

It is the case that a dispensation for defect of birth was given to Hamilton (*Dowden, Bps.*, 89), but the usually accepted version of the story is that he was the natural son of the first Earl of Arran.

"On the 21st of February, 1497-98, he (James IV) set out from Stirling intending to visit the Isles. . . .

"At Ayr he was joined by Lord Kennedy, and remained there till the 7th of March, fitting out one or more ships for his expedition, and awaiting the arrival of mariners from Leith. Several boats and their crews were hired for the conveyance of the king's retinue—one for the Laird of Fast Castle and Sir John Ramsay, another for the Abbot of Dunfermline's 'folks,' Sir Patrick Hamilton and the Laird of Cockpen. . . .

"Preparations being completed, a sea-mantle and other equipments furnished for the king, and a bed fitted up for him in the ship, he sailed on the 8th of March." (*Accounts of the Lord High Treasurer*, i. clxiv.)

"Item, James Wilsonis bote and his marinalis, feit sic like to the Abbot of Dunfermlynis folkis, Schir Patrik Hammiltoune and the Lard of Cokpen. iiij li. (£4.)" (*Ibid.* 379.)

During George Crichton's tenure of office there are frequent references in the Burgh Records, 1496 to 1499, to William Grant, "indultour" or "Pardonar,"—not to be confused with William Grant, "the laird."

All the references concern his presence as a member of the court, but not one of them conveys the slightest information about him, except the last (334) which describes him as "of St. Anthony's power (*sic*) in Leith and husband of Marjory Patonson."

Clearly he was not a monk, but in what capacity he sat as a member of the court there is nothing to indicate. It is easy to understand, however, that an official resident dispenser of indulgences, " bretful of pardons, come from Rome all hot," was a likely source of considerable income. The practice of commuting penance for money payments had become general long before this.

The Augustinian House of St. Anthony, Leith, the only house of the kind within the realm, was begun by James I, who had been nineteen years in captivity in England where several institutions of the Order existed. It was devoted to the care of those afflicted with erysipelas, then thought to be a form of leprosy, and termed St. Anthony's Fire, which was so prevalent in Scotland that it was a matter of concern for the nation and formed the subject of parliamentary regulations. (*Soc. of Antiq.* 1929-30, pp. 275-7.)

By the special indulgence of the Pope, " all and sundry Christ's faithful, truly confessed and contrite, who shall devoutly visit the said hospital on the feast of the said saint . . . and shall stretch out helping hands for the sustentation and refreshing of the poor, infirm and other persons, shall receive seven years of relaxation and as many quarantines of imposed penance." (*Scott. Suppl.* 12-13.)

In the last year of George Crichton's tenure of office the town was visited with plague, and so serious did the situation become that the Burgh Authorities forbade the sale of victuals to any outside the town—anyone acting to the contrary to be apprehended by the alderman and bailies, and the victual confiscated, except for small quantities of bread and ale. (*B.R.* 9th July, 1499.)

Visitations of plague were not perhaps so frequent, but possibilities of famine had always to be reckoned with.

" In 1303 there was a great famine in the land—the poorer sort fed on grass, and many were found dead in the fields." (*Hailes' Annals*, ii. 300.)

From the start it had been the practice in every monastery for the almoner to give attendance at the gate at certain specified times for a distribution of broken meats and a dole of money to travellers, or others, who were in need. But, with all the resources they had behind them, there is pitifully little evidence of organised efforts on the part of the monks to deal with these recurrent tragedies. It has, however, to be said that, after they had been dispossessed and these resources fell into other hands, there is even less evidence of their being voluntarily applied to philanthropic or charitable purposes of any sort.

Robert Blacader

According to Dr. Chalmers (i. 192-3), quoting Hay's *Scotia Sacra*, Robert Blacader, Abbot of Dunfermline, died in the course of a journey to Syria in 1500.

There was a Robert Blacader about this time, a brother of Sir Patrick Blacader of Tulliallan, who became Bishop of Aberdeen and Archbishop of Glasgow, but a comparison of dates does not confirm the idea of identification. Dr. Chalmers suggests that there may possibly have been two ecclesiastics of the same name about the same time.

Dowden in his notes on the bishop says nothing about his ever having been Abbot of Dunfermline.

Herkless and Hannay (*Archbps*. i. 193), quoting Brady (i. 178) say that on 3rd June, 1500, James Stewart was made Commendator of Dunfermline, which had become vacant through the translation of Abbot George. And later : " George Crichton was translated to Holyrood (Brady i. 182) and James Stewart, on the same day, from Holyrood to Dunfermline."

It looks as if Hay had slipped up in this matter and Dr. Chalmers had simply taken his word for it.

James Stewart.   1500—1503-04

He was the second son of James III and Margaret of Denmark. Appointed to Dunfermline on 3rd June, 1500, the sum of 250 florins was offered in his name on 21st August, which shows that, brother though he was to the king, he was not exempt from the usual demand for a year's income from the Pope.

Some of the appointments he held may have been more or less genuine, but the ecclesiastical ones—Abbot of Arbroath, Abbot of Dunfermline, and Archbishop of St. Andrews—were merely held *in commendam*, to enable him to draw the revenue attached. So far as Dunfermline was concerned, his tenure of office can have been of very little account, the duties being undertaken doubtless by the prior, but, to judge by a letter addressed to him by the king, he must have been there on 31st October, 1502.

His record of office as Archbishop of St. Andrews, and those of Alexander Stewart, James Beaton and Andrew Forman, are so exhaustively set forth in *The Archbishops of St. Andrews*, by Herkless and Hannay, that there is no need to dwell upon them here, except in so far as the interests of Dunfermline are concerned. Their comment on James Stewart is as follows :—

" James Stewart is in truth but one of a wilderness of names. . . . By his tenure of great offices, for which he was in no special way fitted, he simply serves to illustrate a phase in the degradation of the Church of Scotland."

He died in 1503-04 at the age of 28, and was buried at St. Andrews.

James Beaton. 1504—1510

The youngest son of the Laird of Balfour, his advance in office was unusually rapid—Provost of Bothwell in 1503, Prior of Whithorn, Abbot of Dunfermline and a Lord of Session in 1504. His appointment to Dunfermline was subject to certain conditions, and, though these were not unduly serious, he petitioned for tenure *ad vitam*, and in 1506 received an extension of time wherein to hold the living without assuming the habit or making profession, for, though in priest's orders, he was not a monk.

During his first tenure of office in Dunfermline—he had a second innings from 1522-1526—the same sort of question arose in connection with Stirling as Andrew of Kirkcaldy had to deal with at Perth. Eventually an agreement was entered into in 1507 whereby the abbot and convent contributed the sum of £200 for building that portion of the Church of Stirling which was afterwards known as the East Church, together with an allowance of " fourtie schillings usuale money " for the upholding of " all ornaments necessar baith for holy dais and wark dais that thai aucht to have "—the provost and bailies thereafter becoming responsible for the maintenance of both choir and ornaments.

Twice, in the course of the year 1505, James Beaton, as Abbot of Dunfermline, sent a present of a horse to the king, the Lord High Treasurer's Accounts showing a payment of 5s. in the one case, and 14s. in the other, for "bridilsilver." Bridle-silver was the present given to the servant who delivered the horse to the king, varying, it would seem, according to the value of the horse.

From the same source we gather that the king, James IV, bought a horse at Dunfermline that had evidently taken his fancy, and paid well for it.

"1508—last day of April, in Dunfermline.—To ane callit Mure for ane hors quhilk ran up the staris of the cors (Cross)—£26 13s. 4d." (iv. 21.)

"1504-05—To ane fischair of Dunfermlyn that brocht gret pikis to the king—3s." (iii. 132.)

"1504-05, 23 Feb.—To Alexr. Kers, to lous (return) the Kingis stope (stoup, flagon) quhilk wes taen quhen he wes Abbot of Unresoun—£13 4s." (iii. 127.)

"It was, I think, peculiar to the Roman Catholic Church that, while they studied how to render their church rites imposing and magnificent by all that pomp, music, architecture and external display could add to them, they nevertheless connived, upon special occasions, at the frolics of the rude vulgar, who, in almost all Catholic countries, enjoyed, or at least assumed, the privilege of making some Lord of the revels, who, under the name of the Abbot of Unreason, the Boy Bishop, or the President of Fools, occupied the churches, profaned the holy places by a mock imitation of the sacred rites, and sung indecent parodies on hymns of the Church." (*Sir Walter Scott: The Abbot.*)

"1505-06—To priests in Dunfermline 42s." Reason not given. (iii. 71.)

"1504—Relic of St. Duthus from Dunfermline to Tain—5s." (ii. 467.)

No explanation is offered of this last entry, but we know that Tain was a popular resort of pilgrims in pre-Reformation days, and that James IV visited the saint's shrine there several times, the last occasion being in 1513, barely a month before his death at Flodden. We know also from the Treasurer's Accounts that a "silver-gilt relique of St. Duthac" was made by his command in 1507-08, to replace the old relic that had been broken.

Does it not look as if the monastery at Dunfermline had been called on for a " spare " to meet the needs of the pilgrims to Tain until a new one could be provided ?

In 1508 Beaton became bishop-elect of Galloway, whilst retaining Dunfermline, and James IV suggested that he be transferred to the more lucrative See of Glasgow, so that he might be able to resign Dunfermline in favour of Alexander Stewart, the king's own natural son, then Archbishop of St. Andrews (*Dowden, Bps.*, 339)—Beaton's appointment, as the king is careful to point out, being only " pro tempore."

Alexander Stewart. 1510—1513

The exact date of succession is uncertain. Beaton appears in office as early as 22nd February, 1504-05, and continued till 17th June, 1510. (*Douglas book, Sir William Fraser*, iii, 194.)

And yet it is on record that Stewart was provided *in commendam* January, 1508-09. (*Vat. Transc. Reg. Ho.* iii, 187.)

In spite of the fact that there was an " aetas legitima," he was only 14 years old when he was appointed Archbishop of St. Andrews, and not much older when he became Abbot of Dunfermline.

Erasmus, who was his tutor, gives him an excellent character, but he got little chance to show what was in him, being slain, with his father, at the Battle of Flodden in 1513. It is worth recording that not only was the Abbot of Dunfermline slain on that occasion, but that the prior, Adam Forman, brother of the better known Andrew Forman, who was acting as standard-bearer, was taken prisoner. (*Crawfurd* 59-60.) He must have regained his freedom, for he was again acting as prior in 1525. (*H. & H.* ii, 6n.)

James Hepburn. 1513—1516

Appears as *postulate* 26th November, 1513 (*Acts of Parl.* ii. 281) and continues as such till 7th January, 1516 (*A.D.C.*, p. 68).

Dr. Chalmers, however, is mistaken in representing him as son of Adam, Lord Hailes. He was the son of Alexander Hepburn of Whitsome (*Dowden's Bps.*, 167.)

By arrangement with Andrew Forman, who also claimed the office, he resigned in his favour and became Bishop of Moray in succession to Forman. Arrangements of the sort were not uncommon about this time.

Andrew Forman.   1516—1522

Born about 1465 of the family of Formans settled at Hutton, Berwickshire, he was attached for a time to the household of the Earl of Arran, and from that passed to the service of the king, finding favour also with the Pope.

On the death of Alexander Stewart at Flodden, he became Archbishop of St. Andrews, and is credited with having been one of the best statesmen of his day; but historians differ widely in their estimate of his character.

So highly did Pope Julius II rate him that he is said to have intended to make him a cardinal. This is borne out by a notarial instrument recorded in the *Formulare* (No. civ. f. 89), according to which Forman, along with the prior and convent, appointed procurators to promise a payment of 5,000 ducats to the bankers for the Roman Court. Because of the death of that Pope, the proposal did not materialise, but he was Archbishop of Bourges, and Commendator of Pittenweem, as well as Abbot of Dunfermline—probably holding all three offices at one and the same time.

Another instrument (No. cx. f. 90) contains an acknowledgment of his indebtedness for 500 marks Scots to a creditor " who had granted him possessions to be sold, in his urgent necessity, for the payment of his debts to the Roman Court on account of the bulls (in connection with) the said archbishopric and abbacy. If he does not repay the 500 marks by Easter, he binds himself to the payment of double."

In addition to Adam, Prior of Dunfermline and Standard-bearer at Flodden, he had another brother, Robert, who was Dean of Glasgow (*H. & H.* iii. 167). He was buried in Dunfermline Abbey.

James Beaton.   1522—1526

Though now Archbishop of St. Andrews, he reappears as Abbot of Dunfermline, 20th January, 1523-24.

The following incident illustrates the legal controversies which constantly arose when a great benefice changed hands :—

" Andrew Forman, as Commendator, had let certain lands to his brother the Dean of Glasgow, for a period of nineteen years, and Beaton sought to invalidate the transaction. The case was taken to the Court of Rome, which named two churchmen as arbiters.

" Hew Spens, the provost of St. Salvator's in St. Andrews, acting as sub-delegate, cited Robert Forman; and he, on his way to the church, was roughly handled by one of Beaton's servitors, accompanied by many armed men.

" An excellent opportunity was afforded for a counter-appeal to Rome, and Forman took instruments that there was no ' safe access ' to St. Andrews, that, before the citation, Beaton had resigned the commendatorship, and that Spens was not an impartial judge, being an official of the archbishop." (*H. & H.* iii. 166-7.) Soon after he became archbishop, Beaton founded the New Divinity (St. Mary's) College and began to build it, though he did not live to complete it. He is also credited with having built fourteen bridges.

Officially he was responsible for the trial and martyrdom of Patrick Hamilton, almost at his own door, but it is generally felt that his nephew, afterwards Cardinal Beaton, had quite as much to do with the matter as he had.

(*Note.*—It has commonly been supposed that no native of Scotland was ever elevated to the college of Cardinals before the celebrated Beaton, but George Innes, born in Scotland in the fourteenth century, of the Order of Trinitarians, was by Pope Urban VI created Cardinal of Saint Laurence in Lucina. He declined the honour, but Pope John XXIII, who had himself been legate in Scotland, and from personal acquaintance knew the worth of Father Innes, prosecuted the design of his predecessor. He renewed the creation of cardinal, and at the same time laid his injunctions on him to accept the dignity. This done, he called him to the Council of Constance, where he assisted until its termination in the year 1418. (*Archaeologia Scotica*, ii. 130.))

Since James Beaton was abbot and archbishop at the same time, it goes almost without saying that his duties at Dunfermline must have fallen largely into the hands of the prior, but in the year 1525 he spent some considerable time in Dunfermline. (*State Papers*, iv. 407.)

George Durie. 1526—1560

If Beaton continued beyond 1526, it can only have been as *usufructuar*, for George Durie, his nephew and successor, Archdeacon of St. Andrews, was granted Dunfermline Abbey,

23rd May, 1526, under papal provision, "with reservation of fruits, regress and collation of benefices" in favour of his predecessor in office—the tax paid to the Pope for the appointment being 250 florins. (*Brady*, i. 178.) For further particulars concerning Durie, see *History of Carnock*.

Among MSS. of the Earl of Rothes at Leslie is a feu charter by George, Commendator of Dunfermline, setting in feufarme a part of the lands of Stenton, with a licence to the tenants to dig for coals at their own expense, paying to the convent every ninth load. And if they made any sinks or holes to find coal and did not find it they were bound to fill these up at their own expense. This is dated 12th January, 1555.

About this period there seems to have been an alarm lest the coal should be quickly exhausted, and an act was passed in 1563 restraining export, and frequently repeated.

Smithy coal was permitted to be exported in 1565 by Act of Privy Council.

Durie's active connection with the monastery ceased in 1560, but, from a reference in Laing Charters (No. 1090), dated 5th December, 1563, where Pitcairn was acting for Durie, it looks as if he had still some interest. The story that Durie was canonised has no foundation in fact.

Robert Pitcairn.   1560—1583-84

Said to have been the son of a sister of George Durie, and, like him, had also been Archdeacon of St. Andrews.

He was the first of the commendators following the Reformation, and unlike his successors, is said by Bellesheim to have espoused Protestantism. This assertion would seem to be confirmed by his application to the Kirk Session for a "Heighe seat" in the parish kirk. He held office till, at least, 14th March, 1583-84 (*Reg. Ho. Charter No.* 2715b) and is mentioned as deceased 22nd March, 1584-85 (*Yester Writs, No.* 848). In 1583 he had been denounced as rebel for his share in the Raid of Ruthven. His name is associated with occupation of the Abbot House in the Maygate, Dunfermline, and with the following inscription on its doorway:—

> "Sen Vord is Thrall and Thocht is Fre
> Keep Veill Thy Tonge I Coinsell The."

After his death, John Fenton, described as " Comptroller-Clerk " was appointed Administrator of the Abbey, 8th November, 1584 (*Indexes P. to B.*)—though what exactly was the nature of his duties is not specified.

Patrick, Master of Gray. 1585—1586
Was something of " a dark horse," a man of considerable ability but was eventually banished from the kingdom, and his estates forfeited. Though reputed a papist, he went in 1584 to church at Berwick with Lord Hunsdon and astonished him by his obvious familiarity with the prayer-book and usage of the Church of England. (*Cal. Scott. Papers*, vii. 366.)

George, Earl of Huntly. 1587—1589
This is the man who, to gratify his revenge, attacked the House of Donibristle and burned it to the ground, killing the " Bonnie Earl o' Moray," 8th February, 1591-92.

Henry Pitcairn. 1587—
Is styled commendator in 1593, though not strictly one of the number. Curiously enough, there is a reference to his having received a gift of the Abbey on 26th December, 1582, in succession to Robert Pitcairn, but it is not unusual to find a certain amount of confusion of this kind.

In 1589 James VI presented the Abbey to his consort as a marriage gift, and this was confirmed by a crown charter in 1593.

In the same year it was perpetually annexed to the Crown by Act of Parliament.

MONKS OF DUNFERMLINE

According to the *Registrum*, the monastery started off in 1124 with a membership of thirteen, brought by King David from Canterbury—symbolical of Christ and His disciples.

From the same source we gather that by 1230 the number had increased to fifty, and in a Kineddar Charter of 1321 we hear of an addition of two to the number, with provision for their maintenance.

Despite a tendency to magnify the number of monastics, and the fact that, with the possible exception of Arbroath, it was the most renowned monastery in Scotland, it is doubtful if Dunfermline had at any time many more than fifty full-fledged monks.

In addition to the regulars, there were chaplains, whose duty it was to serve at the various altars, though monks too sometimes performed that duty. Dr. Chalmers reckons the number of altars in the Abbey as 15. Dr. Henderson brings the number up to 20; but Dr. Erskine Beveridge is a little doubtful about one or two of the 20.

There were also several Chapels in Dunfermline and its neighbourhood, each served by its own chaplain :—

" The Chapel of St. James, the Apostle, North Queensferry, given in 1323 by William, Bishop of St. Andrews, to the Abbey, for the service of which the monks shall find two chaplains to celebrate divine worship, and shall also provide a chalice, vestments, books and ornaments suitable to a chapel." (*Dalyell*, 36.)

The Chapel of St. John, the Baptist, stood at Garvock, its lands being mentioned in *R.M.S.*, 6th September, 1584, and *Reg. Dunf.* 486.

The Chapel of St. Catherine, the Virgin (of Alexandria, that is, not Siena), stood a little to the north-west of the Abbey, beyond the street known as St. Catherine's Wynd.

The Chapel and Hospital of St. Leonard—near the old St. Leonard's School.

St. Mary's Chapel—on the south side of the Netherton, at the east corner of Grange Road. According to Dr. Henderson

(*Annals*, 512, 585), one of its walls fell in 1783, and the last vestige was removed in 1814. "Rent of Pitrenny granted for Chapel of St. Mary at Dunfermline in 1388." (*Exch.* iii. 166.)

This chapel is to be distinguished from the Lady Chapel in the Conventual Church, to which reference is made *c.* 1320. (*Reg.* 357.)

" St. Ninian's Chapel (sometimes referred to as St. Ringane's) between the High Street and West Queen Anne Street, not far east from Collier Row (now Bruce Street). ' Fundit and erekit within the burgh of Dunfermlyn be vmquhill of gud memour Mastir Johne Cristisone (Vicar of Cleish), and Schir Johne Brovne, Chaplane of the said chapell.' " (*B.R.* xxvii-xxx.)

Dr. Chalmers also refers (i. 160) to a St. Michael's Chapel, probably in the vicinity of Broomhall House. There may have been, but no reference can be traced to it either in the *Registrum* or the Burgh Records.

Including tradesmen and servants, the total number of men connected, one way or other, with the monastery must have been considerable.

As for lands and other properties gifted to it, the following list has been compiled by Professor A. R. Macewen (*Hist.* i. 175-7), but he is careful to point out that it is far from exhaustive, that, as a rule, only one gift of each type has been quoted, and that charters which are not undoubtedly genuine have not been taken into account :—

" Broomhill, Pitcorthy, Petbachly, Pitnaurcha, Bolgie, Kirk-aldyshire, Inveresk, Lauar, Inveresk Minor, Hailes in Edinburgh-shire and lands in Kinglassie, Raith, Humbie and other parishes on both sides of the Forth. To these he (the king) added Kinghorn, Inveresk Major, with mill and fishings, dwellings (*mansurae*) in Edinburgh, Berwick, Stirling and Perth, the church of the burgh of Perth (St. John Baptist's) and a rent of 100 shillings secured on property in England, these properties being freed from all burdens except military service, an eighth part of all payments and fines due to the Royal Court of Fife and Fothrif, a tenth of rents paid to the king in the same district, a tenth of the game brought to Dunfermline, half of the hides and fat of all beasts killed in the royal kitchen on the occasion of banquets held at Stirling and anywhere between the Forth and the Tay, one ship free of duty at all ports, and the right of taking wood for building and fire from the king's forests, all the offerings laid upon the Great Altar of the church, every seventh seal caught at Kinghorn after deduction of tenths, and a tenth of the salt and iron brought to Dunfermline for the king's use. Further, it was ordained that Holy Trinity should be exempt from subjection and payment to any secular or ecclesiastical power and should enjoy the same liberties as the Church of St. Andrews.

" In the same year, by a separate deed, a tenth of the provisions brought to the king's house at Perth was secured to the Abbey.

" In 1130 the abbot and monks were set free for ever from all work on castles, bridges and other undertakings. A tithe of the pennies of the king's census at Stirling was assigned to the abbot.

" The Abbey was gifted with the harbour dues of Musselburgh and with a ploughgate in the parish of Liberton and the houses inhabited by the wife of Roger Cass, reserving her liferent. The abbot's own ship with its cargo was exempted from all dues.

" In 1133 there was a gift of a tithe of the flour, cheese, barley for brewing, pigs and cows, and of payments in specie due to the king from Fife, Fothrif and Clackmannan.

" In 1135 the king enacted that the people of Newburn shall not be subject to any other court than that of the Holy Trinity and its abbot, at which the king's ' judex ' shall always be present to see that justice is done.

" In 1136 a fishing in the Tweed and a toft in Berwick were assigned to the Church of Holy Trinity.

" In 1140 a saltpan beside the king's saltpans within Stirling territory was given to the abbey, the workers to be protected by the king's Peace; also, certain lands in Morayshire, with their pertinents, and freedom to hunt in the woods, these lands too to be held under the king's Peace.

" In 1143 the property of Carberry in Midlothian was given to Holy Trinity. Between 1147 and 1153 a toft in Haddington free from all dues and servitudes, the right of taking building-material from the king's woods, the ' villae ' of Nithbren and Belacristin (reserving the rights of the Culdees), and the churches of West Calder and Kirknewton, with the lands adjacent to these churches, were gifted to Holy Trinity, the Abbey and the monks; also a toft in Haddington, bestowed by the widow of the king's son, a church at Dunkeld and five properties near Coupar Angus.

The North Porch.   Part of Abbot de Bothwell's Scheme.   This was placed in front
of the original Norman Doorway.

" By a special confirmation, Robert, Bishop of St. Andrews, recognised the right of Dunfermline Abbey to ' possess ' ten specified churches with all their pertinents, including in two cases schools, free from all servitudes and secular dues, with reservation of episcopal right and due."

" This one Abbey," Professor Macewen goes on to say, " in addition to possessions in its immediate vicinity, acquired lands as far north as Elgin and as far south as Berwick; houses in widely scattered burghs; trading rights, fishing rights and hunting rights; exemptions from taxation, from specific dues and from body-services; a proportion of some payments due to the king, varying from a half to a tenth; numerous churches with their endowments and the offerings of the faithful at the local altar."

We have seen that not a few of the Abbots of Dunfermline attained to power and position in national affairs, but with regard to " other ranks " (obedientiaries) it is surprising, and not a little disappointing, to find that so few names stand out.

With a membership of 30 to 50, over something like 400 years, all of them having the advantage of a Grammar School education, and five per cent. of them supposed to have spent four years at a University, it might have been thought that not a few would have left their mark. They may in fact have done so, but the evidence is not outstanding.

It is not easy, one admits, to see clearly across a chasm of four or five centuries, but here and there a figure does emerge dimly from the mist.

In the first half of the twelfth century—very soon, that is, after the foundation of the monastery—there was a monk of Dunfermline of the name of **Andrew** who so commended himself to the authorities that he was nominated to the bishopric of Caithness in 1130—the first appointment to that See. Unfortunately, the revenue from the diocese was so scanty and precarious that, to make life possible, he had to be given in commendam the church of the Holy Trinity at Dunkeld. (*Cupar* i. 321.)

In 1153, King David died and was succeeded by Malcolm, a boy of 12 years old. The Earl of Fife had been selected as his guardian, but he died the following year, and the government of the country fell largely into the hands of the young king's mother, the chancellor of the kingdom, and Andrew, Bishop of Caithness. In addition to doing "his bit" in national affairs, he is credited by his contemporaries with being an authority on the geography of Scotland.

It was he who gave to Dunfermline (*Reg.* 123) the lands of Bendochy and Coupar-maculty (now Couttie, N.W. of Coupar)—a gift that led to trouble *c.* 1221 between the monasteries of Dunfermline and Coupar-Angus—but the lands remained in the possession of Dunfermline till the Reformation. The Church of Bendochy was, however, restored to Coupar. (*Charters, Coupar-Angus,* i. 74.)

One of the few things that can with confidence be said about him is that he was more fortunate than his immediate successors in the bishopric, for he died at Dunfermline, 29th December, 1184—at peace, so far as one can judge, with all mankind— whereas John, the second bishop, being in a castle which was stormed and captured by the Earl of Caithness, had his tongue cut out (*Dowden, Bps.,* 232); while Adam, the third bishop, a foundling, it would seem, laid at the door of a church, was as the result of a dispute between him and his flock, stripped, beaten, stoned, mortally wounded with a fork and burned. (*C.P.L.* i. 89.)

About the same period there was a Prior of Dunfermline, Richard Mongal by name, of whom Fordun speaks very highly (i. 441).

Unfortunately we know little or nothing about him, except that he was the author of a small work entitled *Lives of St. Bernard and St. Abelard,* and that he died about the end of 1148 at St. James of Compostella, in Spain, where he had gone on pilgrimage.

Another misty figure that emerges is **Arnald (alias John) Blair.**

"Born in the county of Fife, in the reign of Alexander III, and educated with Sir William Wallace at the school of Dundee, he went to France, studied at Paris, and entered into holy orders. . . .

"On his return to Scotland, he retired to the Benedictine cloister of Dunfermline. But when Sir William Wallace was made governor or viceroy of the kingdom in 1297, he was called out of the monastery and made his chaplain; and, being an eye-witness of most of his actions, he composed the history of his life in Latin." (*Mackenzie's Scots Writers.*)

It is a pity that this story cannot be accepted unreservedly. It is not seriously questioned that John Blair may have acted as chaplain to Sir William Wallace and written the story of his life. There is, moreover, documentary evidence that three sons of Sir Alexander de Blair, Adam, David and George, were members of the monastery of Dunfermline c. 1278. (*Reg.* 213.)

But, according to the *Book of Wallace* (ii. 257) the statement by Dr. George Mackenzie that John Blair entered the monastery of Dunfermline under the name of " Arnald " rests on no historical basis.

About the beginning of the fifteenth century we encounter another figure—this time with a little more flesh and blood.

Dr. Henderson, with his usual partiality for anything and everything connected with Dunfermline, describes him as **William Brown,** monk of Dunfermline, " the eminent theologian and poet." (*Annals*, 167.)

Brown was, no doubt, a promising student in his day, being one of those selected for a University course. His knowledge of theology is more or less vouched for by the fact that he took his degree as a Bachelor of Theology—a somewhat unusual accomplishment at the time. His claim to recognition as a poet rests on the more doubtful ground of a disputed reading of a line in Dunbar's *Lament for the Death of the Makars.*

The Maitland MS. runs :—

" In dunfermling he (Death) hes done rowne
    With maister robert Hendersoun."

The Bannatyne MS., on the other hand, renders it :—

" In dunfermling he hes taen Broun
    with Maister Robert Henrisoun."

No satisfactory explanation has yet been offered of what " done rowne " means. But " taen Broun " is quite intelligible, and the association of the two names by Dunbar is natural, seeing that the two men were not only contemporaries but both connected with Dunfermline.

Lord Hailes in his *Ancient Scottish Poems* supports the Bannatyne reading and includes in his reference a poem by Broun on *The Judgment of God.*

Dr. MacLean Watt also supports the reading " taen Broun." " Dunbar," he says, " was sick, and was thinking things over seriously, probably hearing the far-off sigh of the tide of the

Eternal on the shadowy shore, and he, in thought, mentions some whom he considers of the immortals, and lo! death has taken them.

" Regarding some of those mentioned by him there is little or nothing known, so that such a criticism does not justify the attempt to sweep Brown aside, particularly when in the Bannatyne MS. there is a poem by a man of the same name." (*Private letter*.)

There are in fact two poems in the Bannatyne MSS., one immediately following the other, which seem to have a good deal in common, though only one of them is signed by Brown.

Mr. N. F. Donald, English Master at Dunfermline High School, who has examined both poems carefully, while admitting that the contiguity of the two in the Bannatyne MSS., the similarity in theme, and the correspondence in metrical irregularity are facts that must be reckoned with, is unable to say definitely whether or not both should be attributed to Brown.

There is, he says, about the poem signed by Brown a flavour of the morality *Everyman*, and he singles out for favourable notice the image used in the following line :—

" Trymland for dreid As dois the leif on trie."

The poem, running to seventeen stanzas of 8 lines each, is too long for reproduction, but Mr. Donald suggests, as typical of the age, two stanzas :—

> " ffra hevin to hell Throw erd and air
> That hiddouss trump sa lowid sall sound
> That throw the blast I you declair
> The stanis sall cleive erd sall redound
> Sall no man respect get that stound
> ffor gold for riches or for rent
> ffor all mon cum ouir see and sound
> And present thame to Iugement.
> Gif ye haif keipit Iust and richt
> The law ellyk to riche and peure
> With blyth hairt in the Iugeis sicht
> Ye may appeir I you assure
> Haif ye misgorvernit ocht your cure
> Sair may ye dreid the hard torment
> Off hellis fiyre that sall Indure
> perpetuall eftir Iugement."

As an example of the often used image of the shepherd and his flock the following stanza is also worth repetition:—

" Ye men of kirk that care hes tane
      of sawlis, for to wetsche and keip,
      Ye will be tynt and ye tyne ane,
      In your defalt, of Goddis scheip;
      Be walkand ay that ye not sleip,
      Luke that your bow be reddy bent,
      The wolf about your flok will creip
      Ye mon make compt at Iugement."

And for general application:—

" Be gude of lyfe, and bissie ay
      Your gud examples for to schaw,
      stark in the faith, and luk allwey
      That na man cryme unto you knaw,
      Let ay your deid follow your saw
      And to this taill ye tak gud tent
      Say-weil bot do-weil is nocht worth a straw
      ffor you to schaw in Iugement."

(*Note.—bot*, a contraction for be-out, *without*.)

For further particulars concerning William Brown, see pp. 192, 201.

About the same period as William Brown, a monk of Dunfermline is credited with having painted a portrait of Joan of Arc. The story is interspersed with too many suppositions and conjectures to be quite convincing, but is interesting none the less. It is recorded as follows in Robert Brydall's *History of Art in Scotland* (p. 45):—

" At the trial of the unfortunate Maid, she was questioned as to whether she had ever seen, or caused to have painted, a portrait or image of herself, and replied that at Rheims she had seen in the hands of a Scotchman a picture resembling her in armour, kneeling on a cushion in the act of presenting a letter to the king.

" There appears in the royal accounts of France for the year 1420 the name of Hames Poulvoir, a painter who was then probably at Poitiers, and with more certainty at Tours, between 1428 and 1431.

" It was this Poulvoir who painted the white banner of Jeanne d'Arc—*semée* with *fleurs de lis*, with a world and two angels, and the motto " Jhesus Marie." His daughter was a friend of La Pucelle, and she was married at the cost of the *bourgeois* of Tours.

"When it is considered that the name of Polwarth is a well-known Scotch one; that the name of Poulvoir is not native French, and not unlike Polwarth; and also that Hames is the ancient Scoto-French form of James—we may believe that a Scottish artist was the author of the portrait described by Joan in her examination,—a not unreasonable supposition to anyone familiar with the transformation of Scottish surnames in old French history.

"Another of these strangers, if not the same, followed La Pucelle in all her campaigns, and did not quit her till he had witnessed the barbarous tragedy at Rouen, and afterwards ended his life as a monk in the Abbey of Dunfermline.

"It is known that this monk was familiar with, or left some account of, the life of the heroine, the existence of which is as yet undiscovered; and it is supposed that the Dunfermline monk, the painter of the white banner and the thus mentioned portrait, was the same individual."

To round the story off, the author adds the following note :—

"The same Dunfermline monk is mentioned, after returning from France, in the Preface to the Marchmont and Bodleian MSS. of Fordun, as compiling twelve books of that history at the command of the Abbot of Dunfermline."

"*The Book of Pluscarden* (the book apparently referred to in the previous sentence) is thought to have been written by a Dunfermline monk after Pluscarden had ceased to be a Vallis-caulian House and had been colonised anew by the Dunfermline Benedictines.

"Mr. Felix Skene, in his Introduction, gives reasons for attributing the authorship to one Maurice of Buchanan, and the date to 1461." (*B.R.* xxxiii.)

Apart from the abbots, easily the most outstanding name associated with the monastery is that of **Robert Henryson,** the poet. One only wishes that his connection with the monastery and town could be established on an even surer basis. That it was of Dunfermline he was thinking when he wrote :—

"Allone as I went up and doun
In ane abbay was fair to se,"

is not seriously questioned.

It is also generally accepted that he was schoolmaster of Dunfermline in the second half of the fifteenth century. In this there is no inherent improbability, but there is no contemporary evidence in support of it.

What we do know is that he was a Licentiate in Arts and Bachelor in Decrees of Glasgow in 1462, and that he was Notary of Dunfermline Abbey in 1477-78. The earliest reference to him as schoolmaster dates from the beginning of the seventeenth century. (*David Laing, Poems of R.H.*)

Even if he was not a full-fledged monk, it is good to know that he was at least an official of the monastery.

It is not, of course, suggested for a moment that these were the only people of any interest or importance amongst the " other ranks " of Dunfermline during all these years, but contemporary records are few and far between, and details, except in the case of personages of the very highest standing, meagre in the extreme.

Even in the narrower circle of local records it is disappointing, though not altogether surprising, to find how seldom a reference occurs to any of these men. In spite of the fact that they constituted a not-inconsiderable proportion of the community, the Burgh Records, for instance, which are more or less a reflex of the communal life, reveal remarkably few points of contact with them. Such references as there are can be readily enough recognised, as a rule, by the titles appended to their names— *Sir* or *Schir* for chaplains, and *Dene* for monks.

> " All monks, as you may hear and see,
> Are callit denes for dignity.
> Although his mother milk the coo,
> He must be callit Dene Andro."
>
> (*Sir David Lindsay.*)

We read of certain sums received by the Burgh Treasurer " fra Dene Andro Gray to the playte " (memorandum book or tablet), but whether it was on behalf of the convent or on his own account is not indicated.

We read of John Christison, Vicar of Cleish, founding St. Ninian's Chapel, and we have a detailed account of money left by Dene John Spendluff (Spendlaw), " tutor to our Lady aisle," for masses at certain specified altars for himself and relatives.

71

Only once did an entry find its way into the record that had apparently slipped the censor. In the year 1498, at a meeting of the Chapter, the abbot, " through his treasurer and Tom Buquhanan took Alexander Aitton furth of the tolbuth (jail)."

This, in the opinion of the Burgh authorities, was a most unwarrantable interference with the prerogative of the provost.

The monastery, however, had its own place of confinement and its own means of punishment and the abbot, as lord of regality, had ample powers in a matter of the sort. He could demand that any culprit who dwelt within his jurisdiction should be sent back to be judged and dealt with by him, even if he had to find caution that he would do justice within a year and a day on the malefactor.

It is not expressly said that Alexander Aitton was a monk, but the impression left on one's mind is that he had some connection with the monastic community, otherwise the drastic intervention of the abbot is difficult to understand.

The incident is interesting as illustrating the growing tendency of Burghs to assert their independence, but even while they protested, they were not too confident. As late as June, 1491, a Burgh Court was postponed because " the Stewart's Court " had not been held—referring, doubtless, to the Steward of the Court of Regality.

Quite clearly the burgh officials were inclined to study prudence rather than risk a head-on clash.

" The lands belonging to the abbey were held in full regality whence even capital crimes could be tried by a bailie appointed by the abbot. Thus, if any of the men on the territories of the abbey committed a crime, they could be repledged from the supreme criminal courts of the kingdom and brought to the abbot's court.

" As early as the reign of David I it is declared that they shall be bound to answer nowhere but in the court of the Holy Trinity and the Abbot of Dunfermline." (*Dalyell*, 18.)

" In addition to Regality, the Abbot of Dunfermline had an eighth of the fines and escheats of the courts in Fife, both Justiciary and Sheriff, in virtue of early royal grants." (*Exch.* i. lviii.)

Mr. Dalyell, writing in 1809, goes on to say:—

" Many volumes of the records of this judicature were lately found in a garret in Dunfermline, covered with dust. The date of the oldest does not ascend higher than 1582, and the last comes down to the eighteenth century.

"There are several instances of capital sentences pronounced on criminals by the bailie of regality.

"In 1587, Hew Watt, vagabond, is convicted of stealing cattle and condemned ' to be hangit to the deaith on Baldris gallows, or ellis drounit, at will of the judges.'

"In 1583 Andro Stewart, vagabond, is sentenced to be ' brunt on the richt schoulder with the common marking yron of Dunfermline, scourged and banisched.' The trials are by juries, sometimes of eleven or thirteen persons." (*Dalyell*, 19.)

The records must have found their way to the strong room in Dunfermline City Chambers, from which they were recently transferred to the Historical Department of the Records Office, Edinburgh.

The Regality Seal is still in existence. Mr. Dalyell says :—

"The ancient cocquet, or seal of the regality, I fortunately recovered from Dunfermline, and have deposited it in the Advocates' Library."

The letter sent by King Robert to the inhabitants of Bruges concerning it is dated 1322. (*Reg.* 361.)

Dr. Wm. M'Millan, St. Leonard's Church, Dunfermline, describes the seal as follows :—

"The design shows the figure of St. Margaret wearing a long robe falling from her shoulders, and on her head an open crown showing three fleurs-de-lis. She stands against a conventional floral background, having a sceptre in her right hand, and what appears to be a book (perhaps her own Book of the Gospels referred to on page 223). On her right side is a shield, heater shaped, bearing the Royal Arms of Scotland, the lion rampant and the tressure.

"The latter is shown single, instead of double, but this is probably due to ' tear and wear.' On her left is another shield of the same shape, bearing a cross fleury between five birds, these forming the arms attributed to the Queen's great-uncle, Edward the Confessor. Round the circumference of the shield is the following :—*S*(*igillum*) *Cokete Regalitatis de Dunfermlyn*. Small leaves divide the several words of the inscription, and between the beginning and the end is a small cross. It may be noted that the 'L's' in the inscription are inverted, that the 'Y' is doubled up, that the 'T's' are without strokes and resemble the arabic figure '6.'"

The reference to the five birds is based on the story recorded concerning the arrival of St. Margaret in the Firth of Forth.

From the Town Council Seals of Scotland (p. 252) we learn that one side of the Seal of South Queensferry represents Margaret landing. The other bears a cross which is said to symbolise her attachment to the Christian faith. In each angle of the cross is a sea-fowl, and one in the centre. The legend regarding these five birds is that, at the moment when Queen Margaret landed on the Binks rocks, five sea-birds appeared in the air, forming, as they flew, the Sign of the Cross, and the legend further narrates that they alighted on the rigging of the vessel, their position there still having the form of a cross.

The Arms of Queen Margaret assume various forms, the better known amongst them being that of the Seal of South Queensferry, that depicted in the shield of the Confessor in Westminster Abbey and another to be found in the heraldic ceiling of St. Machar's Cathedral, Old Aberdeen.

But in each and all of them there is a cross and five birds, though the birds are variously represented as sea-birds, martlets (imaginary birds without legs often found in heraldic charges), and doves.

The Cokete Seal of Dunfermline would be used in connection with the customs of the burgh. The name to-day is usually given as "cocket" and a seal of that name is still used in connection with H.M. Customs Service.

Reference has been made to the gallows and the branding iron, but these were not the only means of punishment.

Near the tolbooth stood the lear-stane (a kind of pillory), the jougs, the stocks, and the repenting-stool.

So many people seem to think that these were the product of the Reformation. This is quite a mistake. They were there long before the Reformation and there is abundant evidence of their use for disciplinary purposes by the Burgh Court.

As already indicated, the Regality Court of Dunfermline was only one of three such courts under the administration of the abbot, and, to judge by entries in the Records of the Burgh of Kirkcaldy, it would seem that it sometimes sat there.

" 6 June, 1604—The Court of Justiciary, held in the tolbuth of Kirkcaldy by John Louden and James Law, bailies of the said burgh, commissioners depute and constitute be ane noble and potent Lord, Alexander, Lord of Fiwie, baillie principal and generall of the Regalitie of Dunfermline. Sutis callit. Dorathie Oliphant, wagabond, delaitit and accusit as ane sorcerer and dissaver of the peipil for ane wich. . . .

" Thairfor the hail assyss be the mouth of William Lamb, thair chosen chancellor, clenges (clears) the said Dorathie of wichcraft, and fylles her (finds her guilty) of the said abusing of the peepill be formis of charms and using of cures to sik personis as were bewichit . . . ordainis and decernis the said Dorathie Oliphant to be tuken to the tron of this burgh, and thair publickly stand with ane paper on her heid, declaring the caus of her public standing thair, and thairafter to be bainst (banished) the said burgh and haill boundis of the Lordship of Dunfermline, under the paine of death, to be inflictit upon her without deme or law, giff air she be apprehendit within the boundis of the said Regalitie."

" 25 Oc., 1731—The Provost reported that a Regality officer had summoned several burgesses before the Regality Court, contrary to the privilege of the town, and that upon complaint he had imprisoned him, and that there was a protest taken against him for a wrongous imprisonment. The Council approves of the Magistrates' procedure, and gives them full power and warrant to do everything necessary for maintaining the town's exemption from the jurisdiction of Dunfermline."

It is quite clear that, by that time, the situation had completely changed as between the Regality and the Burghs attached to it.

Walcott (Ancient Church of Scotland) tells us that there were twenty-six monks in the monastery of Dunfermline at the time of the Reformation. The names of some of these may be found in Laing's Charters, or in the Burgh Records, but the most complete list is in Yester Writs, 678 and 690, dated 31st August, 1557, and 2nd January, 1559-60, respectively, where the following names appear :—

George Durie (Abbot), John Baxter (Prior), Alexr. Aitken (Sub-Prior), Alexr. Mow, Thomas Burn, Alexr. Stevin, John

Scott, Thomas Jameson, Robert Hogart, Alexr. Summare, James Dundas, Marcus Lun, Patrick Mason, John Durie, Robert Lokard (?), James Reydpath, John Angus, Robert Maistertoun, Andrew Gray, James Thomson, William Smyth, John Henrysoun, William Lumisden, and Alexr. Huniman.

In addition to these, we have from other sources the names of John Murray and William Durie (Doorkeeper).

That would bring us up to Walcott's twenty-six, but it is quite possible that there may have been a few more names which have not been left on record.

It is, however, generally accepted that for twenty years, and more, before the Reformation there was a considerable diminution in numbers in all monasteries throughout Scotland. When the House of Greyfriars at Perth was destroyed in 1559, only eight friars belonged to it. In Culross there were only nine left.

Dr. Chalmers attributes the diminution in numbers at Dunfermline to the fact that the monastery had been greatly impoverished by war. That may be so, but there were other contributory causes. The monastic ideal had by this time largely lost its appeal and the prestige attaching to the habit was growing less.

The cost of living had gone up and the monks themselves were not keen on an increase in their numbers, with its consequent decrease in the '' portion '' allowed to each—to say nothing of the spiritual unrest that was characteristic of the times, particularly amongst the younger men. The fact is that, as the result of King Henry's suppression of the English monasteries, there was little hope left for the future of monastic life in Scotland.

Of some of those who are known to have been members of the Dunfermline community at the time of the Reformation nothing is known beyond their names. Of others a good deal is known, and it can hardly fail to be of interest to know what was their reaction to the historic upheaval that was taking place about them.

Concerning **George Durie**—the last of a long line of Abbots of Dunfermline—there is no room for doubt. He had been a bitter opponent of the new teaching from the start. He had taken an active part in the trial of Patrick Hamilton, had helped to bring Melville of Raith to the scaffold (*K.S. St. And.*

92n), and, even if the traditional story about his having sentenced to death one of his own conventual brethren, John Durie, a near relative of his own, is somewhat lacking in historical authentication, it may be accepted that he would not have hesitated to cast him into prison.

Anticipating the coming of the Reformation, he made provision out of the revenues of the Abbey for his " unofficial " wife and family at Craigluscar, and for other relatives, on a scale that made James VI " grue " when the Crown came to annex them.

After the Reformation, he was warded at Durie, doubtless under the charge of his kinsman, David Durie of that ilk, who was a supporter of the reformed cause, and, so far as one can gather, apart from a visit to France (*R.M.S.* 2083), he remained there till his death, before 1577.

The only member of the abbot's family who seems to have inherited the spirit of active opposition was his son John.

Educated at the Scots College, Paris, and afterwards at Louvain, he joined the Jesuits, by whom he was held in great esteem for his learning and eloquence. Returning to this country, he took such an active part in support of Romanism that his name appears in a list of six Jesuits and seminary priests who were charged by Act of Parliament to leave the country within a month on pain of death. There is little doubt that he was the " Jesuit Durie " who was involved in a conspiracy for the release of Mary and an attack upon Elizabeth about 1586. What became of him eventually is unknown. The other members of the abbot's family, like a good many more, seem to have acquiesced.

Next in importance to the abbot was the prior, **John Baxter.** Even though he was only second in command, yet, serving under a mitred abbot, he must have been a man of some standing, and it is a little surprising, to say the least of it, that the only use the Reformed Church could make of him was to appoint him as reader at a little place like Carnock, 1578-80, doubtless at the same salary as his predecessor, viz., £16 and the Kirk Lands. The Kirk Lands in this case meant next to nothing.

They consisted only of the glebe, and the friar from Scotlandwell who had served the cure at Carnock prior to the Reformation was still alive and in possession of it.

The only explanation that can be offered is that Baxter was no longer young, being one of the twenty-six monks who signed a charter dated June, 1539—thirty-nine years before his appointment as reader at Carnock. So far as can be traced, nothing else is recorded concerning him, but at least it should be said, on his behalf, that, prior though he was, he made no attempt, so far as is known, to make any provision for himself out of the spoils of the monastery—an example by no means followed by all who had previously been under his authority.

The prior's pension was made payable to John Baxter, Senr., and John Baxter, Junr., or to the longer liver of them (*P. to B.* 9th November, 1584, and 9th January, 1584-85)—which rather suggests that the prior was not in a position to cast stones at the abbot in respect of family life, unless, of course, he married after 1560.

Another of the older men was **John Murray.** Like Baxter, he was one of the twenty-six who signed the charter of 1539. When he was appointed Vicar of Dalgety is uncertain, but we know that he was in office there on 5th May, 1548 (*Inchcolm* 208). In 1559, foreseeing the turn events were about to take, he agreed, for a consideration no doubt, to grant a feu-farm of the glebe and kirk-lands of Dalgety to Henry Stewart, a brother of the Commendator of Inchcolm (*R.M.S.* 2487—6th August, 1559). The transaction involved a double illegality.

The granting of a feu-farm of a glebe was forbidden in 1549, and feus of kirk-lands effected after 6th March, 1558-59, were by statute declared illegal. (*Patrick, Statutes,* p. 97). The date of this feu was 6th August, 1559.

The agreement was, however, eventually confirmed, with the reservation of the statutory allowance for a glebe and manse, approximately six acres. (*R.M.S.* 2487—13th January, 1575-76.)

Murray was still Vicar of Dalgety in 1574, but was dead before 1575/6. (*Inchcolm,* 220, 234).

Dene **Alexander Aitken** was sub-prior at the time of the Reformation. On 23rd April, 1569, he was constituted Co-adjutor of Kelso during the minority of the commendator. (*P. to B.* i. 20.)

But on 16th May of the same year, William Lumsden, Sacristan of Dunfermline, was appointed to the same office. (*Ibid.* i. 24 v.)

No explanation is offered for the change, but, from the frequent reference afterwards to Lumsden as Co-adjutor and Administrator of Kelso, there would seem to be no doubt that he actually held the office.

No further reference can be found to Aitken except that his name appears on the list of those who were still alive in 1584.

William Lumsden held the double office of Sacristan of Dunfermline and Vicar of the Parochial Kirk.

As sacristan he would be responsible for the ornaments and furniture of the church and also for the maintenance and repair of the monastic buildings.

As vicar, he would have to arrange for the services in the nave. Quite evidently a man of some standing in the community!

He was the second son of John Lumsden, third of Airdrie—a family which at this time owned the lands of Dales, Inverkeithing. (*Stephen* 160.)

In 1560, the year of the Reformation—probably as the result of family influence and monastic standing—he had himself appointed Parson of Cleish. Quite definitely, however, this did not mean that he proposed to turn his back upon the Abbey and take up duty as a minister of the Reformed Church at Cleish. He did not leave the Abbey and he never took up duty at Cleish. What he did was to enter into an agreement with the Laird of Cleish, in virtue of which he received from the laird an annual payment of £53 6s. 8d., a smaller figure than the teind, leaving the laird free to collect as much more as he could. There was nothing in any way unusual about the arrangement. The collection of teind was seldom easy and all sorts of expedients were adopted to facilitate payment, one of the commonest being that of farming out the teind, that is, appointing a middleman, who agreed to pay a lump sum in the hope of collecting a bit extra for himself. Vicarage teinds, being payable in kind, were even more vexatious and difficult to collect. As for the work of the parish, the best the Reformed Church could do was to appoint a reader, but even for that the parish had to wait seven years.

In other ways Lumsden must have lined his nest well. In 1560 an instrument of sasine is recorded in his favour of half the lands of Easter Pitcorthy, and in 1584 he had a tack of nineteen years of the small teinds of Pitfirrane and Pitconnochie. (*Hall,*

42.) He was also, as already noted, Administrator of Kelso. He did not long reap the benefit of the Pitconnochie tack of 1584, for he died in 1586. It was he who, as sacristan, refused to do anything about the repairs needed for the parish kirk. (*Page* 226.)

John Angus was Precentor of Dunfermline Abbey for some time before the Reformation, and was still in office when the crisis came. Thanks to researches by David Laing into books and papers left by a Mr. Wood, who, along with collaborators, of whom Angus was one, took an active part in the preparation of the Scottish Psalter, a good deal of information has become available.

According to Wood (*Soc. of Antiq., Vol.* VII, p. 445) John Angus was born about 1515, entered the monastery of Dunfermline, embraced the Protestant faith shortly after 1543, obtained a pension and also a living in connection with the Chapel Royal at Stirling and died before 2nd March, 1596-97.

Wood evidently knew Angus well and speaks of him affectionately as both " gude " and " meike." The approximate date of his death, as given by Wood, is in keeping with information we have from other sources. Dr. Rogers—who was at one time Minister of the North Church, Dunfermline—in his History of the Chapel Royal, makes no reference whatever either to the pension or the living; but that does not exclude the possibility. The Chapel Royal specialised in music and may well have been interested in a musician of such standing as John Angus. But Wood's statement that Angus embraced the Protestant Faith shortly after 1543 must be accepted with a considerable amount of reserve. That he did eventually accept the new Faith we have reason to believe, though nowhere else is there an explicit statement to that effect. But that he accepted it so early is a somewhat different story. There is no lack of evidence to show that Angus was still an active member of the monastery right up to the time of the Reformation. If, before that date, he had any sympathy with the doctrines of the Reformers, he must have kept it very much to himself. Abbot Durie, while he was still in power, was not the man to trifle with in a matter of that sort.

The Reformation must have found John Angus about half-way through his working-life, and it is not without suggestiveness

West Doorway.   Original Norman Church in its relation to Abbot de Bothwell's Scheme.

that practically all his original and constructive work belongs to the latter stage. That work took two forms—first, the help he gave as an expert in the preparation of the Scottish Psalter—which was certainly post-Reformation, and for which see p. 186—second, the hymns and canticles that he himself composed, ten of which have been recovered :—

The Song of the Thre Childring.
    " O all ye workes of God the Lord, bless ye the Lord. "
The Song of Zacharias.
    " The onlye Lord of Israell be praised evermore."
The Sang of the Blessit Virgin.
    " My soule doth magnifie the Lord."
The Sang of Simeon, callit *Nunc Dimittis*.
        " O Lord, because my heart's desire
        hath wished long to see
        Mine only Lord and Saviour
        Thy Son before I die."
The Simboll or Creide of Athanasius.
    " What man, soeuer he be, saluation will attaine."
The Ten Commands.
    " Attend my people, and give eare."
The Sang of Simeon.
    " Now suffer me, O Lord."
The Lord's Prayer (another version).
        " Our Father which in heaven art,
        And mak'st us all one Brotherhood."
The XII Articles of our Belieff.
    " All my belief and confidence."
Da pacem Domine.
    " Give peace in these our dayes, O Lord."

A first glance at some of the subjects might suggest a pre-Reformation date. But the fact that the music is set to Scots words is quite decisive. Such a combination could have had no place in pre-Reformation worship. The reference to the Creed need occasion no surprise. For many a day every communicant in Scotland was expected to be able to repeat the " belief," and the Reformers were as familiar with the Creed of Athanasius as we are with the Apostles' or the Nicene.

One would like to think that John Angus continued as Precentor to David Ferguson, who, one imagines, would have found him in many ways a congenial spirit. The situation would not have been in any way unique, for Ed. Henryson, Precentor in pre-Reformation days in St. Giles, Edinburgh, continued as precentor in the same church after the Reformation, and he and two of his sons in succession were in charge of the Sang School in Edinburgh, to the evident satisfaction of everybody concerned. The Kirk Session records of Ferguson's day are unfortunately lost and no light can be looked for from that quarter.

One other thing remains to be said in this connection.

There is a belief on the part of some, based, no doubt, on tradition, that John Angus was the composer of the well-known psalm tune *Dunfermline*. No evidence, it must be admitted, can be adduced in support of this belief. But the tune certainly belongs to the time we are dealing with. It might have been composed by any of the men with whom Angus was associated in the preparation of the Psalter. But not one of them had the same reason as he had for giving it the name it bears.

Whether he continued to act as precentor or not, it is evident that he did continue to fulfil his duties as *almoner*— another appointment he held within the monastery—continued, in fact, for other thirty-five years.

" Edinburgh, 4 Nov., 1595. Gift of office of Almoner of Dunfermline by Queen Anne (on the demission of John Angus, parson of Crieff, sumtyme ane of the conventuall brethren of the Abbey, and last possessor), in favour of said John Angus and Mr. William Angus, his brother-german—or survivor— who during the latter years of his said brother's infirmity and great age has helped him in the said office for the conservation of good order and rule amongst the widows of St. Leonard's Hospital, conform to the privileges of the said office." (*M.S. Char. of Dunf.* ii. 33a.)

" 8 March, 1603—Gift of the Chaplanrie of Sanct Leonard grantit to Williame Wardlaw fer all the dayis of his lyftyme." (*B.R.* xxix.)

Under date 9th November, 1615, Mr. Thomas Wardlaw of Newlands, then almoner, grants a charter of an acre of arable land belonging to St. Leonard's Hospital, with the teind sheaves included, the locality of the land being indicated, and a list of the widows or bedes-women (*vidue seu oratrices*) attached.

6A

On 3rd March, 1621, Mr. Thomas Wardlaw of Logy (possibly the same man) is almoner, and on 6th December, 1636, Mr. Henry McGill, Minister of the Church of Dunfermline. (*Laing's Charters*, 1736, 1856, 2198.)

" 1 April, 1651—Ane supplication being presented by James Espline, Elymosinar of the Hospital of Saint Leonard, situate besyde the burgh of Dunfermline, for himself, and in name of the widows thairof—desyring the charity of the several Presbyteries for re-edifying of the said hospital. The Assembly recommends him to the charitie of the several Presbyteries." (*Minutes of the Synod of Fife.*)

" 20 July, 1651—Immediately after the battle (of Pitreavie), the victorious army, headed by Overton and Lambert, pursued the poor stragglers of the Scotch army to Dunfermline. On the way, the ' rough cavillers ' are understood to have wrecked St. Leonard's Chapel, and also the Chapel of St. Mary in the Nethertown. . . . " (*Annals*, 326.)

" St. Leonard's Chapel and Hospital " were built on " the site now occupied by the older St. Leonard's School and the farm road to its south. There was undoubtedly a burial ground here, and the writer saw many bones exposed about the year 1890. St. Leonard's Well still remains a little to the south-east, and, though now built up, is recognisable. . . .

" It is mentioned in Hutton's MS. Collections, vol. vi. item 120, that the Court Books of St. Leonard's Hospital are extant from the year 1594." (*B.R.* xxix.)

Following the Reformation, John Angus was presented to the Vicarage of Inverkeithing by the Commendator of Dunfermline, 20th August, 1562, with collation and institution by the Bishop of St. Andrews, 23rd June, 1563—followed by Royal Confirmation 20th May, 1565. (*Stephen*, 272.)

He was also admitted to the Parsonage of Crieff (*Crief secundo*) 4th November, 1595, his brother William, Parson of Kirkinner, being again referred to. (*Fasti.*)

It is very doubtful if either of these appointments implied the assumption of any parochial duty or responsibility.

They were simply the means of acquiring a legal title to draw the revenues attached.

For further particulars concerning John Angus, see p. 186.

Thomas Jamieson. A man of this name became minister of Newburn in 1564—married Janet Clepen before 13th December of that year, was translated to Largo in 1566 and died before 2nd February, 1578-79.

It looks as if this might well be the Dunfermline monk of that name; but there are one or two considerations that make one hesitate. It is not expressly said that the man appointed was a monk of Dunfermline, and it is said that he died before February, 1578-79, whereas Jamieson's name appears on the list of 1584.

Alexander Stevin—signs as witness on behalf of the monastery 1st July, 1550. (*Laing*, 633.)

In a charter of 17th April, 1582, confirming an original of date 1574, Stevin is referred to as " a former professed monk and tutor of the altar of St. Lawrence within the interior (conventual) church of the said monastery," and St. Lawrence's yard and croft are indicated as being near the lower gate of the monastery. (*R.M.S.* 392.)

He was reader at Beath from 1574 to 1579. (*Acts and Decreets.* LXVI., 396.)

" Alexander Stevin, reidare at Baith, his stipend xv li wt. the Kirklands, to be payit out of Sanct Columb's Inche, be the takkisman or parochurs of baith, as the reidare sall chuse." (*Reg. of Ministers.*)

He was also appointed to the Vicarage of Dalgety, 14th June, 1575.

Dalgety and Beath both belonged to the Abbey of Inchcolm and were worked together at this time, under the minister of Aberdour. Stevin seems to have been the first reader at Beath, and succeeded at Dalgety John Brownlow, who had been a monk at Inchcolm. For part of the time during which he held these offices he must have served both places simultaneously. Even readers were scarce and difficult to get, and it was more than eighty years after the Reformation before Beath got a settled ministry.

Stevin's services, however, do not seem to have been found acceptable at headquarters, as is made abundantly clear in a case of disputed jurisdiction between the Kirk and the civil powers, before the Privy Council at Stirling Castle, 31st August, 1579.

David Ferguson, first Protestant minister at Dunfermline, acting as Commissioner for the Kirk in the west parts of Fife, had, it is averred, not only deposed Stevin from his charge and office as reader at Beath, but had admonished him and expressed the intention of pronouncing sentence of excommunication against him for subscribing evidents and letters upon some lands belonging to the Abbey of Dunfermline "as ane of the convent thereof."

Stevin's defence was that this was not an ecclesiastical matter, but civil.

Ferguson was charged to appear personally before the Privy Council with the documents concerned, and both parties appeared on the appointed day.

Ferguson denied that any sentence of excommunication was intended. Stevin had been deprived of his office by the General Assembly and he, as instructed, had intimated that fact to Stevin, but he declined to produce the sentence of the Kirk or a copy of his intimation of it, on the ground that their lordships were "not judges competent thereto."

Their lordships found themselves to be competent judges thereto and ordained Ferguson to produce the documents before a specified date, "under the pane of rebellion and putting of him to the horne."

Further consideration of the action was resumed at a meeting of the Privy Council held at Holyroodhouse, 19th November, 1579.

Ferguson having been summoned to answer for the "sentence of deprivatioun and admonitiounis" pronounced by him against Stevin, and both parties appearing personally, the court decreed that the pursuer be reponed in his office of reader, and the defender discharged from further proceeding against him, "because this mater is thocht to be civile, quhairupoun deprivatioune aucht not to stryke be ony law or custome yit ressavit within this realme."

The process itself is easy enough to follow. The difficulty is to understand the motives that were at work.

Why did the church authorities want to get rid of Stevin? The explanation offered does not sound too convincing—that he had witnessed documents "as ane of the convent." The affairs of the monastery had to be wound up. Deeds of transference had to be signed and witnessed. If it was permissible for the commendator, himself a Protestant, to sign deeds on behalf of the convent, how came it to be such an offence for a reader to witness them ?

After all, the description " as ane of the convent " was little more than a legal fiction. The monastery had been suppressed nearly twenty years before.

What makes the charge still more difficult to understand is that, within the next two years, Stevin, along with one or two others, former members of the monastery, had to appear again before the Privy Council to answer for his having failed to witness a deed " as ane of the convent," after having been charged to do so. He was given three hours to attach his signature. (*Reg. P.C.* III. 399.)

Moreover, the same thing happened after other two years. (*Reg. P.C.* III. 642.)

Cases of the kind need not be taken too seriously. It was a time of great unsettlement and many irregularities. Not only ministers, but even readers, were so scarce that men were sometimes rushed into office without sufficient inquiry, and had to be got rid of later. The reason for dismissal might be anything or nothing—faith, morals, ignorance, a quarrel, or a civil offence of any sort.

While Stevin was still a monk, there would have been no question of civil intervention, and even yet the line of demarcation between civil and ecclesiastical jurisdiction was nebulous and uncertain. But the civil authorities decided that the offence, whatever it was, was of a civil nature, and therefore outwith Ferguson's jurisdiction.

John Henrysoun (Henderson) had been Keeper of Charters and Notary of Dunfermline since, at least, 1550. He was also Master of the Grammar School, and, apparently, had continued in that office for some twelve or thirteen years after the Reformation.

On 14th October, 1573, he brought an action against David Ferguson, Minister at Dunfermline, for deprivation of his office.

Ferguson, he asserts, on the instructions of John Douglas, Archbishop of St. Andrews, had charged him to abstain from further teaching in the said school under threat of excommunication. He claims that he had not only been lawfully appointed to the office, but had satisfied the Kirk as to his beliefs and had

behaved himself in his office honestly in conversation and life,
" never teaching or utherwyse moving onything to the sklander
of the Evangell," as he is prepared to make good in evidence.
In any case, the action was in its nature civil and profane, and
neither archbishop nor minister was competent to deal with it.

The archbishop and minister were charged to appear before
the Council on a certain date, but neither appeared, nor any
other to represent them. Wherefore the Regent, " with avise
of the Lordis of Secreit Counsall, findis that na sic forme or
ordour of sentence of excommunicatioune suld be gevin or
pronuncit aganis the said Johne in maner foirsaid . . .
without prejudice alwayis to thame to persew him utherwyise
for removing fra the said charge." The finding is dated at
Holyroodhouse, 14th October, 1573. (*Reg. P.C.* II. 288.)

Henryson's case is unusually involved and difficult.

Not only have we his own protestations of fidelity to the
Reformed Church, we have also to reckon with the fact that he
was at the time, or very soon afterwards became, both vicar and
reader at Cleish. There was no particular significance attaching
to his appointment as vicar. The Church had little or nothing
to do with such appointments, and acceptance did not necessarily imply obligation to perform the duties. But the readership was quite a different matter. A reader could only be
appointed by the Church, and acceptance of the appointment
certainly carried with it obligation to fulfil the duties. So
that it does seem as if there was some substance in Henryson's
claims.

On the other hand there is the plain fact that Henryson
never quite severed his connection with the monastery. Not
only, like some of the others, did he continue to witness deeds
" as ane of the convent." He was " collector " for the monastery for more than twenty years after the suppression. (*Reg.
P.C.* III. 399—4th July, 1581.) That office did not necessarily
mean a great deal in itself, but he was under no sort of obligation to continue in it, and the fact that he did so was not likely
to increase the Church's confidence in him.

The very nature of his duty as schoolmaster helped to increase
the difficulty. If a former monk or priest conducted a service
according to Roman rites, it was an easy matter to prove the
charge against him. But a schoolmaster, without committing

himself to anything that would justify a charge, might easily arouse suspicion on the part of the Church, and yet the Church be unable to do anything about it.

The result was that, not infrequently, there was trouble with schoolmasters who had been appointed to office prior to the Reformation.

In 1566 Thomas Kynneir was appointed parish minister of Crail and offered " to tak the scoile in teiching," provided the present teacher willingly removed. But the present teacher would not, and neither Kinnear nor his successor could do anything about it. (*Churchyard Memorials of C.* 31.)

One thing is clear. Nobody who knows of the brave stand made by David Ferguson on behalf of education in that famous sermon of his preached before the Regent and nobility at Leith, at a time when the cause had none of the popular support behind it that it has to-day, would readily suspect him of countenancing or condoning anything that was likely to be prejudicial to its interests.

" For the scheulis are the seid of the Kirk and Commonwealth, and our children are the hope of the posteritie, quhilk being neglectit, thair can nothing be luikit for bot that barbarous ignorance sall overflow all."

John Henryson died in 1581—so that he was collector for the monastery up to the last year of his life.

" **John Durie** was born at Mauchline, a little village in the country of Kyle, and trained up a little in letters in the town of Aire; after which he was sent to George Durie, his cousin, Abbot of Dunfermline, and placed by him among the monks of that Abbey, where he lived three years." (*Spottiswoode's Hist.*, p. 458.)

It is highly probable that he was a near relative of the abbot, though the connection has never been verified; but if he was a cousin, there must have been a material difference between them in point of age.

The first reference we find to him as a member of the monastic community is when his name appears, 31st August, 1557, as witness to a deed on behalf of the monastery. (*Yester Writs.*)

He cannot have been long, however, within the precincts before he became suspect in respect of the new teaching, and, with a man like George Durie, such a suspicion was apt to develop very quickly into action. As already indicated, the story of his having been condemned to be immured between two walls until he died may be somewhat lacking in authoritative confirmation, but there can be little doubt that prompt and drastic action would be taken.

Whether he escaped, or lay in prison till the Reformation, we do not know.

The first story recorded of him after his departure from the monastery is difficult at first to understand. It seems that he had been arrested in Edinburgh on a charge of assembling the Queen's lieges for the purpose of an attack on two men, but was " repledged " by authority of his kinsman, David Durie, son of the laird of Durie and East Luscar, who was the Bailie of Regality of Dunfermline, Mr. William Scot of Balwerye, a friend of the family, becoming surety " that justice sall be ministrat and done."

The charge is detailed as follows :—

" CONVOCATION—WOUNDING—MUTILATION.

" Oct. 30 (1563).—Dene Johnne Dwrie, Monk in Dunfermling, was ' replegit be Dauid Durye, sone and apperand air of the Lard of Dwrye, baillie of the Regalitie of Dunfermling, who assigned the penult day of November, delatit of the Conuocatioune of our souerane ladeis liegis, to the nowmer of xxiiij persones, bodin in feir of weir, &c., vpoun the xxiiij day of July instant, vndir scilence of nycht, and setting vpoune Dauid Murray in Kerse, and Antoune Ruderfurd, vpon THE HIE STREIT OF EDR, quhair thai were gangand to thair beddis, to the Chalmer of the young Abbot of Dumfermeling, in sobir and quiet maner, &c. ; and thair Invading thaim for thair slauchteris, and crewalye Hurt and Woundit the said Antoune in four sindry pairtis of his heid, in his craig (throat), in his right leg, at the kne, and diuerse vtheris pairtis of his body, to the greit effusion of his blude; and mutilat and maid him impotent of his said rycht leg; and left him lyand for deid; And als, crewalye Hurt and Woundit the said Dauid Murray in his heid and diuerse utheris pairtis of his body, to the greit effusion of his blude; and Mutilat and demembrit him of his left arme."

89

"James and Archibald Mowbray, brothers of John M. of Barnebowgall, Robert and James Bertane, brothers, and Patrick Thomsoun, son of Thomas T., burgess of Edinburgh, Richard Thomesoun, son of Edward T., baker there, and Thomas Hendersoune, 'Maister of the Fense-scule,' were denounced rebels, &c., and all their moveables escheated, for art and part of the said crime, and their cautioners unlawed for their not entering to underly the law, &c." (*Pitcairn's Criminal Trials*, i. 436.)

David Durie, Bailie of Regality, whose wife was a sister of Sir George Douglas of Lochleven, turned Protestant with his wife's people. This was much resented by the Queen's party, and more than one skirmish took place on the streets of Edinburgh as the result of the feud. (See *History of Carnock*, 322.)

John Durie himself was not expressly charged with the attack, but with the "Convocation."

The next we hear of him, he is acting as exhorter at Penicuik in 1567. Following that, he became minister at Colinton in 1569, was translated to Leith in 1570, and became one of the ministers of St. Giles, Edinburgh, in 1573, where he would doubtless reside at St. Giles Kirkyard, the Abbot of Dunfermline's "lugeing" in the High Street having been already requisitioned for John Knox.

"Abbots Lodging, Edinburgh—John Durie, tailor, removed 'for the eis' of John Knox, minister, with promise that as soon as the bailies and council can provide the said minister with another lodging, he will regain possession." (*Edin. B.R.—4th September*, 1560.)

"John Durie and others—Sasine for themselves and in name of the ministers, of the 'mans, duelling housis and yairdis within Sanct Gelis Kirk yaird.'" (*Ibid.—27th March*, 1579.)

The following notes concerning him are taken from the Diary of James Melville, who afterwards became his son-in-law:

"1574—About the sam tyme cam to St. Androis, to visit Mr. knox, Jhone Durie, fellow-minister of Leith with Mr. David Lindsay, wha was then for stoutness and zeal in the guid cause meikle renouned and talked of. For the gown was na sooner af, and the Byble out of hand (frae the kirk) when on ged the corslet, and fangit was the hagbot, and to the fields!

" 1579—Jhone Durie was of small literature, bot haid sein and marked the grait warks of God in the first Reformation, and bein a doer baith with toung and hand.

" He had bein a diligent heirar of Mr. Knox, and observer of all his wayes. He conceivit the best grounds of maters weil and could utter tham fearlie, fullie, and fecfullie, with a mightie spreit, voice and action. The speciall gift I marked in him was haliness, and a daylie (and nightlie) cearful, continuall walking with God in meditation and prayer.

" He was a verie guid fallow, and tuk delyt, as his speciall comfort, to haiff his table and house filled with the best men.

" Ther ludgit in his house at all these Assemblies in Edinbruche (for comoun), Mr. Andro Melvill, Mr. Thomas Smeton, Mr. Alexander Arbuthnot—thrie of the lernedest in Europe— Mr. James Melvill, my uncle, Mr. James Balfour, David Ferguson, David Home, ministers, with sum zelus, godlie barrones and gentilman."

Probably no better testimony could be offered to his life and work than that which is to be found in the minutes of the Town Council of Edinburgh :—

" That license micht be grantit be thame to Jhone Dury, minister, to pas to the westland for making of amity and reconciliatioun of dyueris deidly feudis standing in thai pairtis." (*Edin. B.R.—27th October,* 1581.)

The Town Council, it may be added, were willing, if the Kirk agreed.

Durie and David Ferguson, minister of Dunfermline, were on the friendliest possible terms personally, but in their attitude towards the king there was a material difference.

David and King James were " cronies "—it amounted to nothing less—and, fond though he was of a practical joke, David was at all times careful not to offend the king.

But Durie was uncompromising.

In the course of a violent sermon preached in St. Giles, in 1579, he referred to the king in terms that were very far from complimentary. The king, taking advice of his council, summoned him to his presence, instructing him to bring his manuscript with him. Durie appeared, but refused to submit his manuscript.

He was therefore ordered to enter into ward in Edinburgh Castle on Saturday next. Saturday was an awkward day for a minister to go to jail; so Durie gave up his manuscript, and the matter appears to have dropped for a time.

But only for a time. Soon he is in trouble again—this time a tirade against Popery and the Court. He is cited to appear before the Privy Council and ordered to leave Edinburgh.

Before doing so, he consulted the Assembly, which advised him to keep to his charge till he was removed by force, but, should he be so removed, to go peaceably. On express orders from the king, the magistrates were reluctantly obliged to exercise compulsion.

" About nine o'clock, after supper on a summer evening, he was seen making his way to the Cross of the town, in company with Mr. Lawson and Mr. Balcanquhal (his fellow-ministers in St. Giles), and two notaries, and there, under the shadow of his own church, he went through the curious ceremony of placing a piece of money in the notaries' hands, in token that he left his charge against his free will.

" There was a little crowd round them as the party went through this strange performance, who, it is said, were much moved, though the wife of a shoemaker cried out that if any would cast stones she would help.

" After this, John Durie went forth at the Neather Bow and St. Giles for some time knew him not." (*St. Giles*, *J. Cameron Lees*, p. 166.)

But changes took place at Court which made it possible for Durie to return, and then took place that stirring scene referred to later (page 187), when a crowd of 2,000 people met him at the Nether Bow and escorted him back to St. Giles, singing as they went, words and tune alike familiar to them, the 124th psalm, in four parts.

Again we quote from Dr. Cameron Lees :—

" It must have been a stirring spectacle, that great bare-headed multitude singing opposite the door of St. Giles that psalm, in the rugged metre which has come down to the present day.

" Few more picturesque scenes have occurred in connection with our church's history. When darkness came down on the town on that memorable night, two or three hundred citizens kept watch at the back of the church for the ' saftie of the ministers,' and, though the authorities besought them to go home, they kept their watchfires bright, and remained singing psalms till break of day.

" Next day Lennox left the town, and they needed to watch no longer."

In November, 1583, Durie was again discharged by His Majesty from his place in the city, and at a meeting of Town Council, held on 21st February following, two of the elders of St. Giles appeared, stating that he was in need, and asking something for him from the town. The council found that they owed him nothing, and as the king had declared that :

" He will nocht that the said Jhonn Durie return agane or serve or mak any residence here, they discharge the said Jhonn Durie of ony stipend to be payet to him hereafter. And in respect of the kirk's request they grant unto him the sum of fyftie punds for the transporting of his wyfe, familie, and household geir from this toune, provyding he binding the guid toun na furder in tyme coming, quhilk sum they ordain John Broun, collector of the kirk annuells, to delyver to the said Jhonn Durie's wife."

Following this final banishment from Edinburgh, he joins his son-in-law, James Melville, at St. Andrews, and, after being nearly drowned in the River Lunan, which was in spate, is by him escorted to Montrose, where he was to remain in ward.

There he succeeded John Craig, one of his old colleagues in St. Giles, who had been translated to Aberdeen, and remained there till his death.

" Pension of seven score pounds to himself, his wife and Josua, his son—and langer liver of them—considering the greit, lang and ernest travellis and labouris sustenit be his (the king's) lovit orator, John Durie, . . . besydes the greit chargis and expensis maid be him thir mony yeirs bygane in advancing the publict effayres of the kirk and remembering the greit houshold and famelie of barnis quhairwith he is burdynit." (*Acts of Parl*. III. 551.)

He died 29th February, 1600, and was buried at Montrose. (*Edin. Tests. Vol.* xxxiv—*2nd July*, 1600.)

" The haill course of his lyff that I knew was an unweireing and constant occupatioun in doctrine, prayer and praise. The

mair I think on him, the mair I thank God that ever I knew
him." (*Melville's Diary*, 463.)

If his cousin, Andrew Durie, Bishop of Galloway—Bishop
Stottikin, as Knox called him—made the name of Durie to stink
in Scottish nostrils, it cannot be questioned that John did much
to redeem it. He not only constituted the greatest contribution the monastery of Dunfermline made to the cause of Reformation in Scotland, he has a right to be reckoned among the
outstanding churchmen of his day.

He was survived by his wife, Marion, daughter of Sir John
Marjoribanks, Provost of Edinburgh, and had issue :—

Joshua, minister of Inverkeilor.

Robert, minister of Anstruther.

Simeon, minister of Arbroath.

Christian, married George Gledstanes, Archbishop of St.
Andrews.

Elizabeth, married James Melville, minister of Kilrenny.

——— married John Dykes, minister of Kilrenny.

" 1544—**Mr. John Davidson,** an eminent divine, was born
in the parish of Dunfermline this year. At a very early age he
was sent to school in the Abbey, completing his scholastic
education there.

" He became a monk of the Order of Benedictines. Afterwards he embraced the Protestant faith, and became celebrated
as a divine and a poet." (*Annals*, 196.)

It is quite clear, however, that Dr. Henderson has slipped up
here. John Davidson, of Prestonpans, to whom he refers, was
not born till some five years later, and would not have been
more than eleven years old at the time of the Reformation.

What seems to have misled him is that there was a chaplain
of the same name belonging to the monastery, attached to one
of the altars in St. Peter's, Inverkeithing, who, on behalf of
the monastery, signed as a witness, 9th March, 1567-68.
(*B.R.* 220.) (For this John Davidson, see *Hist. of Carnock*,
274, 275, 334.)

A somewhat disappointing record from the Reforming
point of view—a few readers and vicars of somewhat doubtful
allegiance—the one clear gain, John Durie.

A particularly disappointing record when compared, for
instance, with that of St. Andrews :—

"In January, 1571-72, fourteen of those who had been canons of the Priory of St. Andrews are mentioned as Protestants, twelve of them being then parish ministers of the Reformed Church; and, besides these, other thirty-one of the clergy had joined the Reformers by the 17th of March, 1559-60. Many members of the University forsook their former faith, for the first General Assembly deemed twenty-one 'in St. Androes' qualified 'for ministreing and teaching,' and, with few exceptions, these were professors or regents; so that, as Principal Lee has well said, 'this city was at that time the chief nursery of the Church.'" (*Reg. K.S. St. And.* vii.)

But Dunfermline had not the history of martyrdoms that St. Andrews had, nor had John Knox been living and preaching in it.

What happened to the clergy of the old regime who did not attach themselves to the ministry of the new?

Is there any substance in the picture drawn by Wordsworth in his *Excursion*?

> "That violent commotion which o'erthrew,
> In town and city and sequestered glen,
> Altar and cross, and church of solemn roof,
> And old religious house—pile after pile;
> And shook their tenants out into the fields,
> Like wild beasts without home."

A few, quite naturally, sought sanctuary on the Continent, where they would be free to continue the practice of their faith.

But that sort of escape was available only for the very few.

Speaking generally, the majority of the superior clergy were little, if any, the worse, financially, of the upheaval. Many of them in fact gained materially, and at no time was there so much as a suggestion of reprisals.

They had two-thirds of their benefices secured to them, with possibilities of increase by means of feus, etc., while the lands and revenues, which had hitherto been at their disposal only during their tenure of office, were so often diverted to become the absolute possession of themselves or their dependents.

On a somewhat lower level, there were so many cases, as we have seen, of monastery officials being presented to vacant charges belonging to the monastery for the sole purpose of securing a legal title to the revenues, without the least intention of fulfilling any of the duties.

It would be easy to write with pungency upon the iniquity of such a proceeding, were it not for the fact that cases are not unknown of ministers of the Reformed Church, for whom no sufficient stipend was available, being inducted as prebendaries or chaplains to altars, with no intention, needless to say, of fulfilling the conditions attaching to these offices.

As for the inferior clergy, it is a somewhat different story. There are too many references to needy monks and nuns to make it possible to say that none were unprovided for.

At the same time, it is only right that such provision as there was, should be made known.

The first General Assembly, held in December, 1560, appointed " that all such as hes been in the ministrie of the Paip's Kirk, good and well-conditioned persons, that they shall live upon the almes of the Poore."

It was further enacted that " priests, friars, monks and other kirkmen, that had their pensions and livings allotted to them for their services, should retain or brook the said pensions if they would be professors of the truth and leave their papistrie, otherwise all should be taken from them for their obstinacie."

In view of that provision, we are not surprised when we come upon an entry like the following—even though the recipient did have considerable difficulty in getting possession of the so-called gift :—

" 16 June, 1577—Gift by Robert, Commendator of Dunfermline and the convent thereof, to John Durie, Minister of Christis Evangell, sumtyme ane of the convent of our said Abbey, and to Josua Durie, his son, and longer liver of them for their lives, of a pension of £64 13s. 4d. in place of his portion due to him from the said Abbey before the dispersioun of the brethren thereof, to be lifted starting at Whitsunday, 1577." (*Yester Writs*, 799.)

As for the reservation about " leaving their papistrie, otherwise all should be taken from them for their obstinacie," one can only say that it is not at all difficult to find numerous instances in the records of neighbouring parishes of pensions continuing to be paid to the clergy of the Old Church up to the day of their

General view of Monastic Buildings as seen from Pittencrieff Glen.

death, even though they never joined the Reformed Church—the only expression of feeling being that some of them lived a long time.

So far as the former members of the monastery at Dunfermline are concerned, the position is quite clear.

" The Commendator agreed to pay them £50 yearly, plus 20s. for coal, with their chambers and yards, while the monks, on their part, agreed to renounce their portion and petty commons.

" The Commendator found that he could not collect the ' commons ' for want of the register thereof. The court decreed that the brethren shall produce the register." (*Acts and Decreets*, xxxvii. 30.)

In the case of Culross, the value of the " chambers and yards " was estimated at £10.

On 4th November, 1566, we find William Durie, his son Robert, and survivor, being continued for life in his former office as porter of the Abbey, at a salary of £4 per annum and three chalders oats (*Registrum Assedationum, Dunf.*, 1557-85, f. 98v.) and on 22nd March, 1584-85, John Gib was appointed keeper of the " place and yairds " of Dunfermline Abbey. (*P. to B. Vol.* ii. 1578-87.)

On 22nd December, 1584, the king, at Holyroodhouse, ratifies and confirms all survivors in continual possession of their pensions, and, as many of them were now aged and infirm, he decrees an augmentation of £10—the survivors being indicated as follows :—

Alexr. Aitman, John Angus, Alexr. Huniman, Thos. Burn, Thos. Johnneston (Jameson), Wm. Lumsden, Andrew Gray, Alexr. Stevin, John Durie, and William Smith.

In the case of John Baxter, John Durie and William Durie, it is to be noted that the pension was made payable to the man and to his son, or longer liver of them.

What is still more unexpected is that in 1584 we find quite a number of cases where, the original pensioner having died, the pension is " gifted " to people who, so far as one can gather, had no connection with the monastery. (*P. to B.*)

To make assurance still more sure, we have an Act of Parliament, dated 29th July, 1587, which provides as follows :—

" And Mairattour, it is speciallie providit that, notwithstanding of the annexation of the temporalities of benefices to the Crown, yit the conventuall brether of the Abbay of Dunfermling sall nawayes be preiugit nor hurt anent the livingis, portionis, pensionis, yairdis and dewties of the said abbay, bot that thai and everie ane of thame may peaceablie brouk, joyce and vplift thair portionis, pensionis, livingis &c. during thair lyftymes.'' (*Holyrood*, *Act of Parliament* re *Annexation of Temporalities.*)

Contrasting such provision with the pittances that were generally paid to readers and ministers, one may be pardoned for coming to the conclusion that the loaves and fishes were as much in evidence in the case of the retired Romanist as in that of his Protestant successor, on whom lay the burden of responsibility and work.

Another thing that stands out is that the Reformed Church took somewhat longer to establish itself than is generally thought. It is not merely that Roman rites continued to be observed in not a few churches for a considerable time. For years afterwards, vacancies were not infrequently filled, with royal confirmation, by men who were completely out of sympathy with Protestantism.

There are frequent references to '' remanent monks.''

This does not necessarily mean that they all continued to reside within the precincts, though it is only reasonable to suppose that, in view of the free provision of '' chambers and yards '' quite a few of them would do so. But when Walcott tells us that in 1580 '' there were Benedictines watching within barred doors beside the shrines of St. David and St. Margaret '' (*Ancient C. of S.*, *p.* 22), we can only conclude that he is romancing.

MINISTERS OF DUNFERMLINE

David Ferguson.   1560-1598

There is no reason to question the traditional belief that Ferguson was a native of Dundee. Dundee was one of the centres of reforming activity, associated, in particular, with George Wishart, and the first recorded reference to Ferguson locates him in Dundee.

His occupation is variously described as that of glover, skinner, sutor. The idea of his having been a skinner is given some countenance by one of the practical jokes attributed to him.

" Having on one occasion presented to the King and Council a petition for an augmentation of stipend, he was mortified by having it returned to him with the unpromising words, ' Sicut ante.'

" Some time afterwards, the King, passing through Dunfermline, saw the old minister going through the ungraceful process of dressing hides, and asked somebody if he had lost his wits ; whereupon Mr. David overhearing the question, promptly replied that he was endeavouring to fulfil His Majesty's commands by returning to his original trade and thus gaining his bread *sicut ante*, ' as before.' James is said to have engaged to have his petition more favourably backed when it next came before him." (*Laing's Tracts*, viii.)

Nothing is known of his parents, and even the date of his birth is quite uncertain. Spottiswood gives the year 1533, but Wodrow thinks that it must have been some ten, or even twenty, years earlier. James Melville, in his notice of proceedings of the Synod of Fife, of date February, 1597-98, refers to him as " the auldest minister at that time in Scotland." On Spottiswood's conjecture he would have been only 65.

That he had the advantage of a University education is more than doubtful. On the other hand, it would be a mistake to think of him as in any way uneducated. He had certainly some knowledge of both Latin and Greek, and the valuation of his library (£100) after his death would seem to indicate for those days an unusually well-read man.

The first recorded notice of him is as follows :—

" 7 July, 1558.—Item, the said day, to David **Lindsay,**

Rothesay herauld, passand of Edinburgh, with letteris, to summond George Luvell, David Fergusone, and certain utheris personis within the burt. of Dunde, to tak ourte of thame that thai sall compeir befoir the justice and his deputies in the tolbuith of Edinburgh, the xxviii day of Julii instant, for thair wrongus using and wresting of the scripture, and disputing upoun erroneous opinions, and eiting of flesche in Lenterone and utheris forbidding tymes, contrair the actis of parliament— iij li vs.'' (*Compot. Thesaur.*)

(*Notes.*—George Luvell was, or became, a Burgess of Dundee. The sum of £3 5s. referred to represents the herald's fees and expenses for serving the summons. No record can be discovered of the outcome of the summons.)

The next we hear of him is his appointment as minister at Dunfermline, July, 1560. It was quick work, only some four months after the passing of the Act legalising the Protestant position.

Although Knox's views respecting the Sacraments were some-what " higher " than those generally held in the Church of Scotland to-day, it is doubtful if he believed that any special grace or Apostolic descent of authority was received from the laying on of hands. What he, and his fellow-workers, were principally concerned about was the Call of the people of God.

In this case, there was as yet no congregation in being to issue such a Call, and no court of the Church to deal with it.

Ferguson's appointment, like that of a few others, was the outcome of a meeting in the Great Kirk of Edinburgh, when provision had to be made at once for some of the more important and populous towns.

The people present at that meeting knew the men they were calling and their record of work already done. And that, for the time, was held to be sufficient. Afterwards, when the courts of the Church came into being, more rigid rules were adopted for the sustaining of Calls, trial of gifts, and due appointment.

But that could not be yet.

It was a staggering situation with which Ferguson must have found himself confronted. The only part of the Abbey buildings that remained in any measure intact was the Parochial Kirk, and very soon it was found to be in a somewhat precarious condition.

A commendator had been appointed some two months earlier and was probably already in occupation of the Abbot House. There was no manse or glebe, no stipend, no office-bearers, no congregation as such. That many of the parishioners were well disposed towards his coming goes without saying, but he would not be long amongst them without realising that that did not apply to all ; that there were not a few who still retained their attachment to the old ways and did not welcome change, and that there were some who were more or less hostile.

Commenting on the proceedings of the Synod of Fife, May, 1596, James Melville records Ferguson's own recollection of the start as follows :—

" And sa David Fergusone, Pastor of Dunfermline, a reverend father, spak verie pleasandlie and comfortablie of the beginning and succes of the Ministerie : Namlie, how that a few in number, viz. :—onlie sax, whairof he was ane, sa mightelie went fordwart in the wark but (without) feir or cair of the warld, and prevalit, when there was na name of stipend hard tell of ; when the authoritie bathe Ecclesiastik and Civill, opponit themselves, and skarslie a man of name and estimatioun to tak the cause in hand."

One of the first problems calling for attention was that of finding a house to live in. The vicar who was responsible for the services in the Parochial Kirk being himself a monk resident within the monastery, there had never been a manse. In the Inventory drawn up at the time of Ferguson's death there is a reference to a house for which he had paid rent, but where it stood there is nothing to indicate. It was not till 1627—sixty-seven years, that is, after Ferguson's ministry began—that the minister's right to a manse and glebe was established.

" Whereas we ar informed that the Manse and gleib of the Church of Dunfermeling have been designed to one Mr. Henrie McGill, present minister ther, and that the possessours of the gleib tak exception against the designation vnder cullour of our interest thervunto, thereby intending to defraud that church of that which is justlie due vnto the same : Therfoir it is our will and pleasure that, calling befoir yow our Advocats, yow consider of our interest therin, and if yow find that the possessours have no further cause than what is pretendit vnder cullour of interest therin, we think it reasonable that the said church be in no worse case than vther churches in the lyk nature ar, and as the Law hath provyded for them. Whythall, the 8 of Febry., 1627." (*Reg. of Royal Letters*, I. 127-8.)

The letter, admittedly, makes pleasant reading, but it would be unwise to jump to the conclusion that the manse would materialise immediately. Some 30 years later—23rd March, 1658—there is an entry in the records of the Kirk Session to the effect that there was no session this day because of a meeting for the designation of a manse for the minister; and that, so far as can be traced, is the last explicit reference to it for many a day to come.

On 17th April, 1660, we find the following entry :—

" The session considering yt the most parte of the Kirkyaird has been useless these many yeirs by gane—And the necessitie yr is in drying of it yt it may be a sufficient and commodious buriall place—And having taken the aduyse of skilfull men who think fit yt the Kirkyaird may be made dry if yr were *a gutter under the graves*, and ane open cast for covoying the water away under Mr. William Oliphant, minister his hous, to caus it to run in to his gutter under his hous—The session eftir long deliberation yrin, have resolved, etc."

which would seem to indicate that Mr. Oliphant's house was to the south of the graveyard, on the ground now known as the Bee Alley Gardens; but, according to the *Fasti*, Mr. Oliphant was minister of the Second Charge, which never had a manse. (See page 124.)

Wherever this first manse of the First Charge stood, it cannot have been for very long in occupation as a manse, for when, about 1800, the question of the provision of a manse was raised again, the general impression was that there had never been a manse. Nobody within living memory, it was said, had ever heard of such a thing. It was only after protracted search that the Rev. Allan M'Lean discovered that there had once been a manse on a site that had been part of the former monastic precincts, and on that based his claim for another.

" Where there had once been a manse in a Royal Burgh with a landward parish attached to it, the minister is entitled to insist upon a manse being provided for him, although his predecessors had accepted a sum of money for manse rent in place of it." (*Digest of Session Cases*, re *Dunfermline Manse*.)

Possession of the present manse was obtained in September, 1816.

The Second Charge never had either manse or glebe.

Another pressing problem, and one of even greater urgency, was the ensuring of a stipend to live on.

Control of the Abbey revenues was now in the hands of a commendator, and there was nothing to be looked for from that quarter. It was not till 1567, seven years after Ferguson's appointment, that provision was made by Act of Parliament for a third of the teinds to be paid to the ministers of the Reformed Church. In this Act it was expressly stipulated that the thirds were to be paid to the ministers " aye and until the Kirk come to the full possession of their proper patrimony, which is the teinds "—a clear recognition by the legislature of the Church's right to the teinds. But even this provision, as a glance at contemporary records abundantly makes clear, did not work at all satisfactorily.

The allowance was not only meagre at the best, but often quite elusory.

In fulfilment of the provisions of this Act an order was issued by the Privy Council requiring all the beneficed clergy in the kingdom to produce their rent-rolls, that the value of the ecclesiastical property might thus be ascertained, and the superintendents were at the same time required to make up lists of the ministers and readers of the Protestant Church, that calculations might be made as to how much would be required for their support.

When the rent-rolls had been produced, as they were after considerable hesitation and delay, it was found that the thirds of all the benefices in the kingdom amounted to £73,880— which would suggest that the total annual revenue of the Roman Church had been in the neighbourhood of a quarter of a million—a tremendous sum of money in those days.

The Commission appointed to modify stipends consisted entirely of Protestants—the Earls of Argyll, Morton and Moray, with the Justice Clerk, the Clerk-Register, the Laird of Lethington and the Laird of Pitarrow—but, Protestant though they were, they proved parsimonious to a degree, and, out of the seventy-three or seventy-four thousand available, they assigned to the ministers £24,231, leaving a balance of over

£48,000. This should, according to plan, have gone to the Crown, but only a fraction of it was handed over. The only redeeming features in the allocation were two entries—one, the sum of £1,018 given to houseless monks and the other, a sum of £754 3s. 11d. given to a number of enfranchised nuns.

Looking back upon it all in after years Ferguson plaintively comments :—

" The greatest number of us have lived in penury, without any stipend—some twelve months, some eight, and some half a year—having nothing in the meantime to sustain ourselves and our families but that which we have borrowed of charitable persons until God send it to us to repay them."

So far as Dunfermline was concerned the development was much as follows :—

On 24th February, 1567-68, the Privy Council ordained that letters" be direct, yit as of befoir, to command and charge the said Collectouris that thai and ilk ane of thame compeir before the Lordis Auditouris of the Chekker and thair mak compt of thair intromissioun of the fruits of the lxvii yeir, within uther sex dayis nixt efter thai be chargeit thairto, under the pane of Rebellioun."

Sir William Murray of Tullibardine, Knight Controller, however, was able to report the receipt of certain sums from the Collector for Fife, " togidder with the third of Dunfermling, baith money and victuallis." (*Reg. P.C.* I. 611.)

That, of course, was all to the good, but it by no means followed that the minister's financial anxieties were immediately at an end. Innumerable difficulties had to be overcome, as a rule, before anything was paid at all.

At a Convention of Estates at Holyroodhouse, 23rd September, 1586, complaint was lodged by the Master of Gray, Commendator of the Abbey of Dunfermline, against certain ecclesiastical commissioners who were attempting to encroach on his prerogative or " at the least thirll him to the payment of certane ministeris stipendis to be modifeit be thame."

This, he asserts, is against all equity and reason. The minister's right to such provision is based on service in the Parish Kirk and within the parochial bounds assigned to him. If the boundaries of the parish have not yet been determined, his claim falls to the ground. In any case, the minister's claim in law extends only to the third, which is in other hands than his.

The two-thirds which are within his control are already " swa exhaustit and dismemberit with pensionis and utheris burdingis, alsweil be Actis of Parliament as utherwayes " that any further encroachment on them will completely dissipate them.

The Lords, finding " the ressonis of the letters abone specifeit to be relevant " discharge the defenders " of all proceding againis the said complenare." (Reg. P.C. IV. 102.)

It was not till the reign of Charles I that provision for the minister became a first charge on the teinds of the parish. From that time forward, payment could more or less be depended on.

It must not be forgotten that, great and many as must have been the calls upon Ferguson's time and strength arising out of his work at Dunfermline, it was not the only sphere of his labours. For a time at least he had also the oversight of Rosyth and Carnock. No doubt in both places he had the assistance of a reader, but, even with that assistance, the calls upon his time must have been considerable.

For his work at Dunfermline and Rosyth his stipend amounted to £160, with £40 added to it after November, 1572. For his work at Carnock he had an allowance out of the thirds of Scotlandwell, the teind of Carnock being attached at that time to the Hospitium there. The curious thing is that the reader at Rosyth was paid out of the third of Dunfermline, the teind at Rosyth being apparently unavailable. Compared with the salaries of others in similar positions, £200 per annum may not seem unduly low, but it was a long time before he got that length.

Ferguson's reputation as a preacher rests largely on a " Sermon preached before the Regent and Nobility at Leith, 13 Jan., 1571-72," during the Assembly, dealing with the provision for Reformed ministers, schools and the poor. It may not have been, as Laing in his Introduction to Ferguson's Tracts remarks, a courtly composition; but when the next General Assembly proposed that it should be published, it was submitted to the revision of five of the most eminent ministers, all of whom expressed strong approbation, and John Knox, one of the number, then on his death-bed, gave it the following emphatic recommendation:—" John Knox, with my dead hand but glad heart, praising God that of His mercy He leaves such light to His Kirk in this desolation.''

A more ambitious publication was a book of his '' writ in defence of the Reformation, in answer to ane Epistle of ane Renat Benedict, a French Doctor,'' printed at Edinburgh, 1563.

Should there be doubts about Ferguson's scholarship, a perusal of this treatise ought to dissipate them.

But, perhaps, the most characteristic production of his pen was his historic collection of Scottish Proverbs, under the following title :—'' Scottish Proverbs : Gathered together by David Ferguson, sometime Minister at Dunfermline ; And put *ordine alphabetico* when he departed this life, Anno 1598. Edinburgh, Printed by Robert Bryson, and are to be sold at his Shop at the signe of Jonah, 1641.''

Nearly everybody who came in contact with him comments on his ready wit and pawky sense of humour and it is no exaggeration to suggest that in this collection he has not only given us something we could ill have spared, but in the compilation of it he has done a good deal to refine and enrich the Scottish language.

The answer to Renat appears to have been accompanied by an original portrait of the author, which, unfortunately, cannot now be traced.

Ferguson was a member of nearly every Assembly that sat up to the day of his death, and there were few committees appointed to deal with matters of delicacy and importance on which he was not called upon to serve. The fact that he was three times Moderator of the General Assembly speaks for itself. The record has not often been exceeded, and no minister of Dunfermline since his day has occupied the chair.

Valuable as his contribution to the Church was in all these ways, there was still one other field in which he played a part that, for his time, places him in a category almost by himself— his personal relations with King James VI. The portrait of him which accompanied his Answer to Renat is said to have borne the inscription :—

'' Mr. David Ferguson, Minister of Dunfermline, and Chaplain to King James VI.''

No confirmation can be found of any such appointment, but few Scottish ministers, by their personal relations with the monarch of their day, can have served their Church so well as David Ferguson did—William Carstairs, perhaps, or Norman Macleod—but the number must be small.

Whoever was responsible for his call to this ministry, there cannot be the shadow of a doubt that the choice was amply justified. In the prosecution of Stevin and Henryson there may be little to suggest unusual wisdom or ability, but it must not be forgotten that in both these cases he was acting, not on his own initiative, but on instructions from headquarters.

The general impression one receives is that of a man of a pleasant and kindly nature, with a keen sense of pawky humour, grown wise as the result of long experience of men, both high and humble, tolerant in non-essentials, but capable of a great upsurge of feeling against wrong-doing in any shape or under any guise.

John Row, of Carnock, his son-in-law, knew him well.

A man of academic distinction, like his father and his son, Row was naturally inclined to look askance at any preparation for the ministry which did not include a University education.

But that did not prevent him seeing and appreciating accomplished facts.

" Albeit he was not a graduat in a colledge, yet the Lord so wrought with him and by him that, being placed in a verie idolatrous and superstitious part of the countrey (in those dayes) to be their minister, by the power of God's Word, whilk he preached both with great boldness, wisdom and holiness, and by the blessing of God on his pains, he brought that people to verie good order, knowledge of the trueth and obedience to the discipline of the Kirk."

In 1615—seventeen years, that is, after Ferguson's death—there is a reference in the Synod Minutes to the " largenes of the congregatione of Dumferling having more than two thousand communicants." Starting, more or less, from zero, it was a considerable accomplishment to have brought the Communion Roll to anything like that number.

At the time of the Great Fire, nine years later, it is estimated that there were 200 houses in Dunfermline, with a population of about 1,600. The number of communicants in the Burgh was 700. The other 1,300 must have resided outside the

Burgh boundaries, but the old parish at this time was still intact, no portions being yet disjoined.

Shortly after settling in Dunfermline, David Ferguson married Isobel Durham, by whom he had nine children—five sons and four daughters. His eldest son, William Ferguson, A.M., survived him. His daughter, Margaret, born 31st May, 1562, was married to Mr. David Spens, minister at Orwell, 18th June, 1581; his daughter Grizzell, born February, 1575-76, was married to Mr. John Row at Carnock in 1595; and his youngest daughter, Isobel, was married to David Ramsay (a layman) before 22nd April, 1598, when her father made his will, the day before his death.

The following figures are taken from the Inventory at the time of his death :—

His buikis of theologie and humane histories	£100	
In poiss of reddie gold - - - -	118	
Reddie money - - - - - - -	52	
Vtenceillis & domiceillis with the abulzie-mentis of his body - - - -	20	
	————	
Summa of the Inuentar - -	£290	
Dettis awin to the deid,		
(Teind and Money Stipend unpaid) -	259 3	4
	————	
	£549 3	4
Dettis awin by the deid :—		
House rent due at Whitsunday and sindrie terms preceiding -	£20	
William Angus, seruand, half-year's fee - -	4	
Janet Burne, seruand, half-year's fee - - - -	4	
Helene Reid, seruand, half-year's fee - - - -	4	
	————	
	£32	
	32 0	0
	————	
Restis of frie geir the dettis deducit - -	£517 3	4

His wife had evidently predeceased him.

Apart from " thrie crounes of the sone to the appoticarie and utheris quhilks ministrat curis to him the tyme of his sicknes " and a double fee to be paid to each of his servants at Whitsunday, he left everything he died possessed of to his family.

" Magister William Ferguson of Balbeuchlie, physician, was admitted burgess (of Dundee), 21st May, 1592, by the privilege of David Fergusone, minister of Dunfermline, his father. . . .

" William Fergusone was born at Dunfermline in 1563 and settled in Dundee. He entered the Town Council in 1601, and served almost continuously till 1626, frequently holding the offices of Bailie, dean of guild, and kirkmaster. . . . He died on 26th March, 1627.

" A splendid monument was erected to his memory in the Howff, Dundee, and still exists, though much defaced." (*Compt Buik of David Wedderburne*, S.H.S., p. 56n.)

Dr. Ferguson was twice married :—(1) Katharine Wedderburn, daughter of Alexander Wedderburn and Janet Myln, and sister of David Wedderburn. (2) Eupham Kinloch, by whom he had a son, William Ferguson, merchant, who married Helen Duncan, daughter of Katharine Wedderburn by her first marriage. (*Ibid.*)

" Magister David Ferguson, great-grandson of David Ferguson, minister of Dunfermline, was also a burgess of Dundee. . . .

" This succession of burgesses carries back the connection of the family with Dundee for over 150 years." (*Burgess Roll of Dundee.*)

Dr. McMillan has kindly supplied the following information with regard to what has come to be known as the Ferguson Mazer (a cup or goblet made of maple, or other hard wood, usually highly ornamented) :—

" Perhaps the most valuable bit of Scottish plate to be lost and found was the Ferguson Mazer, which was exposed for sale in London about 1931 and withdrawn after a bid of £6,000 had been made.

" After the death of the late Laird of Kilkerran, in the parish of Dailly, Ayrshire—General Sir Charles Ferguson—a number of things were removed from the house and thrown into the ' coup.' Among these was an old-fashioned ' band-box ' containing some old militia forage caps, for the Laird had served with that force. A day or two later an old woman visiting the ' coup ' found that the mazer had been under the forage caps, and had it not been for her interest in the contents of the ' coup,' and also, be it said, her honesty, then this most valuable asset might have been lost to the house of Ferguson.

" Though not an ecclesiastical vessel in the ordinary sense, this mazer had a church connection, for it was originally in the possession of David Ferguson, the first Reformed minister of Dunfermline. Indeed, it is quite possible that it had been used at the Communion there, for we know from many sources that such mazers were among the earliest cups to be used at Communions in the Reformed Church of Scotland."

It is deeply to be regretted that the K.S. Minute Book of Ferguson's day is lost beyond hope of recovery. Nothing can quite compensate for that loss. Here and there, however, as in the records of the Synod and the General Assembly, we have glimpses of the sort of questions that bulked largely in those days.

The Reformation was in many ways thorough-going and complete, but it could not have been easy for the new Church to eradicate immediately beliefs and practices that were so long established and so deeply rooted. It must have taken a considerable time, for instance, for people who had all their days been accustomed to the ornate worship of the pre-Reformation Church to become acclimatised to the austerities of post-Reformation worship.

It is not to be wondered at, therefore, that attempts were sometimes made to modify that austerity.

Early in 1612 the congregation gathered for worship in the nave must have been astounded to see a Crucifix painted on the chancellor's seat. The minister at the time, who was not too popular, immediately became suspect, and the question of what was to be done about it was referred to the Synod.

" The mater, being ryplie in all the circumstances considered and pondered (by the Synod), wes found to haue giffen gryt offens to the haill countrey, and that the causer, as also the paynter, of that idolatrous monument, and the minister foirsaid, haue highlie offendit." (Selections, Synod of Fife, p. 43.)

The suspicions of the Synod centred upon Chancellor Seton, and he was cited to appear, with the minister and the painter.

At the September meeting the archbishop reported that he had " acquainted the king's majestie with the offens upon the paintrie of my lord chancellar his desk," and intimated " his heiness ' will that the kirk insist no further in process against his lordship, seeing his majestie thoght the offens sufficientlie removid." The only thing that did happen was that the minister was suspended from the exercise of his office; but it certainly created something of a sensation for the time being.

Another matter that caused considerable ferment locally was the burial of the Laird of Rosyth in the Kirk of Dunfermline, in 1577. The pre-Reformation Church attached considerable importance to burial in consecrated ground. But, from the start, the Reformed Church, not without reason, set itself against burials in churches that were still used for worship. Ferguson, when he heard of what was contemplated, warned the young laird that it was forbidden by Act of Assembly. When the family persisted, he lodged his complaint with the Assembly, which ordered John Durie to warn Mr. James McGill, the Clerk Register, to appear. He, in his defence, pleaded that " the Provost and Baillies of Dunfermline agriet to burie the said Laird of Rossythe in the kirk; that he was not the causer thereof, submittand himselfe allwayes to the judgement of the Kirk, if any offence be found done by him."

No further action seems to have been taken in the matter, but it certainly gave rise to considerable trouble at the time.

The curious thing is that the same thing happened with the same family as late as 1660, and very little was heard of it.

From the Kirk Session Records of that year, 24th April, we gather that the ministers, Mr. Kay and Mr. Oliphant, being informed that it was the intention of the friends and kinsmen of the Laird of Rosyth to bring his body to the kirk, went there between four and five in the morning and found that one of the bailies had taken the keys from the church officer the night before. The bailie said that he had given the keys to the town officer to ring the 5 o'clock bell in the morning. The town officer, when he arrived, refused to hand over the keys. Thereupon a servitor of the Laird of Buchanan and a writer from Edinburgh came upon the scene and with the aid of five or six men forced their way into the church. The ministers protested, but they could do nothing else.

We are so apt to forget the history of this practice.

In the light of medieval teaching and belief, prayers for the dead were not unreasonable, and from that it was a comparatively easy step to the desirability of burial where these prayers were being offered. Monastic life being accepted at the time as the highest expression of religion, and prayers for the dead being offered there almost unceasingly, burial in a monastery church became pre-eminently desirable, and fabulous sums were sometimes paid for the privilege. The right of sepulture was, in fact, one of the most fruitful sources of revenue a monastery possessed.

After the Reformation, no such prayers would have been tolerated, and, that being so, one would have imagined that burial in a church would lose a large measure of its appeal. But the lairds of Rosyth had been for long stewards of the Regality of Dunfermline, with a right, apparently, to burial in the nave, and it is clear that they bitterly resented the withdrawal of that privilege.

On the other hand, few nowadays would question the cogency of the Reformed Church's contention that a place devoted to public worship could not fittingly be used for the disposal of the dead.

The pre-Reformation Church was much more easy-going in respect of Sabbath observance than its successor, and it is not to be wondered at that the question soon became acute as to what sort of occupations should be forbidden during times of worship, and what sort of recreation was permissible in the afternoon.

With regard to the first, the Assembly decreed in 1576 that: "salt-pannes, mylnes, and uther labouring, quhilk drawes away innumerable people from hearing the word of God, sould not be permittit, and the violators to be debarrit from the benefites of the Kirk, quhill (until) they make their repentance, and the continuers therein to be excommunicat."

With regard to the second part of the question, a previous session of the same Assembly refused "to give libertie to the Bailzie of Dunfermling to play upon the Sunday afternoone ane certaine play quhilk is not made upon the canonicall parts of the Scripture, in respect of the Act past in the contrair."

From the wording of the refusal one might be tempted to conclude that, if the play had not been based on the Apocrypha, there would have been no objection raised. But that is by no means certain.

" 21 July, 1574—The said day, anent the supplicatioun gevin be Mr. Patrick Authinlek for procuring licence to play the comede mentionat in Sanct Lucas Euuangel of the forlorne son, upon Sunday, the first day of August nixt to cum, the seat (session) hes decernit first the play to be revisit be my Lord Rectour, Minister, M. Johnne Rutherfur(d), Provost of Sanct Saluatour Colleage, and, gyf they find na falt thairintill, the same to be play(it) upon the said Sunday, the first of August, swa that playing thairof be nocht occasioun to wythdraw the pepil fra heryng of the preaching, at the howre appointed alsweil eftir nune as befoir nune." (*K.S.R. St. And.* 1559-82, 396.)

The matter came, however, before the Assembly.

" In his answer concerning Robin Hood's plays, Hamilton (Commissioner for St. Andrews) admitted that ' certane servands and young children plaid them certane days,' but, he added, ' alwayis the kirk baith prevatlie in thair assemble, and I publiclie in tyme of preching, dischargeit (forbade) the samen, as it is notorious knawn, and desyrit the magistrattis to tak ordour thairwith.'

" He further stated that ' Ane clark play wes plaid be the scollouris of the grammar-scull, bot not at the tyme of preching, and yit for causes moving us we dischargeit the mais (ter again ?) to play the samen.'

" A fortnight later, 7 March, 1574-75, the General Assembly again met at Edinburgh, and considering that ' the playing of clerk playes, comedies or tragedies, upon the canonical parts of Scripture inducit and bringeth with it a contempt and profanation of the same,' concluded ' That no clerk playes, comedies or tragedies, be made of the canonicall Scripture, alsweil new as old, neither on the Sabboth day nor worke day, in tyme comeing; the contraveiners hereof (if they be ministers) to be secludit fra, and if they be utheris, to be punischit be the discipline of the Kirk.' " (*Ibid.* 397.)

Another question of widespread interest was as to whether or not, in view of the difficulties attendant on the payment of stipend, even after it was decreed, it was permissible for a minister to leave his charge on the ground that he could not live on what he received. The answer of the Assembly was as follows :—

" Seeing that our Master Christ Jesus pronounces that he (such a man) is but ane mercenarie who, seeing the wolf coming, fleeth for his own safeguard, and that the very danger of lyfe cannot be ane excuse for sic as shall fall back from Christ, we nowayes think it lawfull that sic as ance put their hands to the plough shall leave the heavenly vocation and return to the prophane world for indigence or povertie ; lawfully they may leave an unthankfull people and seek where Jesus Christ his Evangell may bring forth better fruit : but lawfully they may never change their vocation."

Towards the close of Ferguson's ministry, the Scottish Parliament met in Dunfermline, and the General Assembly of the Church of Scotland very nearly did so.

" About the end of November (1585) warning was maid, according to the ordour of the Kirk be the last Moderator, athort the countrey to the breithring, to convein in General Assemblie, conforme to custome befor the Parliament at Dunfermling, na uther meit town being frie of the pest. The breithring frequentlie (in numbers) furthe of all partes resorting thither. The portes of the town war closit upon tham be the Provost for the tyme, the Lard of Pitfirren, alleaging he haid the King's expres command sa to do.

" Therfor the breithring, commending the wrang to God, the righteous Judge, convenit sa monie as might in the fields and, comforting themselves mutualie in God, apointed to meit in Linlithgow a certean dayes befor the Parliament." (*Melville's Diary*, 226.)

It cannot be said with certainty where David Ferguson was buried. Traditional belief has it that the old tombstone on the west side of the walk, half way between the North Gate and the Porch, is his. It is probable enough. Unfortunately the inscription has become quite indecipherable.

It seems such a pity that the memory of men like David Ferguson and John Durie, who served their day and generation so faithfully and so well, should be allowed to slip into oblivion.

8A

John Christison—Reader at Dunfermline

The office of reader is an old one in the Church of Scotland and came into prominence in the days following the Reformation owing to the scarcity of qualified ministers.

A number of smaller churches would be grouped together under the charge of a minister, assisted by one or two readers.

In the absence of the minister, the reader would read, not only the lessons, but the prayers as well ; and if he happened to have the additional qualification of an " Exhorter," he would also preach, but he could not lawfully marry or dispense the sacraments.

The minister would not confine himself to one church but would visit each one in his group periodically and conduct a service.

In larger centres, such as Dunfermline, there would be both a minister and a reader, the reader fulfilling more or less the duties of a present-day assistant.

In Dunfermline, at least, the practice gradually developed of utilising the reader as Session Clerk, Registrar, and Precentor, so that, even after the office was formally abolished in 1581, appointments on that basis continued to be made.

In Aberdour he seems to have been also schoolmaster, for in a Kirk Session minute of 1671 there is an entry to the effect that " something was given to the reader for instructing poor scholars."

" The office came into public notice as late as 1725, when the Marquis of Tweeddale claimed the right of presenting a reader to the Abbey, even though he could be only a precentor, His Lordship's presentee to have also the registrarship. The ministers (Ralph Erskine and James Wardlaw) resented the claim, on the grounds that they were responsible for the whole service in public worship, and could precent themselves or furnish substitutes ; and when the Court of Session decided in favour of the Marquis, they still adhered to their contention, and officiated more or less as precentors to each other till 1734, when the differences were amicably settled." (*Stevenson, Comm. in Dunf. pp.* 27, 28.)

In the Register of Readers there is a reference to John Burn, who is said to have been reader at Dunfermline and afterwards became minister at Inverkeithing. The explanation is that, as noted elsewhere, David Ferguson was for a time in charge of the parish of Rosyth, as well as that of Dunfermline, the two charges being temporarily worked together. Burn, however, was really working at Rosyth, not at Dunfermline, and became Minister of Inverkeithing in 1570.

The practice of appointing readers was not confined to Scotland, but prevailed also in the Church of England, where, in accordance with the agreement reached at Lambeth in 1561, every candidate for the office had to subscribe the following statement :—

" Imprimis, I shall not preache or interprete, but only read that which is appointed by publick authoritie.

" I shall read the service appointed playnlie, distinctlie and audiblie, that all the people may heare and understand.

" I shall not minister the sacraments nor other publick rites of the Church. . . ." (*Wilkin's Concilia*, iv. 225.)

The first reader at Dunfermline was **John Christison,** a former monk of Culross Abbey.

The name was not uncommon in the district at the time.

There was a " Magister Johanne Christisone," who was Vicar of Cleish from 1464 to 1494 approximately (*Hall*, 173)— evidently a man of some education and standing. The " magister " would indicate that he was a University graduate in Arts. He was owner of some property in Dunfermline and the founder of St. Ninian's Chapel.

There were also two other monks in Culross of the same surname, Robert and Thomas—a John Christison resident in Dunfermline *c.* 1530—and there was a William Christison, who became minister at Dundee in 1560—where John of Culross made his first public appearance in the Reforming cause.

It sounds a Northern name, and it is suggestive that in a Danish case which came before the Kirk Session of St. Andrews, the help of William Christison, minister at Dundee, had to be invoked, there being no one at the University who could speak Danish. (*Reg. K.S., St. And.*, xxxvii. 48n, 49.)

It is probable that these, or some of them, were of the same stock as the monk of Culross who became reader in Dunfermline Abbey.

John Christison must have left Culross before 1560, for, on the day that Ferguson was summoned to appear before the justice and his deputies at Edinburgh, he and Paul Methven,

William Harlaw, and John Willock were likewise summoned to stand trial before the Justiciary Court at Stirling for usurping the ministerial office, for administering, without the consent of their ordinaries, the sacrament of the altar in a manner different from that of the Catholic Church during three several days of the late feast of Easter, in the burghs and boundaries of Dundee, Montrose, and various other places in the sheriffdoms of Forfar and Kincardine, and for convening the subjects in these places, preaching to them, seducing them to their erroneous doctrines, and exciting seditions and tumults.

As the preachers were resolved to appear, George Lovell, burgess of Dundee, became surety for Methven, John Erskine of Dun for Christison, Patrick Murray of Tibbermuir for Harlaw, and Robert Campbell of Kinyeancleugh for Willock.

So many, however, expressed their intention of accompanying the preachers to the place of trial that the Queen Regent became apprehensive and besought Erskine of Dun to dissuade them, authorising him to promise them in her name that she would put a stop to the trial.

(*Note.*—This account of the interview between the Queen-Regent and Erskine of Dun may be open to question, but that she did break faith with the congregation a fortnight later is certain. (*Macewen. Hist.* II. 101n.))

When the day of trial came, the summons being issued by orders of the Queen, the preachers were outlawed for not appearing, and all persons were prohibited, under the pain of rebellion, from harbouring or assisting them.

The gentlemen who had given security for their appearance were fined. (*McCrie's Life of Knox*, I. 257.)

The next we hear of Christison he is minister at Fetteresso in 1560, with Dunnottar and Glenbervie also in his charge, removing to Glenbervie before 28th September, 1570. (*Fasti.*)

We know also that he became reader in Dunfermline in November, 1570, and continued in that office till 1574. It may seem a little surprising that a man who had been inducted to a charge of his own should give it up for a readership. But it was one thing to get admitted to a charge and quite another to secure the teinds belonging to the parish, or even any share of them; and, with all his fine qualities, Christison, as we shall see, had a keen enough sense of money-values.

" Mr. John Christieson, reider at Dunfermling, his stipend xl lib. to be paid as follows :—the thrids of the vicarage thereof xx merks, and out of the thrids of Dunfermling, be the Abbotes, Chamerlain, takkisman, or parochinar of Dunfermling xx merkis." (*MS. fol. Adv. Lib. Edin.*, 1574.)

After leaving Dunfermline he became minister at Logie (Dundee), being admitted to that parish before 1576, with Liff and Invergowrie also in his charge, and, presumably, he remained there till his death, before 30th June, 1615.

Another John Christison, possibly enough a grandson of the reader, was admitted to the charge of Liff, 30th July, 1673, on appointment by Archbishop Sharp. He was deprived by Act of Parliament following the Restoration, but afterwards received into communion. (*Fasti.*)

John Christison's first marriage, 30th April, 1570, is recorded in the Register of Dunfermline, as is also the birth of his first child, William, 25th January, 1572-73. There is nothing in these entries to enable us to identify him beyond question, but he was certainly living in Dunfermline, as reader there, when the child, William, was born. If we accept the entries as referring to him, he must have been three times married :—

(1) Bessie Keir, 30th April, 1570.
(2) Janet Davidson (died before 12th February, 1609) (*Fasti.*)
(3) Christian Westwood. (*Forfar Inhibitions*, 17th July, 1615.)

Janet Davidson was a sister of John Davidson (page 94), Minister of Prestonpans, a native of Dunfermline and educated there, and one of the outstanding figures in ministerial circles at the time.

The Davidson family consisted of :—

(1) Janet, married John Crystesone, minister at Liff.
(2) John, afterwards minister at Prestonpans.
(3) Lawrence.
(4) Catherine, married John Law.
(5) Isobel.
(6) Bessie, married Henry Clerk, burgess of Dundee.
(7) Helen, died before 1610—had a son, James Law.

After a dispute between John Christison and the Davidsons over the executry of Janet Davidson, Christison undertook to pay Davidson 400 merks. (*Reg. of Deeds*, 170, fol. 180, 12th February, 1609, Regd. 26th April, 1610.).

James Christison, burgess of Edinburgh, had given a bond for £50 to John Christison, and £10 of liquidat expenses, in case of failure. Christian Westwood, after her husband's death, took action against James Christison for the recovery of the £50. (*Forfar Inhibitions*, 17th July, 1615.)

The last reference that can be traced concerning him is a disappointing one :—

" Edinburgh, 4th June, 1612.—Complaint by Sir thomas Hammiltoun of Byris, King's Advocate, for his Majesty's interest, as follows :—On the 7th of March last he had obtained decree before the Lords of Council and Session against the following persons for contravening the Acts of Parliament forbidding the taking of more than 10 per cent. interest for money given out by them, viz. :— . . . Mr. Johnne Crystesoun, minister at Liff . . .

" These persons were therefore declared liable to the pains ordained by the said Act of Parliament, viz. : confiscation of all their movable goods and punishment in their persons ; and this second portion of their punishment is at the discretion of the Lords of Council.

" Those who did not appear were denounced as rebels for their non-appearance." (*Reg. P.C.* IX. 385.)

(*Note.*—One must keep in mind the very strong prejudice existing at the time both in England and Scotland against interest in any form or at any rate.)

John Christison was not the only reader in Dunfermline, but owing to the loss of the Kirk Session Records prior to 1640, it is not possible to give his immediate successors. We know, however, that John Walker was reader from 1604 to 1640, and that he was succeeded by Robert Anderson.

Following the General Assembly at Perth in 1618, when the Five Articles were adopted, both John Murray of Dunfermline and John Row of Carnock not only declined to conform but actively opposed the change. The two were very friendly and Row preached often in Dunfermline. John Walker, who was reader at Dunfermline at the time, reported the substance of Row's preaching to the authorities, with the result that

Row was confined to his own parish for two years, and Murray was deposed. (*Row's Hist.*, 476.)

"25 Aug. 1640—Mr. Robt. Anderson was ordainit be the minister and elders to read the prayers both morning and evening, alsweill on Sabbath as weik dayes . . . and ordainit the bookes of baptism, mariage and dead, and session booke to be delyverit to him." (*K.S.R.*)

For further notes on readers see page 189.

John Fairfoul. 1598-1610

In that wonderful record, Dr. Hew Scott's *Fasti Ecclesiae Scoticanae*, too little known even amongst ministers of the Church, there is a more or less detailed account of every minister known to have held office in a charge of the Church of Scotland, and anyone sufficiently interested will find there particulars of the ministers who, since the Reformation, have held office in Dunfermline Abbey.

To round off our story, however, it is desirable that some notice should be taken of them here—much of the information being derived from the above source.

Following David Ferguson, the first minister to be appointed was John Fairfoul. Prior to this appointment he had studied at St. Salvator's College, St. Andrews, had been exhorter at Aberdour, schoolmaster at Dunfermline, and had held the vicarage of Beath and Dalgety. Three years after his appointment he was nominated by the General Assembly " a minister for the King's and Queen's house " (royal chaplain), but was not accepted. Two years later, he was, strangely enough, as it seems to us, appointed by the king " Master of the Grammar School of Culross," while still holding office as minister of Dunfermline. By the Assembly of 1606 he was appointed " constant Moderator of the Presbytery," the members being charged by the Privy Council to receive him as such, 25th January following, within twenty-four hours after notice, under pain of rebellion. What is generally known as the First Episcopacy did not begin till 1610, but for 20 years before that there had been an almost constant struggle between Presbytery and Episcopacy, and at this particular Assembly the Episcopal element seems to have predominated, and the " constant moderator " was a feature of its administration.

In 1609 Fairfoul was called before the Privy Council, at the instance of the chancellor, the Earl of Dunfermline, and charged, on information supplied by his colleague, Andrew Forrester, with praying for the ministers who had been banished in 1606 for attending the Assembly at Aberdeen the preceding year, notwithstanding the king's prohibition of that Assembly.

" At the Assembly of 1605 at Aberdeen nineteen ministers attended and insisted on constituting the Court. Some days afterwards a few other ministers who had been delayed on the way by reason of ' spaits of waters ' arrived. Fourteen of the ministers were brought before the Council, some of them were ' warded ' in Blackness and eight, including Andrew and James Melville, were sent to England. On 13th October, 1606, a Proclamation was issued by the King stating that no minister ' presume at any time hereafter to remember in their sermons and prayers any of these convicted traitors (the imprisoned and banished ministers) . . . neither any way make mention of them either generally or particularly in any of their public exercises either of preaching or prayer, except it be in disallowing of their proceedings : under pain of death to be inflicted with all rigour upon such as will presume to contravene the command of this our present charge.' " (*Calderwood* vi. 583.)

Being found guilty of the charge, Fairfoul was ordered to repair to Dundee, within six days, there to continue during the royal pleasure.

On 8th March, 1610, his place of confinement was changed to West Anstruther. At the same time he was forbidden to attend ecclesiastical meetings without the king's leave, but received liberty, " enduring the tyme of his stay in said parroche, to teache and preache in the kirke thereof."

He became minister there 19th August, 1610.

When Mr. Ferguson died, there were 2,000 communicants on the roll of Dunfermline Abbey, and a movement was set on foot, as we shall see later, to make provision for two ministers. It was a doubtful move, as is evidenced by the fact that it was on information supplied to the Crown by his colleague that Fairfoul was suspended from office and banished to Dundee.

The main difficulty, of course, was finance. Towards the end of his ministry, Ferguson was in receipt of a stipend that was not unduly small as compared with others in a similar position. But there was certainly not enough to meet the needs of two ministers.

And so, for a time, the stipend of the second charge had to be " a voluntar gift, granted by the inhabitants."

In the meantime we shall continue with the ministers of the First Charge, leaving those of the Second to be dealt with later.

Andrew Forrester.   1610-1616

He had been minister of the Second Charge since 1598.

This was the minister who reported Fairfoul to the chancellor and himself got into trouble over a Crucifix which was unexpectedly found emblazoned on the chancellor's seat in the church (p. 110). Fortunately for him, the king put a stop to the process of inquiry, but the evil day was not long delayed.

Having appropriated money from the poor box, and fearing apprehension, he fled from his charge in 1616, on a Sunday, after having announced his text from the pulpit.

John Moray, M.A.   1620-1622

Soon after he was settled in, Moray was summoned before the Court of High Commission, 12th December, 1621, to answer for his non-conformity to Episcopacy, was deprived of office and was ordered to confine himself within two miles of Fowlis-Wester. Failing to comply, he was charged on pain of outlawry, 6th February following, to appear before the Council within fifteen days. A further summons was sent on 24th June, 1624, but, having fallen from his horse shortly before, he could not attend, and his confinement was confirmed " more straitly than at first."

During this confinement, he resided at Gorthie, which belonged to an elder brother—Sir David Moray of Gorthie—on whose death in 1629 he removed to Prestonpans, where he died, January, 1632, aged about 57.

Henry Makgill, M.A.   1622-1642

Nearly all his ministry was under Episcopalian government, but when Presbyterianism was restored in 1638, he conformed.

" 2 Oct. 1638—Mr. William Macgill, Doctor of Physick, and two others admitted to be Honorary Burgesses." (B.R.)

" 4 May, 1639—The Town Council having received instructions from the Committee of War anent the levying of 25 men
furth of the Burgh for going to the South in the present expedition—for choosing the said 25 men the Council elected Mr.
Harrie Macgill, Minister, James Reid, Provost, and 4 others, who
were to report their nominations to next Council day.'' (B.R.)

" 21 May, 1640—The Council ordained Alexr. Drysdaill
(a bailie) to pay 17s. for ane lawing spendit in the Provost's
hous the last Sabbath eftir noone eftir sermone with Mr. Harie
Mackgill, minister, and Mr. Johne Lourie, ane stranger minister,
becaus he refused to keepe thame companie and societie.''
(B.R.)

" 8 Feb., 1641—Peter Law, last Provost, declared that of
necessity for furnishing of the toune's souldiers to this prnt.
expedition he borrowit fra Mr. Harie Macgill xx rex dollars
. . . and was willing to mak compt.'' (B.R.)

Robert Kay.   1645-1665

While many changes fall to be recorded in the course of the
generations, practice and procedure in the Church, in so far
as some things at least are concerned, show very little variation,
and any departure from the normal invites speculation as to
the reason why.

In 1645 both charges in Dunfermline became vacant, and
James Reddy, schoolmaster, was appointed interim moderator.
(K.S.R.)

It has always been the law and practice of the Church that
only a minister could act as moderator in a church court. The
only known exception, if it really is an exception, is that of
Erskine of Dun, who became moderator of the General Assembly;
but even yet there is some doubt as to whether or not he was
ordained.

Reddy, who was a graduate in Arts, had previously been reader
and schoolmaster in Inverkeithing, and may have been a
Licentiate, but there is nothing to show that he had ever been
ordained. Who appointed him is not recorded. The minute
simply bears that he " acted as Moderator.'' In the early
seventeen-hundreds, during a vacancy, it is more than once
recorded that the Session could transact no business " because
there was no actuall Moderator.''

Another unusual case happened about 20 years later.

"13 Nov., 1660—Wm. reid, being called on, compeirit, who produced a testimonial of his marriage with grissell kirk, subscribit only be *mr adam anderson, who married them.* . . . The session think fit to seik the presbyteries aduice therein." *(K.S.R.)*

There was an Act of Assembly forbidding readers to marry, and such a prohibition would seem to imply the existence of the practice. But Anderson was not a reader. He was simply one of the Session. There was, it is true, a reader of the name of Anderson, but that was 20 years before, and his Christian name was Robert.

Dr. Chalmers says: "Mr. Robert Kay of Dumbarton was settled minister of the second charge of Dunfermline, along with Mr. William Oliphant, as minister of the first charge, on the same day, the 15th January, 1645." *(Hist.* i. 423.)

The minute of Kirk Session says: "The 15 day of Jan. 1645 Mr. Robert Kay and Mr. William Oliphant were admitted ministers of the Kirk of Dunfermline." But it says nothing about the charges to which they were admitted. It does, however, put Mr. Kay's name first, and this it does, not on this occasion only, but in every reference it makes to the two of them.

The *Fasti*, on the other hand, is quite definite about it. Mr. Kay held the First Charge and Mr. Oliphant the Second.

After all these years, it may not seem a vital matter, but it might have a bearing on the question left unsolved on page 102— the question of the site of the original Abbey Manse.

If Mr. Oliphant, as Dr. Chalmers says, was really minister of the First Charge, one would be justified in concluding that the house there referred to was the manse. If the *Fasti* is right, the problem still remains unsolved.

Mr. Kay was not admitted till January, 1645, but he preached in Dunfermline Abbey on 5th November, 1643, and signed The Solemn League and Covenant.

In February, 1649, the Presbytery of Dunfermline issued a so-called "Overture for Ordering of Kirk Sessions" to all charges within its bounds and the Kirk Session of Dunfermline incorporated it in its records. About 1841 a certain William Peebles of Dunfermline took an extract of it and sent it to the

Rev. John G. Lorimer, Glasgow, who published it, in modern English, in his book on *The Eldership of the Church of Scotland* (p. 110).

It runs as follows :—

" The Presbytery learning frequently from the brethren of every parish that still profaneness abounded, and that they find very small progress of the power of godliness in the places of their charge . . . therefore do appoint that there be a new election of elders and deacons in every congregation of their bounds . . . and that they be

1st. Men of good report both for knowledge and conversation, free of scandalous walking, such as are known to govern their families well and to have all religious exercises in their families, as likewise attenders upon the public worship at all occasions.

2nd. It is thought expedient that in the most numerous congregations there be about eighteen elders and twelve deacons. In the less numerous there be about ten elders and eight deacons, and in the least there be about six elders and four deacons.

3rd. That magistrates in parishes, having the foresaid qualifications, be chosen elders.

4th. The said elders and deacons to meet together in session with the minister once every week, absentees to be marked and censured, and who shall be found absent without a sufficient reason approved of by the kirk, to be admonished ; if continue to be absent, to be called before the Session to be censured ; and if he refuse to submit, then to be cited before the public to be censured there.

5th. That they have their several wards and bounds, over which in a special manner they watch, and that every first Session day in the month, the minister enquire concerning the behaviour of those under their charge, which is not to exempt them from duty towards the rest of the people as they shall have occasion.

6th. That when it is found any connive at faults, neglect to delate them, or speak in Sessions for offenders, they be censured for the first fault with rebukes and, if fail again in any of these, then to be put a while from the exercise of their office, and if continue, to be deposed.

7th. That the elders visit the families of their bounds four times a year, to know of their Christian teaching, and what obedience they give to the acts of the kirk, and to report accordingly; and the Session call for an account of their diligence herein on the first Session day of the month of February, of the month of May, of August and of November, and that they be reminded of this duty every quarter of the year timeously.

8th. That when there is any sick persons within their charge they visit them and give also advertisement to the minister of any sick persons.

9th. That no sooner any stranger, that is, any from another parish, shall come into their bounds to reside but that they give notice thereof to the session at their first meeting, and that they may have his testimonials or else that he be removed out of their bounds.

10th. That elders join with the minister in the visitation of their several quarters, and that they come with the people of their division to catechising and examination.

11th. That elders and deacons failing in the foresaid duties be censured by the Session, and if they continue in their faults, to be cited before the Presbytery to be censured there."

The extract ends with the Session's finding :—

" Which orders, being read in session, were received and approved, and appointed to be read publicly out of the pulpit."

In 1640, the records show a division of the burgh into six quarters, served by twenty-two elders, while the landward portion of the parish was divided into ten quarters, served by thirty-two elders, besides two for the Abbey—fifty-six in all. And, as usual, the elders were the leading men of the district.

" 19 Oct. 1645—At this tyme meetings were not frequent because of the plague of the pestilence which then was in the paroche, and increasit in the same, so that many died."

" 25 Nov. 1645—And because the number of the poor did increase in this tyme of the plague, many tradismen put to penurie for want of comercing, and handling of geir and money, qlk was then dangerous to use, and little alms collected, thairfore it was thot fitt that meill should be given to the poore for thair present help, and that the presint collections and moneys wch were in the boxe should paye for the said meill, till after that the Lord of His mercie withdraw His judgement of the plague, when other courses may be taine for supplying of the poore, and for restoring of the moneys again to the boxe."

" 1 Oct. 1648—The twa last sabbaths no Sermon nor session was, because of the malignante troupes of Lenrick and Monro's regimentis that came and quartered ymselves in thir bounds and plundert and abusit manie."

" 17 July 1651—being a thursday, cromwell's armie landed heir, who, on the sabbath yreftir, being the 20 day of the sd. month, battell being beside pitreavie, killed and cutt manie of or (our) men, robbed and plunderit all. Everie man that was able fledd for a tyme, so yt yr could be no meeting for Discipline this space."

" 12 Aug. 1651—The boord and seatts of the session hous and the Kirk boxe being all broken, and the haill money in the said boxe being all plunderit and taken away be Cromwell's men, It is thot fitt yt the session hous be repaird and the boxe mendit ; And thairfore Thomas Elder an Jon Duncan are desyred to speak to Thomas horne, wryt, to doe the same, as also to mak a new brod (plate) to gather the offering."

" 19 Aug. 1651—The Session hous being repaired and the boxe mendit, and no money to pay the wryt his paymente is delayed till it be gotten."

" 11 April 1654—This day Mr. Wm. Oliphant, moderator in Mr. Rot. Kay's absence, who should have enterit moderator this month, but was put by the englishes in prison in Inchgarvie, for praying for the king."

To pray for King Charles with Cromwell's troops quartered in the Palace and Queen's House must have required no small courage.

" 25 Apr. 1654—The session referrit to the provost James reid to speak the governor of the Inglishe in the abbay to tak ordor wt. his soldiers for profaining the Lord's day, by drinking in aill houses in the toun in tyme of sermon—and for breaking the glaisin of the Kirk."

The Kirk Session also elected commissioners to supplicate the commander-in-chief of the English for relieving Kay out of the prison in Inchgarvie to his own house, which was granted " until farther order," and that he might have liberty to preach again, " quhilk is thocht fit to be advysit by the Presbytery."

The Second Charge was by this time firmly established, and Kay and Oliphant were the first colleagues on a normal basis.

" 20 Septr., 1662—The Provost produces a supplication subscribed by some gentlemen of the parish to be given in to the Bishop showing the great weakness of Mr. Robert Kay, present minister, for so great a charge, and craving that the place be rendered vacant and that His Grace would assist the patrons to supply the same with habile pastors. The Council subscribed it." (B.R.)

Kay demitted office in 1665 and in March, 1666, was presented to the Kirk of Stow. The Session Records of Stow contain the following comment: " This was the first of the ' curates ' in this parish "—the Second Episcopacy being by this time well under way.

William Pierson, M.A. (afterwards D.D.)   1666-1676
He was translated from Paisley and translated to Stirling.

Alexander Dunbar, M.A.   1676-1678
Son of the Sheriff of Moray and educated at King's College, Aberdeen.

Aberdeen was at this time quite definitely sympathetic to Episcopacy. He died 22nd March, 1678, aged about 40.

Robert Norrie, M.A.   1678-1686
He complained to the Privy Council, 4th May, 1681, against certain Justices of the Peace for issuing a warrant against him to make him account for the fines in the Kirk Session.

John Wardlaw, M.A.
Fasti gives the name of John Wardlaw as minister of the First Charge, Dunfermline, from 1679 to 1686, but this is clearly incorrect, for Mr. Norrie held that charge from 1678 to 1686.

Dr. Chalmers, on the other hand, seems never to have heard of him, which is surprising, for he was not only a local man of some standing, but played an active part in connection with Dunfermline Abbey. He was a son of Thomas Wardlaw, M.A., Laird of Logie, and Katherine, daughter of Laurence Dalgleish. An elder sister, Margaret, married, in each case as second

View of Nave from south-east.

wife, (1) the Rev. Harry MacGill, minister of the First Charge, 1622-1642, and (2) James Reid, Provost of Dunfermline. He was also a relation of James Wardlaw of Luscar, who was minister of the Second Charge 1718-1742.

" Baptised on 20 Oct. 1629, graduated M.A. at St. Andrews University on March 12, 1652, elected minister of the Second Charge, Cupar, on Feb. 6, 1655, called to Kemback on Feb. 17, 1656 and admitted on July 2 following, deprived of office by Act of Parliament of June 11, 1662, and Act of Privy Council of Oct. 1, 1662, and deposed on Oct. 23, 1663, for not submitting to Church Government (Episcopal). Later he was resident in Dunfermline; and on July 16, 1674, he was denounced as a rebel, put to the horn, and had his goods confiscated, for holding conventicles. Subsequently, on Dec. 18, 1679, in answer to a petition by Robert Ged of Baldridge and others for themselves and in the name of other parishioners of Dunfermline, Mr. Wardlaw was allowed by the Privy Council to preach in terms of the Act of Indulgence. About a year later, however, he was again summoned before the Council to answer a charge of keeping conventicles and of exercising the other functions of the ministry without having been licensed; and for failure to compear he was once more put to the horn on June 2, 1681. He died after May 23, 1682." (*Stephen*, 202.)

A thorough-going Covenanter—no doubt of that—and one who, quite clearly, had a following in Dunfermline, but he never had access to the abbey and his services must have been held elsewhere.

Simon Coupar, M.A.   1686-1693
He was accused before the Privy Council, 4th September, 1689, of not reading the Proclamation of the Estates, not praying for their Majesties William and Mary, and for saying, when there came the news of the defeat at Killiecrankie, " that no less could come of them for rebelling against their lawful sovereign," but he was acquitted as this was not proven. He was deposed by the United Presbytery of Dunfermline and Kirkcaldy, 28th December, 1693, for contumacy and contempt of its authority, and this sentence was confirmed by the Synod. Apparently he still refused to budge till he was ordered by the Privy Council to leave the church, 4th June, 1694.

9

John Gray. 1688-1691

The first Presbyterian minister of Dunfermline after the Revolution Settlement.

Though duly appointed and admitted to the charge, he did not get possession of the church, Coupar and Graham, the Episcopalian ministers of the First and Second Charges, still remaining in possession. Gray's services were conducted in the Meeting-house in Canmore Street.

William Gullan. 1692-1694

Ordained in the Meeting-house and conducted services there during the two years of his ministry.

Hugh Kemp. 1701-1704

During his incumbency the parish church was occupied one-half of the day by his Episcopal colleague, James Graham, and the other by himself—in spite of the fact that the Revolution Settlement of 1688 had put an end to Episcopacy in the Church of Scotland.

Thomas Buchanan. 1710-1715

He was seized with palsy at Edinburgh, where he had gone to attend the Assembly, returned and resumed duty, but died 10th April, 1715.

Ralph Erskine, M.A. 1716-1740

" Matriculated at the University of Edinburgh, November, 1699, and is said to have graduated M.A. in 1704 (though his name is not in the list of graduates published by the Bannatyne Club); from 1705 to 1711 he was tutor to the children of the ' Black Colonel,' John Erskine of Carnock, one of his pupils being the well-known author of *Institutes of the Law of Scotland*. He completed his theological curriculum during this period of tutorship and was licensed by the Presbytery of Dunfermline 8 June, 1709. On 1 May, 1711, he was called to the Second Charge here, and on 14 June following to the parish of Tulliallan. He preferred Dunfermline, and was ordained 7 August, 1711; presented by the Presbytery *jure devoluto*, he was translated and admitted to the First Charge 1 May, 1716.

" In the controversy with the General Assembly which led to the Secession of 1733, he adhered to all the protests on behalf of the Four Brethren, being one of the ' Twelve Apostles ' or Representers of 1721. Eventually he joined the Associate Presbytery 16 February, 1737, and was deposed 15 May, 1740.

" He took an active interest in the visit of George Whitefield to Scotland in 1741, but repudiated some of the features of the Revival at Cambuslang. On the question of the Burgess Oath he sided with his brother, Ebenezer, in thinking it a matter for the individual conscience, and, on the separation of the party opposed to the Oath, he issued an admonition to the separatists.

" He was a skilled musician, a lover of the violin, and a religious poet whose sonnets and hymns had an extensive circulation.

" He preached his last sermon on 29 October and died of a nervous fever 6 November, 1752." (*Fasti*, v. 30.)

James Thomson, M.A.   1743-1790

Had previously served for 14 years as Chaplain to the Cameronian Regiment of Foot. During a parliamentary election for the Stirling district of burghs, he accused (in his sermon from Ephesians iv. 25) several persons by name of lying, on which an action was brought in the Court of Session and decided 8th August, 1776, against him, when he was found liable in five pounds to one, and twenty-five to another, with fifty guineas of expenses.

" During my stay in London this spring I (Boswell) solicited his (Dr. Johnson's) attention to another law case in which I was engaged. In the course of a contested election for the borough of Dunfermline, which I attended as one of my friend Colonel (afterwards Sir Archibald) Campbell's counsel, one of his political agents, who was charged with having been unfaithful to his employer and having deserted to the opposite party for a pecuniary reward, attacked very rudely, in a newspaper, the Rev. Mr. James Thomson, one of the ministers of that place, on account of a supposed allusion to him in one of his sermons.

" Upon this the minister, on a subsequent Sunday, arraigned him by name from the pulpit with some severity ; and the agent, after the sermon was over, rose up and asked the minister aloud, ' What bribe he had received for telling so many lies from the chair of verity.'

" I was present at this very extraordinary scene.

" The person arraigned, and his father and brother, who also had a share both of the reproof from the pulpit and in the retaliation, brought an action against Mr. Thomson in the Court of Session for defamation and damages, and I was one of the counsel for the reverend defendant.

" The *liberty of the pulpit* was our great ground of defence ; but we argued also on the provocation of the previous attack, and on the instant retaliation.

" The Court of Session, however—the fifteen judges, who were at the same time the jury—decided against the minister contrary to my humble opinion ; and several of them expressed themselves with indignation against him. He was an aged gentleman, formerly a military chaplain, and a man of high spirit and honour.

" Johnson was satisfied that the judgment was wrong, and dictated to me the following argument in confutation of it. . . .

" I don't think the appeal advisable ; not only because the value of the judgment is in no degree adequate to the expense ; but because there are many chances that, upon the general complexion of the case, the impression will be taken to the disadvantage of the appellant . . . E. Thurlow."

(*Boswell's Life of Johnson, under year* 1776.)

Thomson preached regularly in his turn till his eighty-ninth year, and delivered an action sermon lasting two hours when he was ninety.

He left £100 to the poor of the parish.

" 19 April, 1753—James Wilson, Town Clerk of Dunfermline, compearing before the Session, gave in a Commission from the Magistrates and Town Council of that Burgh to Mr. Colin Angus, Merchant in Limekilns, to represent the said Burgh in the ensuing General Assembly, and craved that the Session would attest it. . . .

" The Session considering that though the said Mr. Colin Angus commonly attends Publick Worship in the Parish Church one part of the Lord's Day, yet he acts so far irregularly as to go for another part of that day to the Meeting House where Mr. Gillespie, deposed by the late General Assembly, preaches, admonished him to behave more regularly for the future, hoping he would do so.

" After this, they unanimously agreed to attest his Commission." (K.S.R.)

" The meeting having considered that this parish for some time past, at least the tenendry and householders therein, have been in some degree opprest by numbers of begging poor travelling in a begging way through the same belonging to distant (?) countrys and parishes, and which will probably increase still more by reason of the present scarcity, unless remedy be provided. They therefore resolve and agree that there shall be badges given to the whole begging poor belonging to this parish and that none shall be served without such badges after the tenth day of May next, and in order that such badges may be given to none but to proper objects, the meeting appoint said badges only to be given by the Magistrates of Dunfermline and Kirk Session at a joint meeting, or as concerted at a joint meeting, betwixt and the said tenth day of May, and recommends it to Mr. James Thomson, minister of Dunfermline, present, to cause make proper intimation of this from the Letteron Sunday next." (H.R., 29th April, 1757.)

Allan MacLean. 1791-1836

After a protracted litigation at his own expense, he obtained a judgment of the Court of Session, 19th November, 1805, which was affirmed by the House of Lords, 9th March, 1812, giving him a manse and grass-glebe.

It was, too, during his tenure of the charge that, after ten years' negotiations with the heritors, the new Parish Church was built.

Mr. MacLean was nine years in the Chapel of Ease (St. Andrew's) and forty-five in the parish church of Dunfermline. He died in the eighty-seventh year of his age, and the fifty-seventh of his ministry.

He was unable to officiate for several of the later years of his life. Mr. John Fernie and he wrote conjointly the second statistical account of this parish.

" Mr. M'Lean left about £2,000 . . . for benevolent and charitable purposes, exclusive of such parochial objects as the heritors were legally bound for, to be applied at the discretion of his trustees. . . .

"A considerable portion of this sum has already been expended in building the schools on his property at Golfdrum, in educating deaf and dumb and blind children belonging to the parish, and in some incidental cases of distress. He also bequeathed his house, garden and two parks there to the kirk Session of the Abbey Church for the education of poor children in the parish, directing a preference to be given to those who are in the suburbs of the town." (*Chalmers*, ii. 322.)

"The MacLean Hospital—This hospital, situated to the eastward of the Prison and Poor House, is a commodious building of two stories, finished in June, 1849.

"It is so named after the late Rev. Allan MacLean, minister of the first charge, Abbey Church, in consequence of a donation of £500 from his trust-funds for its erection. . . .

"It was designed chiefly for maid-servants, and other persons infected with fever or any contagious disease, residing in the town or parish, not in houses of their own, or in houses with defective accommodation, so as to have cleanly and well-aired apartments, support and regular medical and other attendance, either at a small charge or gratuitously, according to their circumstances." (*Ibid*. ii. 322.)

Peter Chalmers, D.D.   1836-1870

He joined the Free Church, May, 1843, opened a place of worship, administered baptism and intimated his intention to dispense the Lord's Supper, but changed his mind, applied to the Presbytery and was again received 21st June, 1843.

He was the author of *An Historical and Statistical Account of Dunfermline*.

For almost 100 years (1745-1843) the office of Presbytery Clerk was associated with the Abbey.

On 9th October, 1745, Andrew Beveridge, described as Preacher of the Gospel and Precentor in Dunfermline, was appointed Clerk in succession to John Louden, minister at Carnock. (No other reference can be found to Beveridge, but it looks as if he had been a "stickit minister.") For a considerable time, prior to Beveridge's death, the work was almost entirely done by Thomas Fernie, minister of the Second Charge.

Fernie succeeded Beveridge in the Clerkship and held office from about 1771 to 1788, when he was succeeded by his son, John, who held office till 1816, and perhaps a little later.

On 1st December, 1819, Peter Chalmers took office and held it till 1843. Probably enough, he would have held it longer had he not gone out temporarily at the Disruption.

James French.   1870-1880

Had previously been Professor of Rhetoric in the Andersonian College, Glasgow.

John Pitt, B.D.   1880-1893

Robert Stevenson, M.A.   1893-1931

Elected to the First Charge 4th July, 1893—this being the first election of a minister by *ballot* in the Church of Scotland.

Author of *Communion and some other Matters in Dunfermline in the Seventeenth Century* (Dunfermline 1900), he died 14th August, 1931.

James W. Baird, B.D.   1932-1940

Admitted to the First Charge 17th March, 1932. The following year the Unification of the Charges was effected.

Robert Dollar, B.D.

Appointed Colleague and Successor 8th October, 1940—the only appointment of the kind in either of the charges.

One minister fled from office, another was ordered to leave by the Privy Council, two were deposed. All the others were either translated to another charge or died in office.

SECOND CHARGE

" At Dunfermline 5 April 1643—Anent the providing of Dunfermline wt another minister, upon the aduertisement given be the moderator of the provinciall assemblie of fyff, sundrie considerable herioters, parochiners, both in brut an land (burgh and landward) came at the tyme appoynted fr yt sessn. It was found that of all that appeared none were unwilling to bear burdens fr mentenance of the sd minister except one . . .

" The assemblie considering the great necessitie of planting the said congregation wt two ministers, and finding so great a consent of heritors, hoping also yt the ryt noble and potent Lord Charles, erle of Dunfermline, the prime heritor wtin the paroch shall liberallie concur to advance so gude a wark; doe heartily approve so pious a design, thanking God for the same, and earnestly exhort the heritors and parochiners both of brut and land to proceed thairin . . .

" Declairing hereby that the patronage, nominatn and presentatn of the sd minister both now and heireftir shall belong to the parochiners and heritors, founders for the sd provision—extract furthe of the registr of the said assemblie and subt be Mr. Jon moreis, clerk thairto." (H. R.)

Andrew Forrester. 1598-1610
The first appointment was an unfortunate one, as will be seen from his record of office in the First Charge, to which he was translated in 1610.

John Moray, M.A. 1614-1620
The second was much better. By the time he was admitted, the Episcopal element in the Church was predominant, but his nonconformity was apparently disregarded, though he had to perform the work of the charge for four years without remuneration. He must, however, have commended himself to the parishioners, for in 1620 he was promoted to the First Charge.

Samuel Row, M.A. 1638-1640
Had been serving as a minister in Ireland, but had to return because of the troubles there. Is sometimes referred to as Assistant to Mr. Macgill in the First Charge, the Second Charge not being fully established till the time of his successor. On application by the heritors to the civil courts, the stipend of the Second Charge, like that of the First, was made payable from the teinds.

William Oliphant, M.A. 1645-1662
Had been chaplain to Charles, Earl of Dunfermline.
Mr. Kay was Episcopal in his sympathies, but conformed to

Presbyterianism. Mr. Oliphant, on the other hand, was an ultra-evangelical Presbyterian and his name is frequently found associated with those of Samuel Rutherford of St. Andrews and Andrew Donaldson of Dalgety. But, as colleagues in the Abbey, they seem to have worked quite harmoniously together.

Mr. Oliphant died July, 1662, " at his dwelling-house in Dunfermline, and was interred at the church there." (*Lamont's Diary*, 152.)

" 12 Nov., 1664—Geo. Walker, an Executor of umqll Mr. William Oliphant, collig. minister at Dunfermline, desired the Council to pay him 200 merks yearly restand be the toune as the sd. decest Mr. Wm. his stipend for the years 1661 & 1662 = 400 merks." (*B.R.*)

Thomas Kinninmonth, M.A.   1666-1668

Alexander Munro.   1673-1676
Said to have been a good scholar, a man of talent, and a keen Episcopalian. Afterwards became Professor of Divinity in St. Mary's, St. Andrews, and, still later, Principal of the University of Edinburgh.

John Balnevis, M.A.   1676-1681

Simon Coupar, M.A.   1681-1686

James Graeme (or Graham), M.A.   1687-1710
Was charged, like his colleague Coupar, with not reading the Proclamation of the Estates, but, declaring that he had not received the Proclamation and was willing to read it, he was acquitted by the Privy Council in 1689.

In 1701 he was deposed by the Synod for Arminianism and neglect of ministerial duties, but reponed by the Commission of the General Assembly. He died in January, 1710—the last Episcopal parish minister of Dunfermline.

For long after the Reformation in 1560 opinion was sharply divided as to whether the government of the Reformed Church should be Presbyterian or Episcopalian, and there were many ups-and-downs, and some never-to-be-forgotten clashes, before the question was finally settled.

It would be both futile and foolish to revive that controversy to-day, but it can hardly fail to be of interest to see how the two systems worked in a Collegiate Charge like that of Dunfermline, where, more than once, one of the charges was filled by a Presbyterian and the other by an Episcopalian; and it will detract nothing from that interest to get the considered opinion of one who was himself for many years a minister of Dunfermline Abbey.

"There is nothing in the Session Books to indicate that the Episcopalian Church differed from the Presbyterian in its Communion service, or indeed in any of the services of Public Worship.

"To the worshippers in the Abbey, Kay the Episcopalian, was much the same as Kay the Presbyterian; and neither by him nor his successors was anything introduced into the Church to which the congregation is known to have objected. The Presbytery, or rather the 'Moderators' were instructed by the Archbishop 'to take notice of the uniformity of ministers in their practice of causing the creed to be recited at baptisms, and of singing of the Doxologies, and of making use of the Lord's Prayer in public.'

"But the use of the Lord's Prayer in public was common to both Churches, and is recommended in the Directory; so was the practice of singing the Doxology, which, according to Commissioner Gillespie, the General Assembly of 1645 purposely left an open question; so also was the recital of the creed at baptisms, which, though not prescribed by the Directory, was authorised by the Book of Common Order, and seems to have been the established usage of the Presbyterian Church in 1641.

"Nor is there anything in the records of the Session to show that the Church, after Episcopacy was restored, had passed from one form of government to another. In almost every detail, the business is conducted, and the affairs of the parish managed, after 1662 as they were before it. The discipline is on the same lines, and follows the same rules. The minutes, which are much shorter (that is not always objectionable), contain no reference to Episcopacy. The Session is there, composed of the Moderator and the Elders. The diligence of the latter is regularly inquired into, anent the visitation of their districts. If catechising is little referred to, the minutes of the Superior Court show that it was a function of the Episcopal system which its ministers could not neglect.

" Some observances, such as Fast-days before the Communion, common to Presbyterians and disregarded by Episcopalians, formed no necessary part of Presbyterian order and were never authorised by the Assembly. Then there was the Presbytery (the people in general knew nothing of the constant Moderator) and the Synod ; and, if they had their Archbishops in addition, who were making their mark upon the country, these seem to have received no encouragement from their representatives of the Abbey in effecting their designs at Dunfermline." (*Stevenson, The Communion in Dunfermline in the 17th Century, pp.* 11 *to* 13.)

In view of the bitterness that developed in the course of the struggle, the picture drawn by Mr. Stevenson may be a little surprising, but, as reflected in the minutes of the Abbey Kirk Session, it is substantially true. The only reservation one feels inclined to make is (1) that, while the Lord's Prayer may have been in use in Dunfermline Abbey, it by no means follows that it was in general use in Presbyterian worship at the time, and (2) that, while the Kirk Session, as a court, had so commended itself in the light of experience, that Episcopalians, little as they liked it, could not afford to dispense with it, Mr. Stevenson would have had some difficulty in showing that they welcomed lay representation in the Synod, for example.

" It is significant to notice how Prelacy is opposed to the influence of the lay element in ecclesiastical matters.

" In 1662, when that system was once more set up in Scotland to gratify the Royal will, the Bishop of Dunkeld wrote to Mr. Bruce (minister of Aberdour), asking him to discharge his Kirk Session, and select five or six godly men to assist him in upholding the fabric of the church, in providing for the poor, and censuring vice and ungodliness. Mr. Bruce does as he is bid, and, setting his Session adrift, appoints six men—whether godly or not we have hardly the means to determine. It is somewhat curious to notice, in this communication, that Mr. Bruce is asked to inform ' his brethren who are next adjacent to him in the same diocese, that they are to do the like, as they shall be answerable.' " (*Ross, Aberdour & Inchcolme, p.* 278.)

Currie of Kinglassie, in his *Vindication*, states that for eight years prior to 1638 (when Presbyterianism was restored) no ruling elder sat in the Presbytery of Kirkcaldy. It has to be remembered, too, that there were invariably fewer meetings of Kirk Session under Episcopacy.

Episcopalian rule came to an end in 1688, but Mr. Graeme continued to officiate in the Abbey till his death in 1710, and his continuance in office did not make things any easier for the Kirk Session.

" 22 Septr., 1706—The Session appoints John Anderson, beddall, to go to Mr. Grame and to desire him in the Session's name not to proclame or marie John Wilson till he satisfie church discipline as to the breach of the Sabbath wherein he is contumatious." (*K.S.R.*)

" 29 Oct., 1706—John Anderson, beddall, being called, the Moderator inquired at him if he went to Mr. Grame & intimat to him the order from the Session that they desyred him not to marie or proclam John Wilson, William Ker and Margt. Hally till they gave bond & cautn to submit to church discipline, reported that he went to him & intimat the sam, bot he sd. he wold do therein as he pleased." (*Ibid.*)

Even after Graeme's death, there was occasional trouble.

" 20 Dec., 1711—Michael Chrystie and Sybilla Espline being cited called compeared and being questioned anent their cohabiting as man and wife answered they were married and produced a Testificate thereof signed by Mr. Wilson, an Episcopal minister, and two witnesses. They were removed and the Session considering the affair and that there were presumptions of guilt betwixt the said Chrystie's son and the said Sybilla as appears by former minutes thereanent They did, and hereby do, Refer the whole to the Presbytery and ordered them to be called in and cited *apud acta* to attend the same, and the Moderator rebuked them Sessionally for their Irregular and disorderly marriage. Being called in, they were cited and rebuked accordingly." (*Ibid.*)

" 16 Aug., 1713—(Andrew Donaldson and Barbara Wilson having pleaded guilty to a charge of fornication) The Session, considering the Complex Case, did Refer the same to the Presbytery. . . .

" After which, the said Andrew desiring again to speak with the Session was allowed to come in and protested that the Moderator and Elders were not Judges competent of such crimes as are alledged against him in regard they are not qualified in terms of Law, neither was he lyable to their censure, he not being of theirs but of the Episcopal persuasion, and therefore declined their Judicatories in terms of the Act of Parliament, and thereon took Instruments in the hands of Henry Elder, notar publick, and in the Session Clerk's hands also.

" To which the Moderator, in name of the Session, answered :

(1) That the Session was Legal in regard the Law had not found them Illegal or unqualified, and that they were still Judges competent of scandal ay and while (until) the Government should find them unqualified.

(2) As to his asserting that he is none of ours, but of the Episcopal persuasion, The Session reckon themselves at no great loss by his separating from them, for his former practice has been a scandal to Religion and a reproach to any Christian Society." (*Ibid.*)

Following the Revolution Settlement of 1688, Presbyterianism found itself in very low water. No wonder! For close on thirty years no student of Presbyterian inclinations could have entered a Divinity Hall in Scotland, with the result that when charges previously held by Episcopalians became vacant there was great difficulty in filling them. So acute did the problem become in this quarter that for a time (1692-1696) the Presbyteries of Dunfermline and Kirkcaldy had to unite to make one effective Court. But so rapid and so steady was the progress made, once the Church found its feet again, that it is now generally agreed that the period between the Revolution Settlement and the Secession of 1733 represents the heyday of Presbyterianism in Scotland.

As the Abbey Records for this period deal in great detail with the problems facing the Church, it is well worth while devoting some time and attention to them, with a view to understanding how the system worked.

One of the first things done, apparently, was to renew some of the former regulations that had fallen into abeyance during the Episcopalian regime.

" 15 Feb., 1711—The Session, considering that the ancient custom of consigning pledges by those who are to be proclaimed in order to marriage is fallen in desuitude during the vacancy, resolve to revive the same and hereby discharge any persons being proclaimed till first they consign six pounds Scots in the Treasurer's hands as was usual in the place, and that the said six pounds be delivered back at the end of nine months after the marriage to all who forfeit not the same." (K.S.R.)

With its usual consideration, however, for the very poor, even when they were at fault, the Session was quite prepared to consider special circumstances.

" 27 March, 1712—The Crowns consigned by David Burley at the upgiving of his name with Helen Burley were shaken out for the use of the poor, but because of his mean Circumstances, they gave him back two pounds Scots." (Ibid.)

" 20 May, 1711—The Session considering that the custom of Elders visiting the Town in time of Divine Worship for preventing people staying unnecessarily at home from publick ordinances and wandering through the streets and fields is much in desuitude They revive the same and appoint the Elders who wait upon the collection on the Lord's Day to visit the whole Town and report to the Session what they find censurable." (Ibid.)

" 26 July, 1713—The Ministers proposed to the Session their design of keeping Exercise in the Kirk upon the Sabbath evenings (Evening Service) in time coming, which the Session cordially went into and appointed Intimation thereof to be made to the Congregation Sabbath next." (Ibid.)

That this was not an entirely new departure is clear from a record of much earlier date.

" 29 Oct., 1643—That day intimation was made to the people of the evening prayers to begin this week following and yrfore they were desyrit to convein frequently yrto, and to have yr. candle in reddines." (Ibid.)

Judged by the amount of space given to it in the Minutes, Provision for the Poor might not seem to have been the Session's chief concern, but it was probably its best bit of work, and the Church at large has every reason to be proud of its record in this respect. No doubt the parish of Dunfermline was a large one, but the number of elders and deacons was not small.

Little difficulty was experienced, as a rule, in assessing the measure of the need, and there is no lack of evidence to show that it was met with a degree of understanding and sympathy that has not invariably characterised the work since it fell into other hands. Apart altogether from those who were regular recipients of relief, the general standard of life was so lamentably low that any untoward happening might easily mean disaster. A man might lose his horse, or a widow woman her cow; the house might be burned down, or the steading; or a man, as the result of an accident, might be incapacitated for life. There was no compensation for injury in these days, no insurance of any kind.

What could anyone in trouble do but apply to the Kirk Session?

As for schemes of public utility, roads, bridges, harbours, where could the promoters turn but to the Church?

If the need proved beyond a Session's resources, the case would be referred to the Presbytery or Synod—in extreme cases even to the General Assembly, which might order a special collection in all churches throughout the land.

Only once in the records of Dunfermline is there a reference to anything of the nature of a Means Test.

" 20 Dec., 1711—The Session taking to their consideration how much the Poors Box is burdened with Monethly and Weekly Pensions and being informed that severals of these who pretend great Straits might be in case to maintain themselves if their Effects were applyed for that end, and when they die their Relations reap considerable advantage by what household furniture they leave behind them, whereby the Session are rendered unable for suitably relieving such as are real objects, They Therefore enact and resolve that after the date hereof They will Inroll none among the monethly or weekly pensioners till first they appear before the Session and give a true account of what Goods and Gear they have and dispone the same to the Session that when they come to die the Session may dispone thereon for the use of the poor at least so much thereof as shall be equivalent to the sums bestowed upon them by the Session. And the Session appoints this Act to be intimate from the pulpit." (K.S.R.)

One rather suspects that this was how the Session came to have a spinet for sale.

"19 April, 1750—The Treasurer and Clerk represented that Mr. Guland, Surgeon in Dunfermline, had proposed to them that he would give Seven Shillings and Sixpence Sterling, and no more, for the Spinet which belonged to the Deceast Mr. Scot. The Session considering that said Spinet has ly'n Several years Useless without an opportunity offering to get it Disposed of, they appointed their Treasurer to give it at the price offered."

Nor must it be imagined that, whether under Presbyterianism or Episcopacy, the Session's beneficence was in any way confined to its own parochial area.

In November, 1631, we read of thirty pounds Scots being collected for " distressed Germans." The following year there is a collection for " the poor captives of Dysart and Kirkcaldy detained in Turkish slavery "—both under Episcopal rule.

Examples of Presbyterian beneficence are as follows :— In 1642, not less than ninety pounds Scots are contributed in behalf of the poor Irish Protestants. Next year other thirty pounds are added for the same cause, and at the same time forty merks are sent to the " captives of Inverkeithing and other parishes." In July, 1647, two hundred merks are sent to " the distressed people of Argyle," and three years after, forty pounds are sent for the relief of Scottish soldiers detained as prisoners, presumably in England.

As for the funds at the disposal of the Session, they came from various sources—legacies, church-door collections, collections at marriages, and proclamation deposits forfeited by misconduct; fees for the hire of the Session's mortcloths, and interest on loans and bonds issued by the Session.

The last-mentioned item was a larger one than might have been expected. There were no banks operating in those days and ready money was a scarce commodity even with people who were by no means poor. It was in no way unusual for the principal heritors in the parish to have dealings with the Poor Box at a price, and even the ministers, paid only once a year, were not unknown to make application to the Session for a loan at the usual rate of interest till the teind stipend became payable, or arrears were recovered.

Next in importance to Provision for the Poor—though vastly more space is given to it in the minutes—was the question of Discipline.

Speaking generally, the cases dealt with fall into two categories—desecration of the Lord's Day and sexual immorality.

With regard to the first of these, people to-day would be inclined to ask if the Session were really justified in spending so much time in dealing with offences such as " having people in the house in time of divine service," " taking off another man's beard on the Sabbath Day," " hoking up a groser busse on the Sabbath," " bringing in of water, and haill sweeping their houses, carrying forth ashes and the like—all which ought to be done on the Saturday before." But every age presents the Church with problems of its own and it ill becomes us to-day with so many unsolved social problems on our hands to comment too freely on the methods adopted by our predecessors in dealing with theirs.

As for cases of sexual immorality, one confesses to a sense of extreme repugnance against their handling of the whole business ; and even yet, though it is now a matter of past history, one cannot read without a shudder the terms employed in the Oath of Purgation, for example, or an Act of Excommunication.

But, again, one has to remind oneself that they were dealing with a question of vital importance both to the Church and to the Nation, that they were, so far as one's knowledge goes, impartial in their handling of it—the chief heritor in the parish, if guilty, being just as likely to find himself on the stool of repentance as the humblest member of the community—and that it is still an open question as to which is the greater offence— to deal over-drastically with such matters, or to take no notice of them whatsoever.

The experience of the Presbytery of Kirkcaldy seems to have been different :—

" It would not be true to say that they administered discipline without fear or favour. They did in practice make a distinction amongst men. Common men answering the brethren in an impertinent way were ordered instantly to be warded, but gentlemen had to be more tenderly dealt with, and were often waited upon at their residence so that they might be brought to a right and proper state of mind.

" On more than one occasion, we find them deciding in favour of a rich as against a poor person." (*The Presbyterie Booke of Kirkcaldie*, p. xvi.)

If they did make a distinction, it can at least be said for them that they were no worse in this respect than the civil law of the period, which allowed an injured husband to slay the adulterer " if he were a mean person."

It might be thought that in thus sitting in judgment upon wrong-doers the elders might be tempted to think their own conduct above question. But that was far from being the case.

" 26 May, 1713—The Session having spent some time in prayer proceeded to their Privy Censures and the Elders being severally removed and the usual Questions anent their walk and Conversation and the faithful discharge of their office being asked, nothing was found censurable.

" The Precentor and Session Clerk being removed, and the Session giving him a good Testimony, he was called in and approven.

" Then the Session considered John Anderson, their officer, and called him in and gave him some necessary Injunctions with respect to the right discharging of his office."

Exactly the same procedure was gone through on the occasion of a Presbyterial Visitation—with the addition that the minister was, in his turn, removed and the elders invited, individually or collectively, to give a frank account of his life and work.

So far as one can judge, the privilege does not seem to have been conspicuously abused, either in the Kirk of Dunfermline or within the bounds of the Presbytery. But, again, the experience of Kirkcaldy was different :—

" One of the lairds in the parish of Kennoway told the brethren that he could ' learn nothing of his minister bot pryd, averice and envie,' and an elder in Ballingry affirmed of his minister that he thought ' his ministrie weak, yea, verie weak, and that he was slow enough in visiting the sick,' while another stated ' that he was of a weak memorie and a slow gift.'

" The parishioners of Kirkcaldy complained that their minister was too credulous ; that he carried things to the pulpit and made indiscreet speeches there, and, judging from specimens given, he most certainly did so.

" An elder in Markinch went the length of swearing in the minister's presence at a meeting of session, and of telling him that he made ' ciphers ' of the elders and ' ledd horss,' and that some of them durst not speak in the session.

" The minister of Auchtertool complained to the Presbytery that the laird of his parish called him ' ane tinkler ' ; that he sought to fee his servant over his head, and that he threatened to hold a meeting of session without the minister's presence.

" These cases are, however, exceptional, and the complainers are nearly all known to have been disaffected persons belonging to the extreme sections of one or other of the two parties into which the Church was at that time divided." (*Ibid.* xvi.)

Sitting accommodation in the church, in the years following the Reformation, proved a vexatious question in nearly every parish in the country, and, as will be seen later, Dunfermline Abbey was no exception. So acute and vexatious did the question prove about the time we are dealing with that there were few meetings of Kirk Session that did not have to deal with rival claims to some particular seat.

" 5 July, 1711—The Moderator, Thomas Mitchel and James Meldrum reported that they had called three Wrights and visited the Craddles (boxed-in seats) and Chairs in the Body of the Kirk who assured them that if the same were turned into pews they would contain upwards of Twenty persons more than at present, which being considered by the Session, they unanimously Referrd the same to the Presbytery for their direction and assistance in making the same effectual by applying to the Heretors and others concerned, being of opinion it would greatly tend to the accommodating of Heretors and others unprovided in seat-rooms."

" 5 June, 1712—Henry Elder cited called compeared and being questioned for heightening and inlarging his seat in the Kirk and putting a Breast to it, whereby those that sit behind and before the same are incommoded, answered that (1) the Complainers have no just ground of Complaint in regard he affirms his seat is no more than what it has been these eighty years bypasst. (2) The Complainers are *in pessima fide* in regard they have no real right nor title to the seats wherein they sit, and therefore he would give no particular answers till all the Complainers should be personally present and produce their Rights to the several seats they are now in possession of, which, he alleged, they could not do.

" He was removed and the Session, considering the Intricacy of the affair and that there was matter of Civil Right in it and a great many persons concerned in the Complaint, They did, and hereby do, Refer the same to the Judge Ordinar to determine therein as he shall see cause. Henry Elder being called in, this was intimate to him."

Rival claims to lairs in the churchyard were another frequent source of trouble to the Session—in some ways rather surprisingly so. In so many cases they were family affairs, the particulars of which are not worth reproducing now, but a case as to the disposal of the grass in the churchyard caused something of a flutter at the time.

"25 June, 1712—The Moderator informed the Session that the Lady Pitfirran had given in to the Justices of the Peace a written Complaint upon the ministers for oppressing the Beadles in their own authority or at most the authority of the Session in taking the grass of the Kirkyard from them. Upon which the Session called in first John Anderson, present Beadle, and interrogate him if ever he had complained thereof to the Lady Pitfirran, who denied the same only confest that being present at the Justice Court when the said Complaint was read he declared to the Justices that the Beadles had always been in use to enjoy the same.

" He was removed and Helen Brown, Relict of James Pringle, late Beadle (whom the Session out of charity had allowed some part of the emoluments since her Husband's death), was called in and interrogate if she had made any Complaint to the Lady Pitfirran anent the Grass of the Kirkyard, denied the same but declared she had right to it and if her sone had been at home she would have possesst the same, but in her son's absence she had given the possession to Robert Strauchan, Gravemaker, for his service to her.

" She was removed and the Session having inspected their records they find that the Session has always taken the ordering and management of the Kirkyard as they saw Cause and being unsatisfied with the carriage and deportment of their Beadles in several respects and also understanding that the Presbytery in May, one thousand seven hundred and eleven, had expressly ordered Mr. Buchanan to take the possession of the Grass of the Kirkyard for his own behoof and preserving the Right to his successors, They did, and hereby do, Refer the whole affair to the Presbytery and called in the Beadles and cited them *apud acta* to attend the same."

(*Note.*—The Court of Session, 27th May, 1836, Stranraer, Lord Moncrieff found that "The grass is the minister's, but is not to be used for grazing.")

There are frequent references to the North Churchyard, which was doubtless in use from very early times (*Anno* 1520— "ecclesie et cimeterij parochialis." *B.R.* 287.), but, after the Reformation, the site of the ruined Conventual Church came also to be used as a place of interment. Colloquially, it is referred to as the "Satur" or "Satyr" Churchyard—probably a corruption of "St. Salvator," the old church being so named in a minute of the Heritors *c.* 1756.

The same ground is also occasionally referred to as the "Psalter" Churchyard, and Dr. Chalmers conjectures that it was so called because it was the site of the choir of the Abbey Church. The balance of probability, however, would seem to be in favour of St. Salvator.

In view of the part played in Scottish history by the Solemn League and Covenant, it is not surprising to find occasional references to it in the Session records.

"29 Oct., 1643—That day the Solemn League and Covenant for reformation and defence of religion, the honor and happiness of the King, and the peace and safety of the thrie kingdoms of Scotland, England and Ireland, was red and intimat be Mr. Robt. Kay, to the haill congregation, that nane pretend ignorance thairoff, bot that they may be prepared to sweare to it, and subscryve the same the nixt Lord's day."

"5 Nov., 1643—That day the Solemn League and Covenant . . . was sworne to be all the congregation in the kirk convenit, and thereafter subtt at sundrie dyetts, as the Booke of the Covenant at lent (length) bears."

"28 Nov., 1644—That it was declarit that James Murray, writer in Edinr., hade gottin 37d. for his fie, and the bookes of the Covenant, and of the last General Assembly."

"3 March, 1644—That day, givin for binding of the Covenant, and a new cover yrto, 46d."

"4 Jan., 1713—The Ministers informed the Session that they had got up from William Walker of Rods the National and Solemn League and Covenants subscribed by this Parish in the year 1638 and 1643, and granted a Receipt for the same, with which the Session were well satisfied and lodged them in Mr. Buchanan's hands to be carefully preserved by him and made forthcoming to the Session for their use when asked for."

" 8 Dec., 1720—The Session understands that the Kirk Bible and the National and Solemn league and Covenants are in Master Erskine's custody."

Mr. Fernie (*Hist. p.* 92) says :—

" Mr. Erskine kept them until his death, when they were transferred to his son, Mr. Harry Erskine, seceding minister at Falkirk; at whose death they went to Mr. Fisher, seceding minister in Glasgow, who transferred them to the seceding session of Dunfermline; thinking they had the best right to their possession." The Covenant is still in the possession of Erskine Church, Dunfermline.

Ralph Erskine, M.A.   1711-1716

"In 1713, two years after Mr. Erskine's induction, while Lord Bowhill was in Dunfermline, in order to the dividing of the area of the church among the heritors, the Presbytery gave in a representation to his Lordship for the consideration of the Lords of Council and Session anent the necessity of a third minister, as the number of the parishioners, amounting to 5,000, was too great a charge for two ministers and the church could not contain above half the people, etc." (*Chalmers, Hist.,* i. 431.)

But the proposal came to nothing.

" On the death of Mr. Buchanan (First Charge), the right of filling up the vacancy fell into the hands of the Presbytery, *jure devoluto,* and Ralph Erskine received a formal call and invitation from that body, with the unanimous concurrence of the parishioners.

" Difficulties arose as to the appointment of his successor (in the Second Charge), and so violent were the animosities that it was considered proper, for the space of at least two years, to suspend the administration of the Lord's Supper.

" First, a Mr. Christie was presented by the heritors and town-council, accompanied by a declaration that ' they would only make use of the presentation, as giving said Mr. Christie a title to the stipend, if the Presbytery go on to call him.'

" Then, after a deliverance by the Synod, and the parishioners being still averse to the presentee, the Commission of the Assembly, to whom the matter was referred, named, with the consent of all parties, a leet of four preachers, out of whom the parishioners might choose one.

" But neither would any of them give satisfaction, and at length liberty was given by the Presbytery to the people to put upon the leet ' whom they pleased,' when the Rev. James Wardlaw, then minister of Cruden, was added, and, with the exception of four or five votes, unanimously chosen, and settled on the 20th of November, 1718." (*Chalmers, Hist.* i. 429.)

James Wardlaw of Luscar.   1718-1742

Admitted as an elder in the parish of Carnock, 1704.

Was one of the Twelve who signed a representation to the General Assembly against the Act condemning the *Marrow of Modern Divinity*.

He was a strenuous opponent of patronage. Ralph Erskine, James Hog of Carnock and Wardlaw were on very friendly terms and like-minded in most things, except on the matter of Secession. Ralph Erskine and James Wardlaw were licensed by the Presbytery of Dunfermline on the same day, 8th June, 1709.

" Thereafter a motion was made by the Preses and the question being put :—If apply the 2nd Minister's vacant stipend to the expense of supplying the vacancy, including Presbytery dinners, and the remainder to pious uses ; or solely to pious uses.

" It carried thirteen against three—to apply the same for paying the expense of supplying the vacancy, including Presbytery dinners, and the remainder to pious uses.

" Against which appointment James Wardlaw for himself and his adherents protested as being contrary to the Act of Parliament, which expressly appoints that vacant stipend shall be applied for pious uses within the parish and seeing that the said appointment of the heritors and Town Councillors in sustaining extravagant bills for eating and drinking is a practice formerly unknown in this place, and which feastings were appointed and consumed by themselves who voted the same without any previous meeting of heritors, or appointment for it, and is not only contrary to the said Act of Parliament but a scandal on Christianity, and further protests that neither he nor any other heritor in the parish who shall adhere to him shall be liable by virtue of former appointment in payment of their proportions of said vacant stipend for payment of said extravagant feasting and drinking; and thereon takes instruments.

" To which protest John Adie of Brieryhill and Alexander Christy of Holl adhered.

" To which William Wilson of Clayacres for himself and in name of his adherents, made answer that as the spending protested against were both necessary and lawful, and done conform to practice in this and other parishes of this Presbytery as well as in most parishes in Scotland, and that same was done at sight, and by consent, of a great many of the heritors and Town Council of this parish without any appeal or opposition by Mr. Wardlaw or his adherents—therefor protests Mr. Wardlaw and his adherers if they delay or refuse to pay their quota, that they shall be liable in damages and expenses.

" To which Mr. Wardlaw replied that the drinkings and feastings were unlawful, especially the expenses of one of the dinners, amounting to £14 10s. Stg., that those dinners were ordered and consumed by two or three of the heritors and some of the Town Councillors, but that the rest of the heritors, though there are upwards of sixty in the parish, knew nothing of entertainments nor had access to know the same, otherwise they would have opposed it; and further protests that those heritors and Town Councillors shall be personally liable to pay the said bills of eating and drinking, which they themselves at their own hand appointed and consumed, and that no part thereof shall come off the vacant stipend." (*Heritors Records*, 12th October, 1744.)

(*Note.*—The Mr. Wardlaw above referred to was Mr. James Wardlaw of Netherbeath, who married the fifth daughter of the Rev. Ebenezer Erskine of Stirling. *Wardlaws in Scotland*, p. 260.)

One of the " pious uses " to which presumably vacant stipend of the First Charge was devoted, was a gift to the Town of Dunfermline of £15 Stg. towards enabling them to make a new clock for the steeple of Dunfermline—it being understood by both parties that the said new clock should be a sufficient one. (*H.R.* 12th October, 1744.)

Thomas Fernie, M.A.   1744-1788

Thomson and Fernie were colleagues for nearly 44 years, and, though unlike one another in some respects, Thomson being a man of robust constitution and remarkably strong voice, and Fernie of a mild disposition and rather feeble voice, they seem to have worked very happily together.

John Fernie.   1789-1816

Son of the above. Like his father, he was for some time Clerk to the Presbytery of Dunfermline, and was author of *A History of the Town and Parish of Dunfermline*. (Dunf. 1815.)

Peter Chalmers, M.A.   1817-1836

" Thomas Carlyle and Edward Irving walked from Kirkcaldy on the Saturday and spent overnight with the Schoolmaster of Inverkeithing (Mr. Douglas). They attended the Induction Service of Peter Chalmers. The preacher was the great Dr. Thomas Chalmers, who had gone two years before to Glasgow to the parishes of Tron and St. John. They walked back to Kirkcaldy on the Sunday evening." (*Carlyle's Reminiscences—Edw. Irving.*)

Peter Chalmers was the maternal grandfather of Sir Peter Chalmers Mitchell.

John Tod Brown.   1837-1844

The Chapel of Ease (afterwards St. Andrew's Church) was erected in 1777 and the North Church in 1840.

During the second local Church Extension movement represented by the building of the North Church, Mr. Brown protested against the unwisdom of setting about the building of a new place of worship without first making some attempt at undoing the consequences of the Presbytery's lamentable oversight, at the time of the erection of the parish church, of the divine principle that " faith cometh by hearing."

At a meeting of Presbytery held on 7th April, 1841, he moved that the whole matter be remitted to the Synod for advice.

Mr. Gilston (Carnock) urged that it was inexpedient to refer the question to any other court as things stood, and moved *delay*—which was carried by 11 to 2. Mr. Brown dissented and complained to the Synod.

The Synod having heard both sides unanimously agreed to remit the matter back to the Presbytery of Dunfermline with instructions to use all diligence in remedying the evil complained of and, if necessary, to report to next meeting of Synod.

Subsequently, the Presbytery heard both ministers of the Abbey, Mr. Chalmers and Mr. Brown, each proposing a different plan.

Mr. Brown moved that a committee of Presbytery be appointed to confer with the heritors on the subject of the unserviceableness of the Abbey Church in its present state, and to press upon them the importance of their consenting that it should be divided into two places of worship, though not at their expense.

Mr. Chalmers moved that the Presbytery, having had under consideration the important subject of the defective state of hearing in the Abbey Church, agree to present a respectful memorial to the heritors of Dunfermline and to the magistrates of the burgh requesting their early and serious attention to the matter generally with a view to the speedy and satisfactory removal of a defect which all must lament, the expense to be defrayed, not by assessment, but by voluntary subscription, and to appoint a committee to prepare said memorial and to take all necessary steps for forwarding the object of it.

Mr. Chalmers' motion was carried by 8 to 3. Mr. Brown dissented and protested for leave to complain to the ensuing General Assembly. But apparently nothing came of it.

Mr. Chalmers' idea, one gathers, was that the pulpit should be moved forward some fifteen feet.

Mr. Brown wanted the church divided into two by a wall two feet thick, with a pulpit on either side of it—the East Church to be fitted with three galleries, the West Church to have some of the seats altered, a session-house provided, and as much of the roof of the nave glazed as would admit light to the church.

Dealt with in this way, the East Church would provide sitting accommodation for 1400, the West Church for 1184. Everybody in either church would see the minister, and the echo would be completely cured.

Roof-lights in the nave! It has had some wonderful escapes in the course of its chequered history, and the issue of this contention must be reckoned one of them. But Mr. Brown was undismayed. "A more reasonable improvement," he said, "never was contended for in any Church court, and never was brought before any body of heritors."

In 1844 Mr. Brown was called to the Presbyterian Congregation, Rodney Street, Liverpool, and afterwards joined the Church of England.

James French. 1845-1870

John Pitt, B.D. 1870-1880

Robert Stevenson, M.A. 1880-1893

Mr. Stevenson was an original member of the Carnegie Dunfermline and Hero Fund Trust, and of the Carnegie United Kingdom Trust.

During his tenure of office of the First Charge, the Abbey was visited by King George V and Queen Mary, accompanied by the Duke and Duchess of York, afterwards King George VI and Queen Elizabeth.

John Fairley. 1894-1902

Translated to Larbert and Dunipace.

James W. Baird, B.D. 1903-1932

During Mr. Baird's tenure of the unified charge the Abbey was visited by the Prince of Wales, afterwards King Edward VIII and Duke of Windsor.

GRAMMAR SCHOOLS

The natural starting point for an inquiry into the springs of education in Scotland would seem to be the landing of St. Columba in Iona in 563.

That Columba himself was a ready writer may be gathered from the time it took him to make that copy of Jerome's Vulgate which led to his having to leave Ireland, and the work done by him and his successors as transcribers of the service books used in the Celtic Church was a definite contribution to education as well as to religion. We have still a catalogue, dating from 1152, of the treasured volumes said to have been the library of the Culdee Settlement on the island of St. Serf, Loch Leven—sixteen in all—mostly Service Books, but including a commentary on Genesis, the Song of Solomon, the Acts of the Apostles, and a collection of the portions of St. Paul's Epistles used at mass (*Prior. St. And. p.* 43). These they would assiduously transcribe, not only for their own use, but for the use of other settlements, and long after the abandonment of St. Serf's there were still people engaged in the manufacture of vellum and parchment in the neighbourhood, who were traditionally believed to have acquired the art from the Culdee monks. (*Monasticon* iii. 98.)

If the books catalogued really belonged to the Culdees, it would look as if they had conformed to catholic usage.

What may well prove to be the first reference to a schoolmaster occurs in connection with a Culdee settlement :—

" 1123—Berbeadh, ' rector of the schools of Abernethy,' witnesses the grant of Loch Leven to the Culdees by Alexander I." (*Prior. St. And. p.* 116.)

There are two directions in which it would seem natural to turn in our search for information as to the rise and spread of education :—(1) The records of the government of the time, and (2) the story of the schools themselves.

As to the first, there is little or nothing available till the closing days of Robert the Bruce. Not that there were no schools in the country until then. We have abundant evidence in charters of the existence of schools at least 200 years before that.

But the long-drawn-out War of Succession must have sadly affected every institution of the sort, and it was only when Bruce had firmly established his position in the country that he felt free to let his thoughts turn to the subject of education. Even then the material available is scanty and uninformative to a degree, though one reference does credit him with a grant " to assist schools at Montrose." (*Grant, Burgh Schools*, 14.)

Otherwise, the references are too personal to convey much information.

" 1329—Concession made to John, son of Adam de Spot, towards his sustenance at schools, at the will of the king, for 3 years—6os." (*Exch*. i. 169.)

" 1329—And to David of Montrose, cleric, help towards schooling—2os." (*Ibid*. 201.)

" 1329—And to Master Gilbert de Benauchtin, a gift of the king for the purpose of study—£14 6s. 8d." (*Ibid*. 210.)

There is nothing in these references to indicate the school they were to attend or the line of study they were to pursue but it is worth noting that the word " school " is so often used in the plural. The first-mentioned was to continue his studies for three years. The second was already a cleric and was apparently to have another year. The use of the title Magister would suggest that the third was already a Graduate in Arts, though there was no University in Scotland at the time to confer such a degree, and the amount of the grant would seem to indicate that he was to continue his studies abroad.

After King David's return from captivity, there are a few more references to schools.

" The customar (Collector of Customs) of Cupar-Fife in 1359, presumably one of the leading burgesses of that place, is designed master of the schools there. . . .

" In the Chamberlain's account of 1364, £4 are paid by warrant of David for the maintenance and clothing ' unius pauperis scholaris, consanguinei domini regis.'

" The youth of the higher classes were not slow to avail themselves of the leave readily granted by Edward to study at the universities of Oxford and Cambridge, and even Scotchmen of undistinguished birth and mature age occasionally took the opportunity of obtaining at the English universities a higher education than was procurable in their own country.

" One of the last-named class was John Barbour, the metrical biographer of Bruce, whose language and versification compare with those of the best English contemporary poets, Chaucer included.

" He was Archdeacon of Aberdeen as early as 1357, and the safe-conducts granted him show that it was after he had held this position for years that he resorted to the universities of England and of France for the purpose of study." (*Exch.* ii. ciii-civ.)

" 1384—In payment, by mandate of the king, of a poor scholar at schools in the town of Haddington—£4." (*Exch.* iii. 120.)

" 1386—To James Stewart, king's son, studying at St. Andrews—£4 13s. 4d. And to Gilbert de Hay, for clothing— 32s." (*Ibid.* iii. 138.)

" 1388—Magister Willelmus de Travernent (Tranent), rector of the schools of Haddington." (*Ibid.* 171.)

For the reign of Robert III there is only one entry :—

" 1396—To Friar Peter going to school—6s. 8d." (*Ibid.* iii. 403.)

Which tends to confirm the impression that sometimes even full-fledged monks and friars were found to be in need of a little further education.

Abbots, too, it would seem, might occasionally be interested in what was being done in schools furth of Scotland.

" 11 June, 1498—Royal Letter of licence granted to Thomas Inglis, Abbot of Inchcolm, ' to pas oure the sey to the skulis for science and knauledge to be had or to the court of Rome in Pilgrimage.' " (*Inchcolm*, 240.)

The first real landmark in the general story of education is to be found in the famous Act of 1496, wherein James IV ordains that all burgesses and freeholders of substance shall send their eldest sons and heirs to school from eight or nine years of age till they be " competentlie foundit and have perfyte Latyne," with three years thereafter at the schools of art and " jure."

No doubt, as Dr. Hill Burton remarks, this was hortatory, rather than legislative, and applied only to a particular class of the community; but it was evidence, none the less, of an increasing desire for education throughout the country. It should also be borne in mind that old Scots Acts were often expressive of what was already established practice.

It was not till after the Reformation that an Act applicable to the country as a whole, and providing for all sections of the community, came into effective operation.

As for the story of the schools themselves, we shall do well to start off with the assumption that a school was an essential accompaniment of a thriving monastery of any size. The first application for admission would, almost certainly, raise the question right away. The chances are that the applicant could neither read nor write, and, until he had learned to do so, he could take no active part in its services. Someone would have to undertake his education—in more than one case there is evidence that the duty fell to the scribe—and, as the numbers increased, the work would develop, till it came to be a recognised part of the routine life of the community.

It is, therefore, rather pointless to inquire as to the exact date on which a particular monastic school began.

At the same time, it is only natural that we should wish to have some idea as to when these first provisional arrangements developed into an organised system forming an essential part of the life of the community.

With regard to the range and quality of the education offered in pre-Reformation days in monastic institutions there is some difference of opinion. At one time it was generally accepted, not only by Roman Catholic historians, but by Protestant as well, that the instruction was of a commendably high order and available for all who were in a position to take advantage of it. In recent years there has been a good deal of research devoted to monastic life, with the result that neither of these claims is now so confidently maintained.

Professor Coulton in his *Scottish Abbeys and Social Life* quotes two Roman Catholic authorities who seem to be content to make a much more sober claim.

" Dom. Ursmer Berliere, the most learned of modern Benedictine historians," he says, " writes :—' The programme of monastic schools was not very vast; the method of teaching did not make rapid progress. . . . The rarity and vagueness of medieval texts do not always permit us to conclude strictly as to the existence of schools for outside pupils in many monasteries.' (*L'Ordre Monastique.*) "

And again :—" The very learned medievalist, Dominican Father Mandonnet, speaks more plainly :—

' The monastic rules, including St. Benedict's, do not provide for either study in the proper sense, or schools in the monasteries.

' In consequence, the existence of such schools should be proved by documents, and not taken for granted. The so-called *Scholae Externae* (for outside scholars) for the use of secular clerics or young nobles existed only rarely and transitorily.' "

As early as 1216, however, we have evidence that in Scotland some provision was made for the instruction of poor children, though it by no means follows that the expression " poor scholars " meant the same thing then as it would to-day.

" Master Patrick, master of the schools at St. Andrews, *together with the poor scholars of that same city*, sued for six measures of barley and the rents which were wont to be given to the monastery in virtue of the composition made between it and the Archdeacon of St. Andrews." (*Reg. Prior. St. And.* 316-8.)

Professor Coulton himself was definitely of opinion that the existence of a school in a monastery could not be assumed. It must be proved.

Professor A. R. Macewen, Edinburgh, was of very much the same opinion.

" The educational function discharged by monasteries in this period has been exaggerated by writers of the romantic school.

" The idea that they were homes of learning and agencies for diffusing literary culture has no foundation, except the hypothesis that they resembled English and continental monasteries of the best class. As a matter of fact, there are only eighteen places in Scotland in which schools or schoolmasters are known to have existed between 1153 and 1286. At least six of these were a direct heritage from the Celtic Church, their teachers and pupils retaining Celtic titles ; two were not monastic but cathedral foundations, and two were connected with local churches.

" Thus there is no proof that more than eight schools were

Processional Door.   South Aisle to Cloister Court.   Detailed photograph.

erected by the new Orders, and of the eight only one (Kelso) had much importance. (*Hist.* i. 200-1.)

In the light of modern research it was inevitable that there should be a reaction against the inflated notions that were current concerning monastic education, and indeed a tendency for the pendulum to swing in the opposite direction. But all the facts of the past did not find their way into the records, and there still remains a good deal of research work to be done on such records as do exist. When that work is nearer completion, it may quite well be found that the truth lies somewhere between the two extremes.

In every efficient monastery some provision would have to be made for novices, generally lads in their later teens, but sometimes grown men, during their year or more of probation. Even full-blown younger monks were often found to be so defective in learning that they needed a grammar-master before they could read Latin with any facility. But this did not necessarily imply very much in the way of learning in the ordinary sense of the word.

" Father Mandonnet," Professor Coulton goes on, " is quite definite on that point. All that the novice or younger monk needed to learn was enough Latin to understand his service-books, enough ritual to go through the ceremonies without blundering, and the rules of monastic discipline and morality."

For these novices and young monks we have (again drawing from the wealth of material made available by Prof. Coulton) interesting details in the *History of the Abbots of Kinloss* by Ferrerius, brought as schoolmaster from Italy by Robert Reid, the reforming abbot of that monastery. Incidentally, in his life of Abbot Crystall of Kinloss, Ferrerius describes how he (Crystall) had begun his schooling at Culross, where there was a monk " firstly, most eminent in religion, and also learned in grammatical elements, in so far as those times permitted, less polished in literature than our own."

Confirmation of the fact that there was a pre-Reformation Grammar School at Culross is to be found in a statement made in 1589 that there had been " in all tyme bygane " a grammar school within the Abbey of Culross, " in the quhilk the youth of the burgh and land of Culross wer instructit in grammar and trainit up in vertue and letters, to the commonweill of the haill cuntrey " and that Mr. William Home is now present master of the grammar-school. (*Reg. P.C.* lix. 115-7.)

In addition to the education of novices, larger monasteries, at least, would have to provide for instruction in singing. The growing popularity of Mary-worship led often to the building of an extra Lady-Chapel in her honour, with extra services, for which the monks found it convenient to hire choristers. In not a few cases it is evident that the song school, thus begun, served also the purpose of an ordinary elementary school.

Finally, there was the obligation laid on every monastery to prepare one out of every twenty of their number for a University education and to provide them with the means of prosecuting it. In the early days this necessarily involved residence " furth of Scotland," but, following the foundation of St. Andrews, a University education became possible at home.

" To this point Scottish students, denied opportunities at home, sought instruction outside the kingdom. In the rare intervals of peace Oxford and Cambridge attracted them to their halls, one of which owed foundation to a Balliol. From the beginning of the fourteenth century that avenue to learning was closed. Opportunely the Franco-Scottish League beckoned to Paris and Orleans, whose famous Universities attracted Scottish students in great numbers. In 1326 a Scots College was founded at Paris which, restricted at first to students from Moray, threw open its gates to all Scotland. The enthusiasm of these pilgrims of learning suggested a home University, while the advantages of an educated clergy, able to confound the heretics, influenced the Church to provide one. Since 1411 Bishop Henry Wardlaw, in his College of St. Mary's at St. Andrews, had afforded lectures. In 1413 a series of Bulls were obtained from Pope Benedict XIII, constituting a Studium Generale or University where instruction should be given in theology, canon and civil law, medicine, and the liberal arts. Forty years later (1456) a second College, St. Salvator's, was established at St. Andrews. Glasgow had already founded a University (1451) and Aberdeen possessed one before the end of the century (1494). As at St. Andrews, the Church was the founder of both." (*C. S. Terry : A History of Scotland.*)

Residence for this purpose " furth of Scotland " involved not only difficulty but sometimes actual danger. In 1248 a

Scottish student of good birth, named Gilbert of Dunfermline, was attacked by a mob of townsmen and so seriously injured that he died shortly afterwards.

It is not strictly accurate, however, to say that, from the beginning of the fourteenth century, the English Universities were closed to Scotsmen.

" In 1359 Edward III granted a licence to Scotsmen to study either at Oxford or at Cambridge, and Oxford, which was at that time full of progressive life, proved specially attractive. In one year (1365) passports were granted to eighty-one Scottish students entitling them to journey to Oxford. Some of them went singly, others in parties of three or six under the guidance of a clerical tutor, who might be a dean or canon and often took several parties in succession. In 1357 and 1373 parties came from Aberdeen, Glasgow, Govan, Tiningham and Carrie." (*Macewen*, i. 296, 296n.)

As to whether or not the monks received special remuneration for their work as teachers, there is not much material to work upon.

" The monks of Arbroath assigned a fixed stipend to the teachers of novices and young brethren." (*Macewen Hist.*, i. 376.)

" At Dunfermline, there was a provision of 53s. 4d., out of the lands of Pinckin (Pinkie) and Keres, at Musselburgh, ' to the Master of the boys at the said Monastery.' " (*Yester Writs*, 678, 31st August, 1557.)

In other cases, the impression is conveyed that the work was done gratuitously. It would be unwise to draw any general conclusion from such scanty information.

A somewhat unexpected method of providing for the education of a young lad with a view to his entering the service of the Church is revealed in the following extract :—

" The rector of a parish church having resigned his charge, no doubt specifying his successor, the Pope granted it *in commendam* to a boy of twelve, with permission to appropriate the residue of the fruits after providing for service during a period of five years, after which he might receive collation (that is, be admitted to the charge)." (*H. & H.*, quoting *Formulare* 138.)

As for the measure of success that attended the system as a whole, there is considerable difference of opinion.

On the one hand, it is undoubted that such learning as there was in Scotland up to the time of the Reformation was almost entirely due to the Church. On the other hand, it is disconcerting to find, even after the invention of printing, so much evidence of the lack of the rudiments of education, not only amongst laymen, but amongst religious teachers too.

Apart from such well-known passages as :—" The Curat his creid he culd nocht reid." (*Gude and Godlie Ballats.*) and :

> " Thanks to Saint Bothan, son of mine,
> Save Gawain, ne'er could pen a line."
>
> (*Marmion.*)

here are two cases from the neighbouring parish of Aberdour :—

In the Bull of Erection (1487) of the Nunnery of Grey Sisters at Aberdour there is an interesting provision to the following effect :—

" It shall be lawful both to the said mistress, and, by her permission, to the sisters living for the time in the said house, to retain and instruct therein young maidens of honourable parentage and willing to be instructed in literature and good arts."

This might well prove to be one of the earliest references to the institution of a special school for girls in Scotland. Unfortunately, when it came to signing a deed on behalf of the nunnery, it was found that not one of the four who constituted the sisterhood could sign her own name—each and all of them requiring the notary's hand to guide them. It may be doubted whether the maidens of noble lineage could have acquired much knowledge of literature and the fine arts from teachers so sadly handicapped. (*The Grey Friars : W. Moir Bryce*, i. 395.)

In the year 1560 a deed was witnessed by seventeen men, described as " the honestest men in Aberdour," and, over and above the minister and notary, only three could sign their names.

" It would be easy to multiply instances of such culpable ignorance, but two must suffice. In signing a charter in 1544, the Prioress and Prioress-elect of North Berwick were constrained to add to their names ' with my hand on the pen '; and opposite the names of the twenty subscribing nuns are the equally significant words ' wyth all our handis leid at the pen.'

And in 1566 the Countess of Huntly (wife of one of the Commendators of Dunfermline) displayed the same disability in signing the marriage contract of her daughter." (*K.S.R. St. And.* 1559-82, 56.)

As regards the progress of education in Dunfermline in particular, we have, fortunately, one or two milestones that we can reckon on.

In the year 1161 we find Arnold, Bishop of St. Andrews, confirming to the Church of the Holy Trinity, Dunfermline, the churches of Perth and Stirling, with their chapels, schools, etc. (*Reg.* 93, *p.* 56.)

There is a Confirmation Charter to the same effect by Richard of St. Andrews, 1168-73. (*Reg.* 96, *p.* 58.)

In neither of these charters, it is true, is there an express reference to a school in Dunfermline, but the disappointment caused by that omission is somewhat modified by consideration of the methods by which the parent monastery exercised supervision and control over the priories and churches attached to it.

When the Priory of Urquhart was founded, it was " colonised " by monks from Dunfermline, and when any material change or new development was contemplated, it was given effect to by an interchange of personnel, such as the appointment of the Sacristan of Dunfermline to be Prior of Urquhart, and the return of the Prior of Urquhart as Sacristan of Dunfermline. There is no reason to suppose that it was in any way different with schools.

Nor should it be overlooked that, while there are not many references of an early date to schools, there are not-infrequent references to the " master of the boys." It is too readily assumed that this means the precentor, who trained boys to take part in the musical services. But time and again there is evidence to show that the reference was really to the monk who was in charge of the primary department of the monastery school.

" In some convents he (the Precentor) was the instructor in music, training the novices and teaching the cloister boys to read. . . .

" ' He was on no account to slap their heads or pull their hair,' this privilege being the right of the master of the boys." (*F. H. Crossley, The English Abbey, p.* 14.)

The standing of the schoolmaster in these early days may be to some extent judged by the fact that Adam, " magister scolarum de Perth," appears as one of the commissaries of Pope Innocent II who were to settle the dispute about the churches of Prestwick and Sanquhar (*Paisley*, 120); that " Alan, Master of the schools of Ayr," was one of the Papal delegates in a cause in 1233 (*Acts. Parl.* i. 96-7); and that " Nicholas, Rector of the schools of Cupar," was one of the obligants for payment of the ransom of David II in 1357. (*Ibid.* i. 517a.)

The next outstanding date is 1254, when Dom. Abraham, a monk in the Abbey, is described as " legum professor." (*Reg.* 121.)

It is not easy to know just how much to read into this somewhat enigmatic definition. Strictly speaking, he cannot have been a professor, for there was no university in Scotland till St. Andrews was founded in 1411, but it is clear that he was something of a specialist in law, or " jure," as it was generally called in those days.

One cannot help wondering whether this definition of status may not have some bearing on the ancient office in schools referred to by Dr. Joseph Robertson in the *Miscellany of the Spalding Club* (v. 72) under the heading " The Ferleiginn, Scholasticus or Lecturer."

Skene has also something to say about him.

" In the latter part of the eighth and in the ninth centuries we find a new functionary appearing in the monasteries and gradually superseding the Scribe. This was the Ferleiginn, lector, or man of learning, whose functions were more closely connected with education." (*Celtic Scotland*, ii. 446.)

He is frequently to be met with in connection with Irish monasteries, and in Scotland he appears in the early part of the reign of David I in connection with the Columban monastery at Turriff and also at St. Andrews.

This official seems to have been of higher rank than even the master of the schools, with powers not only of appointment but of supervision. He is also said to have lectured on philosophy, theology and the higher branches of learning, like the professor of a University. Dr. Robertson illustrates the status of the lecturer by the controversy, already referred to, between the

Prior of St. Andrews and Patrick, master of the schools of the city of St. Andrews, regarding some lands belonging to the *scolocs* (scholars).

Agreement was eventually reached between the parties whereby a fixed annual payment was to be made to the lecturer and his successors for the use and benefit of the scholars—thus exhibiting, according to Dr. Robertson, the three scholastic grades, scholar, master, lecturer, in their proper order and relation.

It should, however, be noted that in the *Registrum* of Dunfermline the word *scoloc* is used, not of scholars, but of the monastery's own " men " (i.e., bondsmen or serfs). One of the families whose genealogy is given has *scoloc* for a surname.

Whether or not the professor and lecturer are one and the same, the fact remains that such an official in Dunfermline at this early date would seem to indicate a considerable degree of organisation in the school.

Reference has already been made (page 29) to the fact that in 1292 Dene Thomas, a monk of Dunfermline, was engaged in the responsible task of transcribing documents of national importance.

The next date is 26th November, 1468, when Richard de Bothwell, Abbot of Dunfermline, tells of the provision he has made " of a house for the habitation of the schoolmaster of the town of Dunfermline and of certain pieces of land and divers rents of the yearly value of eleven marks of the current money of the realm of Scotland, and more, for the maintenance of poor scholars to be taught gratuitously by the said master— alledging that he intends to increase the rents for the maintenance of the said master and scholars." (*C.P.R.* xii. 297.)

This communication is definitely suggestive.

Not infrequently, in early post-Reformation days, the word " schoolhouse " is used to indicate, not the house in which the schoolmaster lived, but the school itself, and it is just a possibility that that is what is meant here. The schoolmaster, if not a full-fledged monk, was almost certain to be an official of some sort in the monastery, and, as such, would not require a habitation outwith the precincts ; but an increase in the number of non-monastic scholars might render desirable the provision of an outside school.

Moreover, he is described as " schoolmaster of the town of Dunfermline." Coming from the abbot in charge of the monastery, such a description seems to suggest, if not a different official from the schoolmaster of the monastery, at least a separate department of his work—in other words, the existence of a school outwith the precincts.

The reference is certainly suggestive, but something a little more definite on one or two points would have been even more acceptable.

The next stage in the story is associated with Robert Henryson, the poet. Traditional belief, unsupported by contemporary documentary evidence, is not, as a rule, satisfactory ground to build upon. But, in this case, the tradition is so definite and the fact vouched for so concordant with probability and so gratifying to local pride that in Dunfermline, at least, it is unhesitatingly accepted that this famous poet was schoolmaster of the monastery in the second half of the fifteenth century. (See page 70.)

Apart from Robert Henryson, the first known schoolmaster is

John Moffat

In the Burgh Records (298) under date 1519, he is styled Schir (indicating Chaplain) Johne Moffat, Master of the Grammar School.

In the year 1525 (168) he is styled Doms (indicating monk) and is further described as " presbitero magistro scolarum ac scole gramaticalis." *Presbitero* is confirmation of his rank as a monk in orders. *Scole* is a loose, but not unusual, reading for *scholae* and the use of the conjunctive *ac* would indicate that his office was a double one—master of the schools and of the grammar school.

On the face of it, this looks like confirmation of the idea suggested by the terms of Abbot Bothwell's provision for schoolmaster and scholars—the idea of a school outwith the precincts of the monastery.

When a later schoolmaster, John Henryson, described himself in 1573 as " Mr. of the Grammar Schole within the Abbay of Dunfermling . . . quhair he and his predecessouris has continewit maisteris and techearis of the youth in letters and doctrine . . . within the said Schole past memor of man," David Laing, a very careful writer, seems to accept this as indicating that the grammar school was within the precincts of the monastery, without so much as a suspicion that there may have been two schools—one without and one within.

Dr. Chalmers and Dr. Henderson were both of the same mind.

According to Dr. Henderson, the grammar school of the Burgh, which had been erected by Ged soon *after* the destruction of the Abbey (1560), was enveloped in the flames of the great fire of 25th May, 1624, and reduced to a ruin. In 1625 a new school was erected on the same site. (*Annals*, p. 290.)

The reference to Ged is based on the following entry in the Old Statistical Account of 1794 (xiii. 443):—

" The present school and schoolhouse are said to be a donation by a Mr. Ged, a Romish clergyman, to the Masters of the Grammar School; by which donation they were obliged to put up prayers for an easy passage through Purgatory to their benefactor."

Does any one seriously imagine that that could be the explanation of the erection of a new school " soon after the destruction of the Abbey " ? By that time, Roman Catholic rites were rigorously proscribed, and any master offering such prayers would very soon have found himself in trouble. On the other hand, the obligation to offer such prayers would have been perfectly understandable and permissible in *pre*-Reformation days.

All these writers seem to have overlooked the fact that in the Burgh Records (280), under date 1525—thirty-five years, that is, *before* the Reformation—in the course of a legal transference of property, the property in question is described as being situated in the Ratonraw (Queen Anne Street) *versus scolam grammaticalem* (opposite the grammar school), leaving no room for doubt that there was a grammar school outwith the precincts of the monastery long before the Reformation. And, as one cannot well imagine the novices and young monks leaving the precincts to receive instruction in Queen Anne Street, the probability would seem to be that the school in Queen Anne Street, though run by the monastery, was intended for outsiders.

One might even go further, without any undue strain on credibility, and contemplate the possibility that this building in Queen Anne Street may quite well represent the embodiment of what Abbot de Bothwell envisaged, some ninety years before the Reformation, when he made provision in his will for " a house for the habitation of the schoolmaster of the town of Dunfermline."

All this raises another interesting question.

Professor Coulton seems to think that monastic schools for outsiders, unless they happened to be almonry schools (schools dependent on benefactions intended for the poor) were definitely unusual.

" Dom. Berliere," he says, " who devoted a whole article to this subject in the Revue Benedictine for 1889, . . . could produce for the whole of Europe, and for eight centuries, only twenty certain cases, and five doubtful, in which monks can be shown to have had a school for non-monastic outsiders ; apart that is, from the Almonry Schools." (*Scott. Abbeys*, 177-8.)

We know that in 1525 the school in Queen Anne Street was under the charge of John Moffat, a full-fledged monk, who was responsible for both schools, the one within as well as that without ; and that the first reference to the Burgh having any interest in it was in connection with the Mortification of 1610.

Either, then, we are driven to the conclusion that this was an almonry school, of which, according to Professor Coulton, there is not much evidence in Scotland, though there might well be poor scholars in almost any monastery school—either that, or a school of the type he finds so very unusual, a school run by monks for the benefit of non-monastic outsiders.

Following John Moffat comes **John Wemyss,** who is described (*B.R.* 270) as " Master (indicating Graduate in Arts) John Wemis, Master of the grammer scuyl of Dunfermline." This would seem to refer to the school in Queen Anne Street, though he may quite well have been in charge of both. Wemyss was neither monk nor chaplain but, like Robert Henryson, notary in Dunfermline Abbey. (*B.R.* 265.)

He was in office in 1530 and 1543.

Following him comes **John Henryson,** who was both monk and notary, so that, quite clearly, there was no rigid rule as to the ecclesiastical status of the man in charge.

John Henryson was in office before the Reformation and for at least thirteen years after it.

Under whose supervision was his work during these thirteen years carried on ?

It goes without saying that, at the Reformation, school work within the monastery would immediately come to an end. But the school in Queen Anne Street was quite another matter. It was not intended for monastics, but for the youth of the community, whose parents presumably were able and willing to pay the fees prescribed.

Nobody wanted to see it closed. Who became responsible for its continuance ?

It is impossible to write with certainty, but one or two indubitable facts stand out.

There were many burgh grammar schools in Scotland long before the Reformation. Aberdeen, in fact, had one as early as 1418.

Edinburgh Town Council had at least the right to close the schools in time of pest :—

" 17 Nov. 1498—All scuillis scail and nane to be halden."

And its general attitude may be gathered from the following excerpts from its records :—

" 25 Jan. 1516-17—The hous of the Grammer Schole in St. Mary's Wynd disponit to the toun be Maister David Vocat, *secundum tenorem fundationis conficiendi.*"

" 10 Jan. 1519-20—Children to be sent to no school but the Grammar School ' to be teachit in ony science bot allanerlie (only) grace buke prymar and plane douatt.' "

" 19 May, 1531—Maister Adam Mwre, maister of the Hie Scule, oblist him to mak the bairnys perfyte grammariarris within thre yeris."

The connection of the burghs with the schools would doubtless arise through their having offered, or been invited, to contribute to the cost of running them, and, having paid the piper, it was a natural development in time to claim some interest in calling the tune.

This was a matter, however, on which the Church was likely to have very definite ideas, and it was only after a prolonged struggle that the burghs attained any real measure of control.

The way things developed in Aberdeen is probably more or less typical.

In 1418 a schoolmaster for the Burgh of Aberdeen was presented by the bailies and the council when the chancellor of the diocese had testified him to be of good character, sound learning and a graduate in arts. The Church was quite willing, apparently, to allow the formal right of presentation to the burgh so long as it was that of a man whom the Church itself recommended.

Some sixty years later, the master had a yearly salary out of the common good of the town until he should be provided with a benefice in the church of St. Nicholas—the town council being presumably the patron of this chaplaincy. The council, now paying the whole of the schoolmaster's salary, took the matter into its own hands in 1509 and not only presented John Merschell to the office but granted him collation as well, institution being given " by gift of a pair of beads."

The Church immediately called the appointment in question and we hear of an appeal to Rome, but how things went we do not know.

In 1538 the town council appointed one man and the chancellor another, but the presentee of the provost and corporation obtained possession in the end.

By 1550 a workable compromise was reached. The burgh was free to make its own presentation and the chancellor confirmed their choice by granting institution.

Where, then, the burghs had been in control of their schools before the Reformation, they naturally continued to exercise that control after the Reformation.

Where they did not have control before, they did in many cases take control at the Reformation, regarding it as part of their civic duty to make provision for the education of the youth of the community.

But this did not always happen, and time and time again we find the Reformed Church, in the midst of a multitude of other pre-occupations, having to take the matter in hand and make what provision it could for the education of the young—the offices of minister and schoolmaster being often held by the same man, sometimes with the consent of the town council, sometimes not.

In 1582 Mr. David Spens, minister of Kirkcaldy—son-in-law of David Ferguson of Dunfermline—made an agreement with the town council to teach a grammar school " be his self as principall, with ane doctor under him, for whom he sall anser."

In 1603 the master of the grammar school of Dundee held also the office of minister, but he resigned the mastership in 1606, because he " was not habile to discharge with a good conscience both the said offices."

What happened at Dunfermline is by no means clear.

The town, we gather, had been in the habit, before the Reformation, of contributing to the expense of the maintenance of the Parochial Kirk; but not a single reference can be found in its minutes to the town council having anything to do with the school in Queen Anne Street either before the Reformation or for fifty years after it.

On the other hand, Henryson, the schoolmaster, himself claims that, following the Reformation, he had satisfied the Reformed Kirk as to his beliefs, and it was the Kirk, when it ceased to be satisfied with his professions, that took steps for his removal from office.

The case, as already noticed (page 86) eventually came before the Privy Council, and the Council found against the Kirk, on the ground that the charges were of a civil nature with which the Kirk was not competent to deal; but expressly added that this finding was without prejudice to the Kirk's right to dismiss him on grounds with which it was competent to deal.

So that it looks as if, for the first fifty years following the Reformation, education in Dunfermline was in the hands of the Kirk alone.

The first appointment of a schoolmaster after Henryson would seem to point in the same direction, the office being filled by John Fairfoul, who afterwards became minister of Dunfermline.

The first reference, as already noted, to the Burgh having any interest in the school is in 1610 when the consort of James VI mortified in the hands of the town council £2,000 (Scots) for the support of the schoolmaster of the burgh and a teacher of music—yielding interest for each of them of £8 6s. 8d. Stg.—the only endowment of the kind in Scotland for a couple of generations.

" To this, in the case of the schoolmaster, the Town Council added from their own resources an annual sum of £9 0s. 10d. Stg., and the fraternity of guildry another annual increment of £5 5s.—in all £22 12s. 6d. This continued till 1833 when the

Town Council executed a trust-deed for behoof of the creditors of the Burgh and the schoolmaster accepted a sum, in full of all demands, during his incumbency." (*Chalmers, Hist. of Dunf.*, I. 438.)

In addition to the headmaster, there was, after the Reformation at least, an assistant, variously described as " doctor " or " usher," but so meagre was the provision for him that vacancies occurred with embarrassing frequency. For this post the town council and Kirk Session were joint patrons—the Kirk Session having mortified a thousand merks (Scots) for the provision of a " doctor." This arrangement continued till 1835 when the Kirk Session " agreed to waive at present the exercise of their joint right of presentation to the ushership, protesting that this shall not be to the prejudice of any rights or privileges claimed by them in reference to the said ushership."

On the whole, it was not too unsatisfactory a settlement of what might easily have proved a difficult problem—the transference of the schools from monastic control.

The Canongate of Edinburgh might well have envied it.

The Canongate had had " Grammar Schools, ane or ma, and that not only since the Reformation of Religion, bot also in tyme of Papistrie and past memorie of man." But William Roberton, schoolmaster of Edinburgh, had purchased of the king confirmation of a gift by the Abbot of Holyroodhouse, while he was still in his minority, and without consent of the convent, on the strength of which " he stoppit and dischairgit their sculis be the space of ane quarter of ane yeir or mair; throw whilk thair haill infantis and children are dispersit and scatterit, as yet they presently remain, to the gret dishonour of God hurt of their commounweill and tinsell of their haill youth."

An application to the Privy Council resulted in a declaration that their lordships " findis thameselffis not to be judges competent to the said mater, and thairfoir remitted the samyn to be decided before the judges competent thairto." (*Reg. P.C.* III. 305-6, *9th September,* 1580.)

It is scarcely necessary to add that the schoolmaster of Edinburgh was not too devoted an adherent of the Reformed Faith.

One rather unexpected result of the transference was the abduction of more than one lad from school.

John Boswell of Balmuto brought an action before the Privy Council against Phillip Moubray, son of James Moubray of Pitliver, for having carried off James Spittal of Leuquhat from the Grammar School of Dunfermline and from the charge of the widow woman in Dunfermline with whom he had been boarded out. By the will of Spittal's father, Boswell was one of three " tutors testamentary."

Phillip Moubray had married a sister of the lad, and she stood next in succession to her brother. Moubray was ordered to restore the lad within a specified period. He failed to do so and did not appear when the case came before the Privy Council.

He was denounced a rebel. (*Reg. P.C.* IV. 418, 11*th October*, 1589.)

A similar case occurred at Stirling.

James Menteith of Randifurde, a scholar in the Burgh School of Stirling, was carried off by his uncle, William, next in succession to the estate. But James, on the death of his father, had been left in charge of the Earls of Argyll and Mar, and action was swift and effective. His uncle was ordered to return him to school. (*Reg. P.C.*, III. 93, 4*th February*, 1578-79.)

This sort of thing would have been inconceivable in pre-Reformation days. Excommunication was then a grim reality which made many a would-be wrongdoer think again.

What about the school itself and its teaching ? How were they affected by the change-over ?

With the same headmaster still in office, as was the case in Dunfermline, it is unlikely that, for a time at least, the change would be very great. The opening prayer would no longer be in Latin, but religious teaching would still bulk large and Latin still continued to be the vehicle of education. The master taught in Latin and the pupils were expected to converse in Latin, not only while in school but in the playground too.

In the grammar schools there was sometimes a boy called " lupus," or wolf, whose special duty it was to report any school-fellow who might be caught slipping from Latin into the vernacular.

In the Universities some held their scholarships on a similar tenure.

It was a narrow and not particularly inspiring programme—Latin grammar and translation every day and most of the day, throughout the whole curriculum. But it was the pabulum on which the Reformers themselves had been brought up, and it was not to be expected that they should change it right away.

Andrew Simpson, who, according to John Row of Carnock, made such a success of his school at Perth that he had 300 pupils under him at the time of the Reformation, was the author of a Latin Grammar which is said to have been in general use in Scotland for more than a hundred years. After that, Ruddiman's Rudiments seem to have held the field.

As the result of a schoolmaster who was well versed in Greek being brought by John Erskine of Dun from France to Montrose, the study of Greek gradually began to appear on the curriculum, and, in course of time, even English came to find a place, though there was strong prejudice against it, and very few, even of educated Scotsmen, knew much about its history or literature, or were familiar with the use of it.

It was not till the middle of the eighteenth century that modern subjects began to get a real place in the school curriculum.

" The credit of leading the van in this reform lies with the town council of Ayr. They boldly faced the problem and set an example to the other burghs in Scotland. In addition to the classics, they introduced into the curriculum of the Grammar School, Arithmetic, Geometry, Euclid, Algebra, Natural Philosophy, Navigation, Surveying and Literature, making it known that their aim was to give the scholars a thorough training for business.

" It should, however, be observed that, whatever changes took place, the teaching of religion always formed an important part of the school training.

" But Perth soon outstripped Ayr and took the lead in making science the foundation of the educational system which it favoured, and it went as far as to build an academy for carrying out its ideas." (*Stewart, The Story of Scott. Education, p.* 84.)

As for the effect of the change-over on schoolmasters, one must draw a clear distinction between those who continued in office and those who entered on it for the first time.

Notwithstanding the discredit into which the monastic life had fallen, there was still a certain amount of social prestige attaching to it, and the monk who continued in office under the new conditions would retain something of it.

No doubt, he would have to reckon with close supervision of his work by representatives of the Reformed Church, but financially, with his pension plus his salary, his position would be more or less secure, and, if trouble arose, he could appeal to the Privy Council.

New appointments were on quite a different footing. The applicants would doubtless have been educated in a monastic or burgh grammar school, but would carry with them nothing of the prestige attaching to a functionary of the monastery. They would have no security of tenure in the office, the bulk of the appointments being only for a limited period and capable of termination on short notice and frequently on very paltry grounds. They would have no redress against injustice, the merest pittance in the way of salary, and no provision whatever for old age or infirmity.

In the case of country schools it was possible for the master to supplement his meagre salary by accepting other appointments, such as precentor or session clerk, or even as gravedigger.

But pluralities of the sort were not encouraged in grammar schools, unless, because of the shortage of ministers, he happened to be appointed reader, but that possibility was available for only a very limited time.

The most unlooked for method of augmenting the miserable salary of the schoolmaster was surely that of organising cockfights in the school—a practice not only permitted but encouraged by the authorities—with payment for admission and the vanquished birds becoming the property of the schoolmaster. It sounds incredible, but the facts are only too well vouched for.

It is not easy to arrive at anything like a reliable estimate of what salaries generally amounted to. Conditions of appointment varied greatly. In some cases free houses were available in addition to the salary. In others the salary included an allowance for house rent. In the year 1627 the Burghs of Ayr, Lanark and Tain paid the masters of their grammar schools £100 (Scots).

That looks comparatively good, but when expressed in sterling as £8 6s. 8d. it does not look quite so good.

Inverness (1634) paid £80 (Scots), Elgin (1622) £66 13s. 8d. (Scots) and Aberdeen (1594) £33 6s. (Scots).

Dundee (1602) paid 200 merks, Irvine (1633) 80 merks. (*Macmeeken, Scot. Met. Psalms*, p. 192.)

It is difficult to believe that it was on such feeble foundations that the proud edifice of Scottish education was built up.

It was the scholars, however, not the schoolmasters, who were clamant in their outcries against the new conditions, and everywhere their protest took the same form—against the curtailment of their holidays. Under pre-Reformation conditions, the school-day began about five or six o'clock, and, for five days in the week, with a break of two hours, continued till about six o'clock at night. On Saturdays it ended at 2 p.m.

Nobody thought very much about that, because they had always been accustomed to it. But in the Roman Church there were lots of Feast Days, when nobody worked. Under the Reformed Church there were no Feast Days at all.

Older folks, in their enthusiasm for the new doctrine, might tolerate that sort of thing. The young folks wouldn't.

Discontent grew and deepened till at last, in Aberdeen and Edinburgh, it led to open revolt against authority.

" Forasmuch as certain scholars of the High School . . . have not only taken upon themselves to hold the school against their master, but have most proudly and contemptuously held the same against my lord provost and the bailies, and, when required, would not render the same, whereby the said provost and bailies were compelled to break in pieces one of the doors and win the same by force, when the said scholars were found with pistols, swords, halberts and other weapons and armour, against all good order and laws, and to the evil example of others. . . . " (*Edin. Burgh Records* IV. 499.)

Eight years afterwards there was another outbreak of rowdyism, again on the score of holidays. The town council had planned to give the scholars a week's holiday in May and another in September, but on the condition that, on each morning of the holidays, they reported to the school. This the " gentry bairns " and others living outside the town resented. On their taking possession of the school, the master applied to the magistrates for help.

A member of the town council, Mr. John Macmorran, came with a party of men to help in getting access to the school, and, on his attempting to force the door, was shot in the head and killed.

In 1604 there was a similar outburst of indignant protest in Aberdeen. Fortunately it passed off without any very serious damage being done.

MASTERS OF THE GRAMMAR SCHOOL

ROBERT HENRYSON—d. circa 1499—A Licentiate in Arts and Bachelor in Decrees, Glasgow, 1462. Notary of Dunfermline Abbey 1477/8.

JOHN MOFFATT—1525—Had been Chaplain of the Morning Service, 1494. Master of the schools both without and within the precincts. A full-fledged monk.

JOHN WEMYSS—1530 and 1543—Notary Public.

JOHN HENRYSON—In office before 1560. Still in office 1573.

JOHN FAIRFOUL—1582 and 1584—Schoolmaster of Dunfermline before 1582 (Fasti). Afterwards Minister of Dunfermline.

JAMES DALGLEISH—1591 and 1598—Witness to Will of David Ferguson.

WILLIAM SMYTHE—Formerly a monk of Dunfermline Abbey and Chaplain of St. Katherine's Altar there—cannot have been long a monk before the Reformation—what he had been doing since is unknown—was succeeded as schoolmaster of Dunfermline, before 21st April, 1618, by

JAMES SIBBALD, probably eldest son of James Sibbald of Kair, minister of Benholme—graduated M.A. (St. Andrews) 29th July, 1611—became minister of Torryburn and Crombie, 18th March, 1629.   (Fasti.)

JAMES REDDIE—1640 and 1642—(Resigned as Schoolmaster, Inverkeithing, 21st May, 1629.) (B.R. Invk.). Calls for the stringent application of "sundrie laudable actes of the said burghe inactit and set doune (1631 & 1632) for restraining and dischairging all persones fra teaching of maill childrene that are able to travell to the comon schoole and have learned the single catechisme" and, in particular, calls for the prohibition of Mr. Robert Anderson, Master of the musick schoole, from doing so. (B.R. 26th February, 1641, 18th December, 1642 K.S.R.).

THOMAS WALKER—1653 and 1664—"20 Dec., 1653—The Session recommendit to Mr. Thomas Walker, Schoolmatr to have his Schollers in reddiness to repeat the catechism everie sabbath betwixt the second and third bell, before noon and after noone ; the one to propose and the uthyr to ansr yt the people may heare and learne, it being usit in uthyr Kirks, and this to begin next Sabbath." (K.S. Rec.). Supplicates the Kirk Session to take to their serious consideration how a competent provision may be had for upholding the grammar school. (K.S. Rec., 11th March, 1656). Referred to as Schoolmaster, 26th November, 1664 (B.R.).

JOHN COWIE—1668—Appointed 14th December, 1668 (B.R.).

WILLIAM KINNAIRD—1670 and 1672—Appointed 3rd December, 1670. Referred to as Schoolmaster, 17th August, 1672 (B.R.).

WILLIAM HAY—1682—"9 Ap., 1682—This day the session peyit to Mr. Wm. Hay, schoolmr. 10 mks., and to Mr. Peter Kennedie, Doctor, 5 mks. for a yeir by gone, viz :—fra witsonday, 1681, to witsonday, 1682, of the annuel rent of the money mortified be umquhl Jon Drysdaill for the use of the poore schoollers." (K.S. Rec.).

PATRICK DYKES—1685 and 1703—"Mr. Robt. Norrie, moderator, gave in seven 14/- pieces, of charitie, given be my Lord Drummond (a schollar) to the poore, all put into the box." (K.S. Rec., 19th April, 1685).

"This day the moderator gave in 8 lib., 8s. givin in charitie to the poore be my Lord Drumond and the rest of the nobles who are schollers, and yt.

for the last sabbath and all preceedings."(*K.S. Rec.*, 13th *September*, 1685).

"Therefore the Counsell unanimously discharge the said John Anderson and Thomas Hanna (private schools) and oyr persons q'soever to sett up Schools within the territories of this burgh, and teach any male children hereafter, *except such as shall be under seven years of age*, and that under the paine of twentie pound scots, *toties quoties*—the one-half of the fine to ye town, and the other half to ye schoolmaster and Doctor." (*B.R.* 13th *February*, 1703). Died in 1704 (*B.R.*).

JOHN HART—Appointed 1705—but only for three months (*B.R.*).

JAMES GRAHAM—1705-1708—Appointed in December, 1705, but died 1st March, 1708. (*B.R.*).

JAMES BAYNE—1729 and 1746—Published a "Short Introduction to the Latin Grammar," 8vo. Edinburgh, 1714. (*Annals*, 393).

"The Councill orders the Dean of Guild, John Scotland, and William Flockart to meet with Mr. Bayne and Mr. Hart, and commune with them about their drawing rent for the Seats of the Scholars loft, and anent their not allowing the Scholars to sit according to their Seniority." (*Burgh Rec.*, 12th *January*, 1730).

Note.—The Scholars' Loft was above the western doorway of the Nave.

GEORGE BROWN—1748—Formerly "doctor," was promoted to be "Master" by 1748.

— RAMSAY—1789—During the last ten years (1790-1800) scholars had decreased from 60 to 20, not from any fault in him, but owing to "the Change of Mode of Education." The Council agree to increase his salary from £17 7/6d. to £25 Stg. (*B.R.* 10th *November*, 1800).

— BATHGATE—1810.

ARCHIBALD HAXTON—1810-1850—The last of the Masters at 1625 school. Excellent teacher and disciplinarian. (*Annals*, 292). A native of Kirkcaldy. Studied for the Secession ministry. Interred in Dunfermline.

1810—In future, presentation of Rector of Grammar School and Precentor of parish church to be granted to competent persons recommended by the Town Council.

Foundations of NEW SCHOOL laid March, 1816—scholars meantime accommodated in Town House.

NEW SCHOOL opened 1817. This represents the third school known to have been on this site.

W. T. BROWN—1851.

Under the Act of 1872 Dunfermline did not rank as a higher-class school, but soon after its appointment the first School Board of Dunfermline took steps to bring the school into line with the requirements of the Act; the first appointment under the new conditions being that of:

JOHN DUNN—1877—later Dr. Dunn, H.M. Inspector of Schools. Following the appointment of Mr. Dunn as Rector, a question arose as to the liability of the Town Council for payment of grants from the Common Good and other sources. The finding of the Court was:—"That an annual grant of £100 be given from the Corporation Funds, but that this grant, although intended to be a permanent endowment so long as the School continues

to be conducted to the satisfaction of the Council, may be withdrawn at
any time, if that condition is not fulfilled."

WILLIAM THOMSON, B.A. (London)—1883-1885—Resigned on appointment as Headmaster, Hutcheson's Higher Class School for Girls, Glasgow,
13th June, 1885.

D. MUNRO FRASER, M.A. (Edinburgh)—1885-1890—On 5th January,
1886, a new (High) School was opened at Priory Lane, with a staff of five
teachers, at a cost of £7,500, which was met by public subscription.

The information concerning the site occupied by the Grammar
School has been supplied by Mr. P. M. Inglis, Dunfermline :—

" When the New High School in Priory Lane was opened
in 1886, Provost Robert Donald purchased the old site and
buildings in Queen Anne Street from the Burgh School Board
for the sum of £800.

" A few years later he sold the ground immediately in front
of the old school, which was used as a playground, to the
Government for the same figure, viz., £800, and it was on this
site that the present Post Office was erected in 1889.

" From 1886 to 1898 the old school was occupied by the
Y.M.C.A. and other religious bodies, free of charge.

" In 1889 the Government found it necessary to extend the
Post Office buildings and, in order to do so, they had to purchase
the old school itself from Mr. Peter Donald of New York, who
had inherited it from his brother, Provost Donald—the price
being £1,350. This sum Mr. Donald very generously handed
over to the Trustees and Managers of Queen Anne Street
Church as a donation towards the re-seating and renovation of the
Church, of which he was a member before going to New York.

" Three old stones with the Burgh Coat of Arms and Latin
inscriptions, and the date 1625, which were part of the old
building, were preserved and built into the extension of the
Post Office, facing east, in 1902."

Mr. Fraser resigned in 1890 to become H.M. Inspector of Schools.

A. B. DON, M.A. (Abdn.)—1890-1898—Retired on grounds of ill-health.

DR. MACDONALD—1898-1919—Appd. Director of Education for Aber-
deenshire.

J. G. LINDSAY, O.B.E., M.A., B.Sc., F.R.S.E., F.E.I.S.—1919-1947—On
7th June, 1939, another High School was opened at Hospital Hill, with over
900 pupils in attendance and a staff of 40 teachers.

   The estimated cost of the plans first submitted was £120,000, but modified
plans were eventually adopted and completed at a cost, including playfields,
etc., of £75,000.

CHARLES H. GORDON, M.A., B.A.—1948-

DOCTORS OR USHERS OF THE GRAMMAR SCHOOL

It is not known when Robert Durie began or John Hart finished, but the dates attached give some indication of the frequency of changes, largely due to the meagreness of the salary paid.

1598	Robt. Durie.		1661	Patrick Mylne.
1640/46	John Hodge.		1665	James Anderson.
1646	Edward Cisholm.		1666	Wm. Walker (Son of the Provost).
1647	Alexr. M'Lean.		1672	Peter Kennedy (died 1704).
1648	Samuel Henryson.		1711	John Hart (died 1748).
1649	Samuel Cisholm.		1746	George Brown (formerly Schoolmaster at Airth) promoted to be Master, 1748.
1650	Edward Cisholm.		1748	Richard Jameson — resigned 1/9/1750.
1650/52	David Niven.		1750	William Hutton — appd. 4th September—resigned August, 1767 (Andrew Thomson being appd. *ad interim*).
1652	John Kay.		1779	John Jesson—formerly schoolmaster in Cupar.
1653	Robert Inglis.			

One of them was charged before the Kirk Session with serious irregularities of life and pleaded guilty. The Session resolved to report the matter to the town council, but delayed his public appearance on the stool of repentance meantime, because " it wald be a means to mak him contemned and vilified in the schoole."

John Hart was a divinity student in 1702. Unfortunately he, too, came under the notice of the Kirk Session, though for an offence less serious than that of the doctor above referred to, and it meant the end of his career in the Church. Appointed presbytery clerk in 1729, he continued in that office till 1743. By this time he had so commended himself to the brethren that when, because of years and infirmity, he had to resign, it was made a condition of the appointment of his successor that one half of the salary would be paid to John Hart as long as he lived.

It appears from the Session Records that, in the case of John Hart, the town council had made the appointment without reference to the Kirk Session. The Kirk Session, having equal rights in the matter with the town council, in virtue of an agreement reached between them, protested against this unilateral action and sent commissioners to interview the town council. At the next meeting the commissioners reported that they had met with the town council, which in the meantime had discovered a copy of the agreement, and that they " were inclined to give all satisfaction to the Session thereanent."

Private Schools lie outwith the scope of the present study, but it would be misleading to make no reference to them.

For long the masters of the grammar school sought to make the education of youth within the parish their own exclusive right, apart from children at a very elementary stage. But the parish was too wide and populous and the accommodation in the grammar school too limited to make that possible. Some of the private schools must have had a sore struggle for existence. On the other hand, it is evident that some of them were definitely successful.

SANG SCULES

Whilst there is no doubt that sang scules existed in Scotland from an early date, it is often difficult, as in the case of the grammar school, to speak with any confidence as to the exact date on which such a school began in any particular community.

The explanation, in both cases, is the same.

Both types owed their origin to a need which was inherent in the very idea of a community called into being for the express purpose of worship. Before a newcomer could take his full part in that worship, he must be able to read and sing, and as very few of them were able to do so at their admission, it followed that, right from the start, some provision had to be made for their instruction.

That there was a precentor in every monastery from the date of its inception, may be taken for granted, and it is difficult to conceive of a precentor filling his role successfully without giving some measure of instruction.

Just when these first provisional arrangements attained to the dignity of a full-fledged school is a matter of comparative unimportance, though, naturally, not without interest.

One thing may be safely reckoned on. As worship of the Virgin Mary developed, with its consequent increase of special chapels and services, the sang scule would attain a standing in the life of the community it had not known before.

Here and there one comes across occasional references to them.

About the middle of the thirteenth century, the Statutes of Aberdeen provide for " singing boys " to be in attendance at the church on great festival days; and in 1494 the duties of the master of the sang scule are defined as follows :—

" To instruct burgesses' sons in singing and playing on the organ, for the upholding of God's service in the choir, they paying him his scolage and dues." (*Edgar* 102-3.)

In Kirkwall (1544), on the other hand, the master of the sang scule was expected to teach gratuitously, not only the boys of the choir, but any of the poor who desired to attend. (*Ibid.*)

In the Collegiate Church at Crail (8th June, 1517) there was a sang scule for the instruction of scholars with provision for a " Parish clerk, skilful in chant and discant . . . to sing at Morning Mass, Vespers &c. . . . and a secular clerk . . . to keep the choir in all honesty." (*Reg. of Crail*, 38.)

The first reference to a school of the sort in Edinburgh occurs in the Burgh Records under date 15th December, 1553.

It names Sir Ed. Henryson as " Maister of thair Sang Scule," and speaks of the school as being " occupiit be him."

In 1554 there is a record of repairs to the school, which was situated in St. Giles' kirkyard :—

" The bailies and counsale sittand in jugement ordains the dene of gild to repair and vpbig the Sang Scule in the kirkyard, as it wes of befoir, sua that the barnis may enter thairto and inhabit samyn." (*Edin. B.R.*, 27th April, 1554.)

This reference to a pre-Reformation sang scule, run and maintained by the Burgh, must be rather unusual. Burghs generally did not take in hand with them till after the Reformation.

In another respect the sang scule in Edinburgh was probably exceptional. It had the same master *after* the Reformation as it had *before*.

Edward Henryson was precentor in St. Giles' previous to the Reformation and continued as precentor in the Reformed Church, the salary then amounting to £60 (Scots, no doubt), plus £10 for rent, and the scholars' fees, which amounted to two merks each per annum.

He was succeeded as master of the sang scule by his son, Gilbert, who was succeeded by his brother, Samuel. Under him the school quite clearly prospered, and he enjoyed a much larger salary than his father had. So great, indeed, was his success that a new school was built for him by the town council, much larger, but on the same site.

After 1616, the interest of the town council in the school began to wane. The building was eventually taken down when the separate churches into which St. Giles' had been divided were combined. (*Edin. B.R.* IV. 407.)

With the Reformation, the great majority of these schools came to a sudden end, and, for a time, preoccupation with other matters prevented the Reformers from giving their attention to the place of song in worship.

There was even a tendency on the part of some to regard it as something that might possibly be profitable, but could not be regarded as really necessary.

Others went the length of questioning whether, in a truly purged worship, there was any place at all for singing, forgetting that it had not only the approval of the Word of God, but the sanction of universal practice.

But neither of these attitudes represents the true spirit of the Reformation. We are on much surer ground when we take our stand on the fact that Parliament, afraid of the effect on national life of the decay of music, took definite steps to ensure that, wherever there were ancient schools, they should be provided with a master sufficient and able for the instruction of youth in the said science of music, as they will answer to His Highness upon the peril of their foundations, and that, by way of encouragement, the king's consort endowed the sang scule at Dunfermline to the extent of £100 per annum, while the General Assembly, in its anxiety to provide psalmody for the people, resolved to lend Lekprevik, the printer, £200 " to help to buy irons, ink and paper, and to fie craftsmen " for printing the psalms. (*Bannatyne Misc.* II. 232.)

So speedy and so satisfactory was the response to these moves that an edition of the Psalter was in circulation by 1564, to be followed soon by others; and in the preface to the edition printed in Edinburgh in 1635—the first published with the tunes harmonised—Edward Miller, the editor, says:—

" I acknowledge sinceerly the whole compositions of the parts to belong to the primest musicians that ever this kingdome had, as Dene John Angus, Blackhall, Smith, Peebles, Sharp, Black, Buchan, and others, famous for their skill in this kind." (*Reg. K.S. St. And.* 41n.)

It has not been possible to trace all the names here mentioned, but most of them can quite confidently be identified.

Andrew Blackhall, a canon of the Abbey of Holyroodhouse, became minister at Ormiston, and afterwards at Inveresk.

Smith, in all probability, is the man referred to by James Melville in his Diary:—" In ther yeirs I learned my music . . . of ane Alexander Smithe, servant to the Primarius of our College, wha had been treaned upe amangis the mounks in the Abbay."

David Peebles, said to have been " ane of the chief musitians of the land," was a canon of St. Andrews, and became a contributor to one of the intermediate editions.

Black and Buchan were the respective masters of the sang scules of Aberdeen and Haddington.

Dene John Angus, the precentor of Dunfermline Abbey (see page 81), was thus one of the leading figures in the production of the Scottish Psalter.

It is not easy to arrive at anything like a just estimate of the comparative contributions to singing in Scotland of the pre-Reformation and post-Reformation sang scules.

That the standard in the pre-Reformation school was high is generally accepted. Some would even compare it not unfavourably with Rome. But, as Dr. Millar Patrick points out, the obligation to use Gregorian settings and the temptation to experiment with what was even more elaborate and intricate tended to make singing a monopoly of the professional performers.

On the other hand, one of the features of the Reformation in all countries where it prevailed was the restoration to the common people of the right, and the opportunity, to participate in the singing of God's praise in public worship.

" The services commenced with the singing of a psalm by the whole vast assemblage. Clement Marot's verses, recently translated by Dathenus, were then new and popular. The strains of the monarch minstrel, chanted thus in their homely but nervous mother tongue by a multitude who had but recently learned that all the poetry and rapture of devotion were not irrevocably coffined with a buried language, or immured in the precincts of a church, had never produced a more elevating effect.'' (Motley, *The Rise of the Dutch Republic*, on the field preachings in the Walloon provinces in 1566.)

Despite the distinction above referred to, the two had points in common, for the New School, as we have seen, owed a good deal of its success to men who had been trained in the Old ; and even some of the psalm tunes that for their simple dignity have been regarded as typically Scottish in a Presbyterian sense have been traced to collections of pre-Reformation days.

The one thing clear is that the country was deeply indebted to them both.

There may have been some substance in the repeated warnings about the art of singing falling into disrepute and decay, but there is little evidence of it in the experience of John Durie, one of the monks of Dunfermline who turned Protestant preacher. Durie was minister at St. Giles' and, for his plain speech about some of the leading figures in Court circles, had been banished from his charge. Soon afterwards, however, he " gat leive to ga ham to his awin flok at Edinbruche ; at whase retourning ther was a grait concurs of the haill town, wha met him at the Nather Bow ; and going upe the streit, with bear heads and loud voices, sang to the praise of God, and testifeing of great joy and consolation, the 124th Psalm :—' Now Israel may say, and that trewlie ' &c. till heavin and erthe resoundit.'' (*Melville's Diary*, 134.)

Calderwood, the historian, confirms the story, adding that the number was estimated at 2,000, that the words of the psalm were known to the singers and that they sang the tune in four parts.

Could the same be said of a crowd of similar dimensions in the streets of Edinburgh or any other city in Scotland to-day?

No specific reference has been found to choirs in early post-Reformation records, but a minute of St. Andrews Kirk Session reveals members of the sang school acting as a choir:—

" Wednesday, the last of October, 1599—The quhilk day, Jhon Sourdy, as master of the hospitall, is ordinit that the auld pepill and bairnis thairintill sall repair to the preaching on the Saboth dayis, and sitt at the west end of the kirk; and Jhon Roull, as maister of the sang schole, to caus the best of his scholaris sitt besyid him self, about the pulpeit, to help to sing the Psalmes on the Saboth dayis; and the parentis and maisteris of sic bairnis and utheris as trubillis the Kirk and kirkyard in tyme of divyne service, or vaiges in this citie tyme of preaching, salbe cited and censurit for thair faultis."

In the records examined there has been comparatively little reference to instrumental music—probably for the simple reason that organs in pre-Reformation days in Scotland were not so very numerous, and that such as did exist at the Reformation were destroyed. But we know that there were organs in use at the service when the body of Queen Margaret was " translated " in 1250, and that instrumental music was re-introduced in the Parish Kirk of Dunfermline in 1882.

" The organ, which it was then (pre-Reformation) the custom to speak of as a ' pair of organs ' was a small instrument, admitting of being easily carried to and fro, such as were called regals or portatives. But it is probable that larger and more powerful instruments were soon after in use in the royal chapel (Stirling).

" In 1517 it was no longer necessary to import organs from abroad, for we find Gilleam, organist, maker of the kingis organs, resident in Edinburgh." (*Accounts of the Lord High Treasurer*, i. ccxxxiii.)

MASTERS OF THE SANG SCULE

Unfortunately there is no detailed account of the sang scule in Dunfermline in the years immediately following the Reformation.

That there was such a school is beyond doubt, the consort of James VI having in 1610 endowed it to the extent of £100 (Scots) per annum.

But the records of the Kirk Session for that time are missing, and, so far, no reference has been found to it in the Burgh Records.

There was, however, in the Church in the days immediately following the Reformation a body of men known as **readers,** whose duties included not only the reading of the Scriptures and of the prayers prescribed, but the leading of the praise of the congregation. It was a temporary arrangement till more ministers became available, and before the end of the sixteenth century it had officially come to an end.

The title, however, remained for very much longer, the main duty being that of precentor, though he might at the same time fulfil the duties of session clerk or treasurer.

According to the first available minute of Kirk Session, 7th July, 1640, the session had to deal with the resignation of

JOHN WALKER—1604-1640—who had been Reader, i.e. Precentor, for 36 years but who, by reason of the weakness of his voice, was no longer capable of performing the duties of his office. There is notice of him in Town Council Minute of 1st November, 1641.

ROBERT ANDERSON—1640 and 1680—Appointed 25th August, 1640 (*K.S.R.*). There is notice of him as Master of the Music School in Town Council Minute, 19th August, 1665.

JOHN CHRISTIE—1687 and 1709—was successor as Church Clerk (Session Clerk) to Anderson, and is described as " Musick Master in Dunfermline."

He became suspect of errors of doctrine akin to Arminianism and his case had to be referred to the Presbytery.

The Presbytery apparently found against him, but the heritors pressed for his restitution to office. On 8th March, 1711, however, it was reported to the Session that the heritors " had passed from insisting any further to have John Christie reponed " and desired that Mr. Jon Brand might be Precentor and Session Clerk, if found qualified.

JOHN BRAND—1711—Under date 27th November, 1729, there is an entry in the Burgh Records as follows :—

" Which day the Council considering that the offices of Music Master and Reader in the church are both vacant, and that it will be for the interest of the town that these two offices be united in the person of one man ; also understanding that the Marquis of Tweeddale is willing to present any person that the council is satisfied with and agreeable to the kirk-session, The Council appointed the two baillies and Charles Chalmer to wait upon the kirk-session and intreat them to concur with the town to find out a man that is sufficiently qualified for both these offices, and that they would join with the town council in desiring the Marquis of Tweeddale to allow the town to advertise it in the Gazett.''

JOHN HART—11th December, 1729. Precentor and Session-Clerk. (*Pby. Rec.*).

ANDREW BEVERIDGE—On 9th October, 1745, Andrew Beveridge, described as Preacher of the Gospel, and *Precentor in Dunfermline*, was appointed Presbytery Clerk. (*Pby. Rec.*). (See page 134 under Peter Chalmers). Died before 1772.

JAMES BAIN—1772—is described as both Music Master and Precentor.

JAMES CHRISTIE—1776-1817—Elected Master of the Song School, Dunfermline, 10th July, 1776. (*B.R.*). Formerly Schoolmaster of Kennoway. A day-school and a music school in the Mason Lodge, top of Bruce Street. Died September, 1817. (*Annals*, p. 504).

JAMES RANKINE—1819—Came from Glasgow. Held both offices, Master of Song School and Precentor of the Abbey Church.

Kept a school for writing and other ordinary branches but only for a time—latterly taught singing, piano and organ—also kept Registers of Baptisms and Marriages, but was not Session Clerk.

In 1835, like the Master of the Grammar School, he accepted a sum, in full of all demand, during his incumbency, instead of the annual salary.

Dr. Henderson expresses great admiration for his life and work (*Annals*, 659). He was buried in the South Churchyard of the Abbey, where there is to be seen a small tombstone with a strung harp cut on it, erected by some of his admirers. Died 21st April, 1849, aged 52.

GEORGE MARTIN—1849—April, 1849, received appointment as Master of the Song School and Parish Clerk. (*Annals*, 659).

JOHN LOCKE—1853—Master of Song School and Parish Clerk of Dunfermline, 13th November, 1853.

THE PRIORY OF COLDINGHAM

Coldingham Priory was erected by Edgar, son of Malcolm Canmore and Queen Margaret, in 1098, and a colony of Benedictine monks was transported to it from St. Cuthbert's Cathedral at Durham as soon as the buildings had been so far completed as to admit of accommodating them. King Edgar was personally present on the day of its consecration and richly endowed it with gifts "for the souls of his father and mother, for the salvation of his own soul and that of his brothers and sisters."

" To begin with, the life of the inmates was most exemplary; the monks employing the time that could be spared from their devotions in the cultivation of their gardens and in the pursuit of agriculture, two of them in the 12th century signalising themselves by the composition of historical works which are preserved and valued at the present day." (*Carr's Hist. of C.*, p. 248.)

But trouble soon developed, and, for the greater part of the Priory's existence, it was seldom far away. For this there was more than one reason.

One lay in the simple fact of its situation. It was not only near the border, but on the main east road between England and Scotland. In a Charter of Protection granted by Henry VI the awkwardness of the situation is frankly admitted.

" The said Priory is so situated . . . our own subjects at one time making inroads into Scotland, at another the subjects of Scotland making inroads into England, going down by the aforesaid priory, very frequently refresh themselves in the same, and in the manors and granges pertaining to it, and destroy and consume the victuals and animals, dead as alive, which were ordained and provided for the support of the prior, convent and their domestics, that they have often neither meat nor drink which they can set before them, on which account the number of monks, who used and ought to serve the Most High in the same is exceedingly reduced and diminished; and it is probable that, for want of food and due support, it will be wholly abolished, so that divine service will necessarily cease in the same."

Fortunately, by a Grant of 1279, " a place of habitation for the monks of Coldingham for ever " was provided in Holy

Island, so that, when trouble threatened, they could seek refuge for the time being there.

Another reason for the unusually checkered story of this priory lies in the fact that, while situated on Scottish soil, it was under the jurisdiction of an English Cathedral. In the days of Edgar, when the border-line was more or less fluid, that may not have been such a serious matter, but in time it came to be a fruitful source of trouble, with unfortunate effects on the life of the community. The possibility of trouble herein contained was later aggravated by the fact that in 1378 the priory was withdrawn from the supervision and care of Durham and attached to Dunfermline, with the result that ecclesiastical as well as national prestige became involved.

As to the reasons that led King Robert II to effect this transfer, there is some difference of opinion.

Dr. Henderson (*Annals*, p. 140) says that it was " in consequence of the great *misrule* and *irregularities* of this Priory," but the charter doesn't say so.

Fordun speaks of the " treacheries, seditions and snares of the English," and further elaborates the idea :—

" The principal motive of the king for bestowing the said priorate on Dunfermline was that a certain monk of Durham, Robert Claxton by name, acting as Prior of Coldingham, was sued and accused before the King and the Three Estates of the Realm for felony, and prying into and revealing the counsels of the King and secrets of the kingdom, and for carrying off the money of the king and kingdom contrary to the prohibition made thereanent, and was convicted." (*Scotichron*. xi. cap. xxiii.)

The *Book of Pluscarden*, on the other hand, explains the transfer as part of the general move for ousting beneficed English from the Kingdom of Scotland. (Vol. II. 113.)

Whatever the reason, Durham vigorously disapproved ; and thus began between Durham and Dunfermline a feud that was to contribute materially to the unsettlement of Coldingham.

As an illustration of the working of this feud, the following facts, based on Dr. Annie Cameron's *Scottish Supplications*, are submitted. Andrew Raybourn, Prior of Coldingham, having been elected to Urquhart, another priory attached to Dunfermline, William Bron (Brown), Bachelor of Theology, monk of Dunfermline, was unanimously elected by the monastery in his place; but an Englishman, of the name of William Drax (Drakis), a monk of Durham, had been, it appears, in unlawful possession of Coldingham for two years. Brown applied for papal confirmation of his election, and got it. (*Priory of C.*, *Surtees*, 91). In the meantime, another applicant, Robert Bowmakare, monk of Arbroath, had obtained possession, or nearly so, of Coldingham, but, through simple ignorance, as he explains, he had not expressed the true value of the said priory— £600 not £200—and had erred in stating that he was a monk of Dunfermline. Bowmakare's claim was apparently bought off on Drax's behalf by the payment of a pension.

In 1420 Brown's Supplication was reconsidered and found ineffective because of a misdescription of voidance (vacancy). (*Scott. Suppl.* 44n.)

Still later he complained to the Pope that he was " inhibited by temporal lords from going to prosecute his cause at the curia." But nothing came of it.

" Drax signalised his appointment by bringing some compatriots to burn down the buildings of Coldingham, whereupon its fruits were sequestrated by Albany. On the return of James (I) Drax seized the opportunity to lay his case before parliament, having perhaps been encouraged to do so in some personal interview with the king at Durham. Judgment was given in his favour as the rightful prior, but parliament at the same time ordered him to repair the buildings which the Englishmen had burned.

" According to Bower, the judgment proved unfortunate, for, comparing him to a serpent in the bosom of the kingdom, he proceeds to tell how Drax caused a notable Scottish sailor, William Alanson, to be taken by the English and to be put to death, even by hanging, instead of the more honourable decapitation, and thus aroused the anger of James against him to such an extent that he did not venture to appear in Scotland for the remainder of the reign." (*Balfour-Melville, James I*, 113-4.)

" In 1431 Broun accepted the priory of Urquhart from Eugenius IV, who then provided Stephen Bryg to Coldingham, ignoring Drax. Drax, however, seems to have retained possession of Coldingham." (*Ibid.* 154n.)

The prior who succeeded Drax was, in accordance with the usual practice, instituted by Bishop Kennedy of St. Andrews, but the election had been carried through against the wishes of the Abbot of Dunfermline, who favoured a monk of his own, and for some time to come neither Durham nor Dunfermline had very much to do with Coldingham, two Canons of Dunbar, of the name of Home, supported by their kinsman, Lord Home, having taken advantage of the opportunity and intruded themselves into the priory.

Another happening that was to have an even more unsettling effect on Coldingham was that in 1487, James III, obsessed with the idea of the new Chapel Royal at Stirling, which he designed to make the grandest ecclesiastical establishment in Scotland, and looking round for funds for its endowment, resolved to withdraw the Priory of Coldingham from Dunfermline, curtail its activities and endow the Chapel Royal with a considerable portion of its revenues. This so incensed the Homes that they joined forces with the other insurgents and James was defeated at Sauchieburn and lost his life when fleeing from the field.

In 1509 the priory was finally withdrawn from Durham and inalienably annexed to Dunfermline by order of Pope Julius III.

Four years later, 12th October, 1513 (i.e., barely five weeks after Flodden), Henry VIII asked the Pope to revoke certain concessions made to the King of Scots, which were injurious to England.

He specially asked that St. Andrews should be deprived of metropolitan honours, that the Priory of Coldingham should be restored to the See of Durham, and that none of the Scottish bishoprics rendered vacant on Flodden Field should be disposed of until he had expressed his wishes regarding them. (*Hay Fleming* p. 166, *quoting Letters and Papers of Henry VIII.*)

Coldingham, however, was not restored to the See of Durham, but continued under the jurisdiction of Dunfermline till the Reformation.

As for the later sufferings of Coldingham caused by its proximity to the English border, it is impossible to give the whole story in detail, but the following extracts from *The Hamilton Papers*, Vol. I, are given with a view to showing what befell it in the closing months of 1542 alone.

" 19 Aug.—The Priory occupied by 300 men under the Master of Works to the King of Scots.

" 25 Aug.—500 men there.

" 25 Oct.—Boats from the English Fleet landed at Colding-ham, ' burnt the corne there and about Aymouth, and also burnt the said Aymouth, and slain a man or twoe, and twoe or thre women, and ane of thayme was slayne, and so the reste paste to thair shipis agayne.'

" 15 Nov.—They left diverse gentlemen with certain of their number at the house of George Home to environ that place so that none should issue out, and proceeded with the rest to Coldingham where, first, they placed a certain number between the Abbey and the town, burning the same with a great substance of corne therein, and also another town called Restone with other steadings belonging to Coldingham.

" In their return homewards, the pile of Ayton was defended by 80 Scots. Howbeit, as the others returned, they all together won the house and barmekyne by fine force, and there slew three Scots, took all the rest prisoners, burned the house and the corn within the same and thereabouts, to the no little hurt and damage of the said Scots.

" The booty for that night included 100 prisoners, 180 nags and mares, 260 head of cattle, 440 sheep, 'with much more insight and stuff of household.'

" 19 Nov.—Since the last raid I (Hertford) made on Colding-ham, 15th inst., I have made another with such horsemen as I could raise from the garrisons of the East and Middle Marches . . . and have burned, spoiled and wasted . . . towns, vil-lages and steadings which, as I am credibly informed, did yearly maintain and keep 140 ploughs at the least. The troops would have burned much more corn had it not been for the snow that fell that night, a foot deep, so that the corn would not burn."

It was during these raids that the priory was burned and destroyed, all save the church, and the reason why the church was not burned was that " having fire in the one end, it smoked so by the dryfte of the wynd toward the Englysh men that it could not then conveniently be burned." They had begun at the wrong end.

It was subsequently ruined by the cannon of Oliver Cromwell who afterwards blew it up, with the exception of one aisle, in revenge for the noble defence made by the royalist garrison.

But in spite of the successes of the English, the hold of the Homes upon the priory was too secure and of too long continuance to be easily dislodged. They had been Bailiffs of Coldingham since 1441, and, following the Reformation, Alexander, Lord Home, who had rendered good service to the king, had the priory and its revenues conferred upon him.

The prior at the time of the Reformation was John Stuart, natural son of James V, who, though a mere infant, was admitted to the office with consent of the Pope. He was still a child when the priory was destroyed by the English. Without a prior in charge and with one disaster following fast upon another, it is easy to understand that there can have been few, if any, monks left in Coldingham when the Reformation came.

The Hamilton Papers describe the population of the neighbourhood as mostly neutral. In addition to the two monks already referred to as historians, the monk Reginald wrote *Miracles of St. Cuthbert*, published by the Surtees Society.

PRIORY OF URQUHART

Unlike Coldingham, Urquhart had an unbroken connection with Dunfermline from the time of its inception to the Reformation, although it is possible that there was an older settlement on the same site before King David's day.

" In 1125 David I transplanted a colony of Benedictine monks from Dunfermline to Urquhart in Moray." (*Chalmers*, *Hist*. I. 204.)

Dr. Henderson says the colony consisted of thirteen monks, but gives no indication of the source of his information (*Annals*, 42).

The figure does not commend itself as likely.

For one thing, it was only the year before that Dunfermline itself started off with thirteen monks from Canterbury, and it scarcely seems likely that it could so soon have been ready for a hive-off of similar numbers to Urquhart. Besides, Urquhart was a small place compared with Dunfermline, and it is doubtful if, even at its best, it ran to much more than a dozen or twenty monks.

What was the object in view in the establishment of this subsidiary " cell " at a distance so remote from the parent house ?

Was it pure missionary zeal, or a gracious response to the needs or wishes of the people on the spot ?

Dr. Chalmers, apparently quoting some unindicated source, probably *Reg.* 17-18, says that " it was founded in honour of the Blessed Trinity and for the enlargement of the House of God and propagation of the holy religion."

Yes, but one may be pardoned for wondering whether there was not to some extent a mingling of political considerations in the choice of the locality. The royal hold on an out-lying region like Moray cannot have been too secure at the time, and it may be that David was not averse to making use of the Church as the best instrument of civilisation at his disposal. Besides, from the terms of the foundation charter, it would seem that Dunfermline Abbey already had lands and interests in Moray before the foundation of the Priory.

How far it succeeded in its intended object would be difficult to determine. The bulk of the references to it, as to other institutions of the kind, in public records, deal, not with its well-being and progress, but with matters in dispute, which so often give a completely distorted picture of the real life of the community.

One thing, in any case, stands out. It was not easy to run a subsidiary house at such a distance.

In the early days, all the documents were signed personally by the Abbot of Dunfermline, who was very zealous in the performance of his duties, besides having a natural interest in the community which he had himself established. But Moray was a long, and in winter a weary, way from Dunfermline, and, with the pressure of other duties and interests, contact was apt to become spasmodic and the door to be left open for other authorities to intervene.

Even under the best conditions there were apt to be border-line " rights " as between the abbot of a monastery and the bishop of the diocese, and with an " absentee " abbot, the possibility of trouble was not likely to be less. Besides, once the members of the priory got the impression that they were out of touch with the monastery, the temptation naturally developed to take the management of affairs into their own hands.

In 1388 the Bishop of Moray, in virtue of his territorial jurisdiction, took upon himself to elect a prior for Urquhart without consulting anybody, though there was already a recently appointed prior in possession. One of the monks, in name of the others, appealed, on behalf of the existing prior, to the civil authorities, with the two-fold result that the king appointed the monk who had lodged the appeal as prior, an office he had certainly not asked for and did not want; while Parliament charged him to demit his office in favour of the man whose cause he had been at such pains to advocate. Four different appointments to the same office within a year—two of them relating to the same man! A delightful comedy of errors, and eloquently suggestive of the difficulties of running a " cell " at a distance so remote.

By the end of the first quarter of the sixteenth century references begin to appear in the Chartulary of Dunfermline to gross irregularities at Urquhart, and about the same time, according to the *Annals of Elgin*, the neighbouring Priory of Pluscarden became suspect, and more than suspect, of scandalous licentiousness.

These stories cannot be lightly dismissed. The same sort of story was current all up and down the country. At the same time, it is not difficult to see that there were other causes at work tending to bring about the union of these two priories.

The clearest account of what took place is to be found in the account, based on a Papal Bull of Nicholas V, by the Rev. S. R. Macphail in his *History of the Religious House of Pluscardyn*, p. 108.

" Nicholas tells us that he had taken action, with a view to a union of the two Priories, because of a petition which had reached him from the Prior of Urchard, John Benale. The petition stated that the Monastery was reduced to *two* monks, while at Pluscardyn there were seldom above *six* resident brothers. The troubles of the time, and the reduced revenues, made it impossible to maintain both Houses in efficiency. The heads of Pluscardyn were far removed in France, and direction could scarcely be expected from so remote a region. It was proposed that, as the buildings of Pluscardyn were more extensive and more stately, the monks of Urquhart should remove thither and unite their possessions and revenues to those of the Pluscardyn House; while the Abbey of Dunfermline should assume the charge of the newly combined brotherhood, and impart to them its dress and rule."

Following the usual practice, the Sacristan of Dunfermline, William de Boyis, was sent as prior of the combined priories, and reported that he found Pluscarden in great need of repair, the neglect of nigh sixty years resulting in the vaulted roofs of choir and crossing threatening to fall—another instance of how rapidly huge structures begin to show signs of decay unless measures are taken to preserve them.

Whether or not the union (4 Id. March 1453-54) accomplished the object intended may be open to question. Certainly the number of monks somewhat increased—one charter being signed by twelve, in addition to the prior. Otherwise, there are few facts available to build upon. Even the names and dates of some of the priors cannot be confidently reckoned on. The last prior, Alexander Dunbar, died in 1560, the year of Reformation, but not before he had alienated a considerable amount of the property, leaving several of a family, of whom three sons were legitimated, 12th February, 1547-48.

Five or six years before the Reformation the lands of Pluscarden passed into the hands of the Setons, in the person of Alexander, " so named by Queen Mary, who gave to him ane god-bairne gift, the lands of Pluscalie, in Murray." (*House of Setoun, p.* 63.)

The buildings do not appear to have been seriously damaged. The monks suffered very little interference, being doubtless provided for much the same as elsewhere.

" About the year 1730 a small yearly allowance was procured from the Royal Bounty Committee, and services were conducted within the ancient, semi-dismantled Priory. By and by the Southern ground-floor was fitted up as a place of worship, and still continues in use as such. In 1843 the congregation connected itself with the Free Church." (*Fasti.*)

" There is not a vestige remaining of the Priory of Urquhart, the whole having been carried off for the purpose of building the farm houses in the neighbourhood, and the place where it stood is now part of an arable field." (*Macphail, p.* 99.)

Robert Arth and Thomas Rose (or Ross) are the only monks known to have been still alive in 1582. In that year they signed a deed together with the commendator (Seton).

In 1586 Thomas Rose alone remained. (*Michael Barrett, Scottish Monasteries* 204.)

PRIORS OF URQUHART

RICHARD—1203 and 1221—(*Moray*, 43, *and Wilkin*, 533).
THOMAS—1226 and 1232—(*Moray*, 23, 30, 76).
WILLIAM—1237 and 1239—(*Moray*, 36, 103, 461).
JOHN—1248—(*Reg.* 97).
WILLIAM DE RATHEN—1260 and 1286—(*Moray*, 138, 279, 284).
WILLIAM DE BUTYRGAK—1343—(*McPhail*, *Pluscardyn*, 105).
JOHN BLAK—1353—(*Fordun*, *ii*. 349).

According to Macphail, the irregular appointment of Michael of Inverkeithing, probably in 1358, as Prior of Urquhart was temporarily acquiesced in, but did not last long.

ROBERT—1369—(*Moray*, 165).
ADAM DE HADYNGTON—1388—(*Moray*, 350/1).
WILLIAM DE SANCTO ANDREA—1416—Appointed Abbot of Dunfermline, 1416, with confirmation 1419. (*Scott. Suppl.* 53). This was a time of rival Popes, leading to much confusion and uncertainty, appointments being made which did not become effective.

Of these, three are noted at this time:—" March, 1416—Robert de Dolas, monk of Dunfermline, of noble birth, for the priory of Urcart in the diocese of Moray, dependent on Dunfermline, value 20 l., old sterling, void by the promotion of William de Sancto Andrea to Dunfermline." (*C.P.R. Petitions*, 605).

" 1416—William de Dalkeith appointed Prior of Urquhart, in succession to William de Sancto Andrea." (*Reg. Vat.* 349, *fol.* 255).

" Richard de Bothwell, monk of Dunfermline, student of canon law for three years. For the priory of Urchart, dependent on Dunfermline, value £60 Old Stg., which, on its voidance by the promotion of William to the Abbey, was given first to Robert de Dolas, and then to William of Dalkeith, monk of Abirbrothok, between whom a question having arisen sentence was given that neither had right therein—notwithstanding that Andrew de Rabuzy (Raeburn ?), monk of Dunfermline, has unlawfully held it for four months. GRANTED. Dec., 1418." (*C.P.R. Petitions*, 610).

The real successor to William of St. Andrews was:—

ANDREW RAEBURN—1416 and 1429—Formerly Prior of Coldingham, from which he had a pension of £20 Scots. (*Copiale*, 493).

" Was canonically elected Prior of Urquhart, held and possessed it for a long time, as he does at present, 2 June, 1419, but doubts validity and supplicates a new provision, which is granted." (*Scott. Suppl.* 65/6, 147, 165, 170).

" 27 March, 1420—Personally promised to pay within a year 50 florins, gold of Camera, for his provision to Urquhart, in Apostolic Treasury, in presence of witnesses." (*Scott. Suppl.* 299).

" A commission of inquiry concerning Raeburn was ordered by Columba, Bishop of Moray, and the Abbot of Dunfermline appointed John Shaw, a monk of Dunfermline, to act as his commissioner and procurator, authorising

him to summon Raeburn to appear in the priory chapel of Urquhart, on 9
February following, to answer for the alleged crimes committed by the
said prior and monks, under pain of deprivation from office and benefice."
(*Reg.* 282/4).

"The Abbot of Dunfermline who had to adopt this painful step for
enforcing monastic discipline was Andrew of Kirkcaldy, provided to that
monastery by Pope Martin V, 13 September, 1427, on the death of William
of St. Andrews." (*Cupar*, 46).

WILLIAM BROWN—1431—Bachelor of Theology, monk of Dunfermline.
(see pages 67, 192).

"In addition to the original founders (primi fundatores) of the University
of St. Andrews, six licentiates, of whom William Brown, then Prior of
Urquhart, was one, were selected to draw up the statutes to govern the
faculty of theology in the university, 18 March, 1428/9." (*Hannay's Statutes*,
112).

(*Note.*—It is possible that Brown may have been acting as Prior of Urquhart
at that time because of the disorders. His formal appointment did not take
place till 1431).

"For annates of Urquhart, £50 Stg., void by the free resignation of
Andrew Raeburn. Collated at Rome, 11 March, 1431." (*Apos. Cam.* 106).

"William Brown charged with having unduly detained possession of the
priory of Urquhart for more than two years, and is to be summoned and
removed." (*Inchcolm*, 165).

JOHN DE SCHAW—before 1433—A licentiate in decrees and bachelor in
sacred writings. As noted above, had been sent as Procurator for the Abbot
of Dunfermline to visit the priory of Urquhart, 17th January, 1429/30. Was
appointed to succeed Brown. (*Copiale*, 425).

Died at the Apostolic See before January, 1433—perhaps two years
before. (*C.P.R. viii.* 467).

WILLIAM DURWARD—1433—A monk of Aberbrothoc.

Evidence that either John Shaw or William Durward actually functioned
as priors is not conclusive, unless a reference in Acts of Parliament, *Scot., ii.*
60a, dated 2nd July, 1445, to one "William, prior of Urquhart," as one
of the Lords Auditors, applies to William Durward, which is by no means
certain.

JOHN DE BENALE—1447-1456—"31 August, 1447—John Venale (Benale)
—50 florins as composition for the annates of the priory of Urquhart and
of the fruits wrongfully taken up from the same." (*Apos. Cam.* 270).

He is referred to as prior by Macphail, p. 224, 12th March, 1453/4, and
in The Familie of Innes (*Old Spalding Club*), p. 56, 10th June, 1454.

WILLIAM DE BOYIS—1456-1476—Sacristan, Dunfermline, 1445-1456.

A licentiate in canon law. Besides reference to him in Reg. 353, 366,
there is one in Moray, 230, 20th May, 1464, and he is witness in a charter
in Reg. Ho., 433, 25th June, 1471.

On admission of John Oll to Coldingham, exhibited a presentation of
himself by the Abbot of Dunfermline, and, on his repulse, appealed to the
Curia. (*C.P.R. ix.* 298).

Was sent to Pluscarden in 1454 to receive professions of monks willing to change from White to Black. Appointed Prior of Pluscarden, Pluscarden and Urquhart being now united, in 1456. (*C.P.R. xi.* 330).

" Pluscarden being void by resignation of John de Benale, the Pope orders the Abbot of Lindores to collate and assign the said priory, which is still void and reserved, whose buildings are collapsed, and on whose fruits, etc., a yearly life-pension of 12½ l. Stg. has been reserved by papal authority to Andrew Hagis, a monk thereof, together with the usufruct of a certain town and certain tithes and courts belonging to it, and also food and clothing for him and a servant—and the remainder of the said fruits, etc., not exceeding 88 l. Stg., to the above William. Mandate St. Peter's, Rome, 1 Septr., 1457." (*C.P.R. xi.* 330).

" A man of energy and ability, he, in Oct., 1463, evinced his determination to prevent the rights of his house at Pluscardine from being violated by the Bishop of Ross, obtaining from the Chancellor of Moray a declaration that the church of ' Dingvalle ' in Ross-shire, with all its fruits, belonged to the priory of Pluscardine. He is there designated as ' Willelmum priorem monasterij vallis Sancti Andree de Pluscardyne.' " (*Cupar i.* 47).

THOMAS FOSTER (Forrester)—1476-1481—" 16 July, 1476—Thomas Fostar, monk of Pluscarden, O.S.B., Moray diocese, principal, for annates of priory of said monastery, accustomed to be governed by a prior (£70 Stg.), to become void by resignation of William Boyis." (*Apos. Cam.* 183).

" Gavin Dunbar, clerk, Moray diocese, annates of priory of Pluscardy (£60 Stg.) to become void by deprivation outwith the Curia, of prior Thomas Foster, *in forma juris*. Promised to pay within six months from day of possession." (*Ibid.* 197).

Foster died before 5th May, 1481. (*Ibid.* 202).

DAVID DE BOYIS—1482-1487—Monk of St. Thomas of Abberbroch—at one time (1449) perpetual vicar of Cleish, and brother of William de Boyis. (*C.P.R. x.* 443 and *Hall, Cleish, p.* 13).

" Annates of Pluscarden (£70 Stg.) void by death of Thomas Frostar, to be paid within eight months." (*Apos. Cam.* 202).

" Quittance for 87½ florins (g.c.) as annates of priory of Pluscarden, 9 July 1482." (*Apos. Cam.* 254).

It transpires, however, that David Boys had not personally paid the 87½ florins with which he had been credited, but had raised the money through agents.

Failing to obtain repayment from him, they applied to the Roman Curia which empowered them to take action in whatsoever courts before whatsoever judges they thought fit. In the event of failure to satisfy his agents, the sentence of excommunication is to be pronounced against him with the usual accompaniments of ringing of bells, candles being lighted and extinguished and cast on the ground.

Whether excommunicated or not, he died before 19th April, 1487. (*Apos. Cam.* 219).

ROBERT HARWAR—1487 and 1508—In 1483 was " terrar " or keeper of the land-rolls of Dunfermline. (*Exch. Rolls and Treasurer's Accts.*).

Was also Sacristan of Dunfermline from that same year.

Annates (£50 Stg.) void by death of Robert Boyis, late prior. (*Apos.. Cam.* 219).

Quittance for 59 florins (g.c.) 18th April, 1487. (*Ibid.* 258).

Annual pension (£9 Stg.) assigned to him on fruits of priory of Pluscarden on occasion of a certain concord, 20th August, 1483. (*Ibid.* 208).

References:—Family of Kilravock (Spalding Club), 171/2; Priory of Beauly (Grampian Club), 118/9.

Mentioned by Macphail as late as 13th October, 1508.

Following Harwar, there is a suggestion of a *James*, prior of Pluscarden, 1519 (*Macphail*, 113, 118n)—but the authority is doubtful.

GEORGE LEARMONTH—1519 and 1529—Appears in Reg. Ho. Charters. Nos. 886 (Dec. 1519) and 947 (7 July 1523)—in Dunfermline Burgh Records, 281 (1526) and in Moray 418 (2 September, 1529).

On 20th May, 1529, he was appointed co-adjutor to the Bishop of Aberdeen. (*Vat. Trans. in Reg. Ho. iii.* 257).

ALEXANDER DUNBAR—1532/3-1560—Appears in Reg. Ho. Charters No. 1083 (2 February 1532/3) and in Acts of Parl. Scot. ii. 594b and 603a (1542, 1554).

On 12th February, 1547/8, his sons, Robert and John, were legitimated. (*Reg. Privy Seal, iii.* 2633).

He died before February, 1561/2, but was probably alive 24th June, 1561. (*Macphail*, 126, 129).

BUILDING, DESTRUCTION AND REBUILDING

" The splendid abbey of Dunfermline owed its inconsiderable foundation to Malcolm Ceanmore; its completion to Alexander I; and its reform to David I. . . . Here the Culdees, with their abbot, discharged their usual duties during several reigns; and David I, who lived much with Henry I of England, upon his accession, introduced among the Celtic Culdees thirteen English monks from Canterbury." (*Caledonia* 438.)

There had been Culdee settlements in Scotland long before the erection of Dunfermline Abbey, and there is evidence of their continuance till the beginning of the fourteenth century, with accounts of occasional co-operation between them and the representatives of the Roman Church. There is also evidence that Malcolm and his queen made an inconsiderable grant of land to the Culdees in Fife. (*Hailes' Annals*, i. 39.)

At the same time it is perfectly well known that St. Margaret was not partial, to say the least of it, to the rites and practices of the Culdees, and it requires some stretch of the imagination to accept this picture of Culdees and English monks worshipping and working together in a monastery founded by her son, whose preference for English ways was quite as definite as her own; and no documentary evidence of any weight has ever been adduced in support of the idea.

It is true that, in an Appendix to the *Registrum* (595), there is a charter by King Malcolm, dealing with the foundation and endowment of the Abbey, which is witnessed by " Ivo, Abbot of the Culdees." But the authenticity of the charter has been seriously contested, and it would ill accord with what we know otherwise of King Malcolm to imagine him asking the abbot who was to be supplanted to witness the deed which was to have that effect.

Bishop Lesley, at least, is quite definitely of opinion that Dunfermline was Benedictine from the start.

Speaking of the " godlie deedes and devote of St. Margaret and King Malcolm," he goes on :—" Throuch quhais requeist lykwyse, king Malcolme erected a fair and magnifik Kirke in the toun of Dunfermiling, with a clostir, of his awin expenses,. and dedicat the samyn to the maist haly Trinitie; Thaireftir he maid this acte: that fra that furth, (it) suld be a commoune buriall to the kings of Scotland; and that the Mounkis of S. Benedictes ordour in that monaster perpetuallie sulde serve god, quhome he enduet with ample and ryche rentis." (*The Historie of Scotland*, by *Jhone Lesley*, *Bishop of Rosse*, *S.T.S.*)

That Malcolm and Margaret built their church on a site previously used by the Culdees is, however, quite a possibility.

According to Turgot, her confessor, St. Margaret, immediately after her marriage, founded a church " in that place where her nuptials were celebrated," and it may well be that it was in the little Culdee church that she was married.

During the excavations carried out by the late Dr. P. Macgregor Chalmers in 1916, the foundations of Queen Margaret's Church, built about 1072-74, were laid bare, showing it to have been a small building of Anglo-Saxon type, with western tower, nave, chancel and eastern apse—the total length being 86 feet.

The erection of this church represents the first stage in the development of what afterwards became known as Dunfermline Abbey.

The second stage arose from the need for finding a place for the monks to worship in while the nave was being built.

So many take it for granted that worship was continued in St. Margaret's Church till the nave was built about it, but a glance at the lines on the floor of the nave showing the foundations of St. Margaret's Church makes it clear that some of the pillars are based on the walls of St. Margaret's Church—leaving no room for doubt that that church must have been demolished before the nave was built.

All the available evidence goes to show that a church for temporary use was built to the east of the nave on part of the site afterwards occupied by the Conventual Church.

The third stage was the building of the nave, the usual order being doubtless followed—the erection of the altar first, and building westwards from it—the start apparently being made in the north-east corner, where the vaulted arch is seen in its least developed from. Mural paintings are to be seen on the ceiling of this vault, representing Four Apostles. They are of early sixteenth century date. (*Office of Works Catalogue*.)

According to the *Chronicle of Holyrood* (p. 35) the nave was dedicated in 1150.

The fourth stage took the form of a development and extension of the temporary church to what is now known as St. Margaret's Shrine. So far-reaching was the change involved that the question arose as to whether or not there should be a new consecration.

The papal decision, however, (1249) was that this was unnecessary, seeing that the " old walls, for the greater part, remained in their original state." (*Roy. Comm., Fife*, 107.)

It was at this stage that the Translation of St. Margaret took place (1250).

" In the 14th century the choir was extended in a north aisle, probably the Lady Aisle, which was afterwards demolished, while on the north side of the nave three of the aisle windows and all of the triforium windows were transformed from Romanesque into Gothic, the wall-head of the aisle being at the same time lowered." (*Ibid.*)

This was the fifth, and last, stage in the development.

It is generally recognised that there are points of similarity between Durham and Dunfermline—which is not surprising in view of the fact that they not only belong to the same period, but that David I and Turgot, Bishop of Durham, were personally interested in both.

The idea is confirmed in detail by Dr. P. Macgregor Chalmers.

" The details and ornaments of the two structures are so closely related that no doubt on this point can be entertained. Further evidence, linking the two buildings together, and furnishing certain indication of the date of the Scots work, has been supplied recently by the discovery of the eastern processional door to the cloisters at the east end of the south aisle of the nave at Dunfermline.

" Workmen were employed preparing for the erection of a monument here, when it was found that the stonework was not of Norman date.

" A portion only of the rubble has been removed, revealing the arch and the capitals of what is probably the most richly decorated Norman work preserved in Scotland. Buried from view in the seventeenth century, the delicate carvings have retained almost their original sharpness. The capitals are sculptured with interlacing foliage and strap-work; a beautiful acanthus-leaf ornament is carved on the abacus; and the arch is decorated with the chevron or zig-zag ornament and delicate diaper work.

" These details are practically reproduced from the beautiful doors in the nave of Durham Cathedral executed about the year 1133.

" When the whole doorway is exposed, it may be found that there is a still closer resemblance to the work at Durham.

" One interesting point remains.

" The decoration of the arch of this door in Dunfermline corresponds with the work on the beautiful church at Dalmeny." (*The Scottish Historical Review*, *January*, 1904.)

The exact date of the commencement of the other monastic buildings is uncertain. Buildings on so large a scale must have taken a considerable time to complete. But it may be taken for granted that they would be in some measure available for use long before the complete scheme took final shape. During the course of erection there is more than one injunction by the king for provision of the wood and other material needed for the work.

Before going further into the story of these buildings, it may be well to give some consideration to the purpose they were meant to serve. The erection of a huge monastery like that of Dunfermline was a great and costly undertaking. There must have been some deep, compelling reason for it. What was it ?

Was it an attempt to evangelise the country by establishing colonies of preachers at strategic centres ? We may dismiss right off any idea of the sort. So far from being the primary reason for a monastery's existence, preaching was one of the least of its activities.

In the Parochial Kirk, intended for tradesmen and servants of the monastery and parishioners in general, there might at times be a certain amount of preaching, though it is doubtful if it ever bulked very large.

In the Conventual Kirk there would be little or none—the so-called *Pulpitum* being used mainly for occasional *ex-cathedra* announcements of one kind or another.

Further, we may rid our minds of the idea that these costly and well-manned structures were primarily intended to serve as civilising agencies or benevolent institutions in the midst of an indifferent and needy people. That they did for a time quite clearly serve these ends is undoubted. But to suggest that that was the object of their existence is quite a different matter.

No—if we are to express in a word the essential purpose of a monastery—the one thing above all others that it stood for— that word must be *worship*. A monastery was erected at the cost of so much toil and treasure to provide a home for religious people whose lives were to be devoted to the worship of Almighty God and to contemplation upon things divine.

Unless we keep this clear in mind, we shall never see monasticism in its true perspective.

A monastery was, in essence, a standing witness to the Eternal and Unseen.

" Imperfect as we may be, we are here, with our litanies, shaven crowns, vows of poverty, to testify incessantly and indisputably to every heart, That this Earthly Life and *its* riches and possessions, and good and evil hap, are not intrinsically a reality at all, but *are* a shadow of realities eternal, infinite ; that this Time-world, as an air-image, fearfully *emblematic*, plays and flickers in the grand still mirror of Eternity ; and that man's little Life has Duties that are great, that are alone great, and go up to Heaven and down to Hell. This, with our poor litanies we testify, and struggle to testify." (*Carlyle, Past and Present.*)

A monastery, then, being in theory a " Religious House ", the main business of whose occupants is to spend their days and nights in the worship of Almighty God, its first requisite is a **Church.** Accept this and it becomes so much easier to understand the part the church played in the life of the community and the vast sums that were expended on it. Without it, the whole conception remains more or less an enigma.

" On the church of a monastery, money, as a rule, was lavishly and ungrudgingly expended. Sculpture and painting, jewels and gold, gorgeous hangings and stained glass that the moderns vainly attempt to imitate, the purple and fine linen of the priestly vestments, embroidery that to this hour remains unapproachable in its delicacy of finish and in the perfect harmony of colours—all these were to be found in almost incredible profusion in our monastic churches. It was the heart of all communal activity.

[By Courtesy of "Life and Work"

North-east corner of the Nave.　　This shows the aisle vaulting in its earliest phase.

" It wasn't that the church was built for the monastery. The monastery existed for the church." (*Dr. Jessop, The Coming of the Friars, p.* 121.)

Almost invariably the church was built in the form of a cross, lying east and west—the long limb of the cross being called The Nave, the cross limbs The Transepts, and the shorter limb The Choir. In the case of Dunfermline, the western limb is generally referred to as the Parochial Kirk, and the eastern limb (not much, if any, shorter) the Conventual Kirk. The latter was the monks' own private place of worship, and it was there that lavish adornment and splendour of decoration were seen at their best.

Next in importance to the church was **The Cloister.**

" Almost as essential to the idea of a monastery as a church was the cloister or great quadrangle, inclosed on all sides by the high walls of the monastic buildings. Its usual position was on the south of the church, to gain as much of the sun's rays as possible, and to insure protection from the northerly and easterly winds in the bitter season. All round this quadrangle ran a covered arcade, whose roof, leaning against the high walls, was supported on the inner side by an open trellis work in stone—often exhibiting great beauty of design and workmanship—through which light and air was admitted into the arcade. The open space not roofed in was called the *garth* and was sometimes a plain grass plat and sometimes was planted with shrubs, a fountain of running water being often found in the centre, which afforded a pleasant object for the eye to rest on. The cloister was really the living-place of the monks. Here they pursued their daily avocations, here they taught their school, they transacted their business, they spent their time and pursued their studies, always in society, co-operating and consulting, and, as a rule, knowing no privacy." (*Dr. Jessop, The Coming of the Friars, p.* 123.)

It may be added that, as time went on, and monks became more self-indulgent, the open trellis work of the arcade was often glazed to avoid draughts and exposure. The idea of monks spending their time, apart from worship, in a cell is quite mistaken—except for the Carthusians, of whom there were very few in Britain.

Curiously enough, there is a reference as late as 1479 to a hermit in connection with the monastery. Witnessing a deed recorded in the Burgh Records (307) he is described as " John Malcum (Malcolm) armyt till our Lady." Unfortunately, there is nothing more recorded of him.

The west side of the quadrangle was usually occupied by the guest chambers. In Dunfermline, however, the space available was so restricted and the fall in ground level so pronounced that there was no room for more than a wall and the guest chambers were erected on the west side of the road passing through the Pends, on a site that later came to be associated with the Royal Palace, the kitchen premises thus serving both the refectory on the east and the guest chambers on the west. The use of the word " palace " as applied to monastic buildings is not at all uncommon, but in this case it came to have a more definite application, for " the property of the monastery was part of the jointure of Anne, Queen of James VI, and the guest-house was adapted as her " palace," in which was born the prince who became Charles I." (*Roy. Comm.*, *Fife*, xlvii.)

On the south side of the quadrangle was the *refectory*, or dining hall; on the east side the *chapter house* and the *dormitories*, or common sleeping-places for the fraternity, with latrines and washing-places in the open air at the south end and a sewer that could be flushed.

Still further east than the dormitories would probably be other buildings, such as a school and an infirmary, though these cannot now be traced.

Outside the walls were the stables and a host of other offices.

When at its best, the monastery of Dunfermline was reputed to be capable of accommodating three sovereigns and their retinues within its ample precincts, but the suggestion that it contained as many as 300 monks and that its precincts covered 360 acres is grotesque. It is doubtful if it ever had many more than 50 monks and the 28 acres indicated on the map in the *Annals of Dunfermline* (p. 182) seems quite generous.

In times of trouble and unrest it was not to be expected that centres of such importance should escape attention, and Dunfermline had its own share of molestation. Three times Edward I of England occupied it, first in 1291, returning 13th August, 1296, and again in 1303. His last visit covered most of the winter, ninety-seven days in all, and on the morning of his departure for Cambuskenneth, 10th February, 1304, he repaid the hospitality he had received by giving orders to his men to destroy the monastery by fire.

A Latin version of the story, from the English point of view, is to be found in detail in *Flores Historiarum* (iii. 311-2) edited by Dr. Luard, Registrar of Cambridge University :—

" Now there were in Scotland two most famous abbeys, very rich in resources and very strongly fortified in the matter of buildings, to wit, Aberbrothock and Dunfermline.

" Furthermore, Dunfermline below its fortifications is exceedingly spacious, comprising three carrucates of land, enclosing in itself many, as it were, royal palaces, in such a manner that three renowned kings with their train were able at one and the same time to lodge there, each one separately, without being subjected to wrongful treatment from either of the others.

" For that reason, because of the enormous capacity of the place, the elders of the kingdom of Scotland had been accustomed to assemble there and to frame plots against the king of England, and frequently in time of war going forth as though from lurking places, they resorted to plundering raids and sanguinary attacks upon the English people.

" Perceiving therefore that the temple of the Lord was not a church but ' a den of thieves ' and, as it were ' a thorn in the eye ' of the English nation, the army of the king sent rope and hooks and levelling everything, cloisters, walls and palaces to the ground, utterly demolished them, only the church being saved from burning and a few houses for the monks who constituted the competent and regular staff.

" Thereafter certain robbers, having united with themselves very many other evil-doers, went forth secretly from the camp of the king of England and came unexpectedly to the celebrated monastery of Dunfermline with swords and clubs. Breaking through the centre of the hall of the abbey right into the chapel, where the ministers of God, two hundred monks, had assembled to pray or to sing the psalms, by sword, bow and missile they threatened with death any of the monks who left his place. They were divided into three companies, one of which guarded their entrance and a second their way of egress, terrifying the servants of God. The remaining company, bent on pillage, shattered the closets and the chests for the religious utensils round the altar, and in the entrance court, everywhere in the treasury of the Lord. And they sacrilegiously carried away crosses, pitchers, pyxes, cruets, censers and vessels for offerings, all of pure gold, and many similar vessels of fine silver, regarding which, merely on account of their great number, mention need not be made of individual items.

" In connection with these, a much bruited report spread abroad that the monks each possessed one jug or flask, cup, spoon and dish of silver. All these the miscreants stole, and carried off.

" Accordingly an outcry was raised and came to the hearing of the king. The king of England, while he was still directing his course thither and when he was still a long way off, saw holy men sitting by the wayside here and there, holding their heads, clad in sacred robes and in raiment made of goats' hair, awaiting the arrival of his most gracious majesty.

" Gazing at them, the king in wonder inquired who they were.

" To him the count of Lincoln said :—' My Lord, these are monks of this place which was plundered the day before yesterday,' Moved by compassion, the king said to them :—' Return into the tabernacles of your house.' Moreover the king was there for several days discoursing and associating with them, and he gave instructions under threat of hanging that an investigation should be made and that, after all its vessels had been restored to the monastery, the perpetrators of the crime should be outlawed for ever.

" And so it came to pass."

The above translation has been kindly supplied by Mr. R. Culbertson, classical master, Dunfermline High School, and no attempt is made to reconcile the story therein contained with that previously given and usually accepted—readers being left to judge for themselves as to the comparative credibility of the two accounts.

King Edward having thus taken his departure, the work of rebuilding was quickly taken up, King Robert the Bruce giving all possible assistance, though, with the enemy still in occupation of much of the country, progress can hardly have been otherwise than slow.

"1329—And to the Abbot of Dunfermline for the fabric of the Refectory—£66 13s. 4d." (*Exch.* i. 215.)

To some it is a matter of surprise that these huge structures should have been erected and repaired so speedily as they were. Skilled craftsmen were bound to have been scarce, particularly when several monasteries or cathedrals were needing attention at the same time, but a monastery like Dunfermline could at least depend on its own bondmen to act as labourers when necessity arose, and they were not without experience.

In 1165 King William declared :—

"When I repaired my castles in Ros, the men belonging to the abbot and monks of Dunfermline assisted me of their own good will at my request, along with other honest men of mine."

But he wished it to be understood that this was not to constitute a precedent. (*Dalyell, Monastic Antiquities, p.* 21.)

A question not infrequently asked about these historic buildings is as to who was responsible for the design.

We know who founded and endowed them. We know, as a rule, who consecrated them. Every mason who worked at them left his mark upon them. But seldom or ever is there so much as a hint as to whose plans and specifications the builders were working on.

This silence on the part of the chroniclers is, to say the least of it, disappointing, but not altogether surprising in view of the scanty information we have concerning notabilities of even later date. It should be remembered, too, that this silence applies only to buildings erected prior to the middle of the thirteenth century. *Gothic England* by John Harvey leaves no doubt as to that. The author of this book has been able to trace the name of only one master-builder (or architect) associated with a specific building in England between 1150 and 1200—Adam Lock. But after 1250 or thereby there were comparatively few buildings of note erected whose architects are quite unknown.

The silence of the chroniclers up to that date is variously interpreted.

The explanation commonly accepted is that the work was carried out by abbots and monks in such a spirit of humility that they deliberately refrained from allowing their names to be handed down to posterity. The work was everything—the artist nothing.

On the other hand, some of the authorities go to the opposite extreme and say that the silence is simply due to the contempt felt by the ecclesiastic for the artisan. The monkish chronicler's one concern was with the glorification of his house.

It simply would not occur to him to mention a temporary employee.

Roman Catholic writers, almost without exception, convey the impression that the work of erection was done by members of the Order concerned.

" Modern writers generally rely, directly or indirectly, on Montalembert's *Monks of the West*, which is a panegyric exaggerated everywhere, and on this particular point inaccurate almost beyond belief. Out of the 50 documents upon which Montalembert professes to rely for his statement that the monks commonly built their own churches, only eight are to some extent accurate in special circumstances, while six say plainly the very opposite of what he claims for them." (*G. C. Coulton, Scottish Abbeys and Social Life, p.* 187.)

Even writers who are not Roman Catholic are occasionally found confirming the belief, as, for instance, Cosmo Innes in his preface to the Bannatyne Club edition of the Kelso Chartulary :—

" That the arts were cultivated within the Abbey walls we may conclude without much extrinsic evidence. The beautiful and somewhat singular architecture of the ruined church (Kelso) itself still gives proof of taste and skill and some science in the builders. . . . Of many of these works the monks themselves were the artists and artisans. . . . "

To which Professor Coulton makes reply :—

" It will be noted that Cosmo Innes here makes no sort of attempt to prove the sweeping generalisation contained in his very first sentence ; he simply takes it for granted. That is typical ; the monastic artist was, in his time, as accepted a legend as the walled-up nun ; and, being more difficult of disproof, it has lingered longer.

" Moreover, there is a kernel of truth in it. The most enthusiastic of medieval handbooks, and one of the most practically useful, is that of the monk ' Theophilus ' (i.e., Roger of Helmershausen at the end of the eleventh century), and, here and there, monks are recorded as painters or metal-workers; more rarely as builders or sculptors. No doubt there were many more of whom we have no record; but, on the other hand, building records nearly always prove, or at least imply, the hired workman, just as he exists nowadays." (*Coulton, p.* 189.)

When experts differ so widely, it is not easy for an outsider to reach anything like a just judgment, but probably Professor Coulton's closing words represent the opinion of an increasing number to-day.

There is evidence of both monks and laymen having been engaged in the work, but the general impression is that the relation of the abbot to the master-mason was pretty much that of the modern client towards the architect whom he employs.

It is quite a possibility, however, that detailed specifications may have been passed on from one House within the Order to another.

Correspondences in architectural detail between Dunfermline and Durham, for example, are confirmed by what is otherwise known of the intercourse between these two establishments, and the similarity of " Norman " or " Romanesque " detail between the churches of Dalmeny, Leuchars and Dunfermline Abbey also suggests what we would describe as a kind of centralised control.

As to the man, or men, responsible for the building of Dunfermline Abbey, one cannot write with any great degree of confidence. But, in a matter of so much natural interest, even the faintest clue is worth pursuing.

In his *Baronage of Scotland*, Mr. Douglas, referring to the lands and family of Masterton, says :—

" This is a local sirname, like many others of great antiquity in Scotland. The traditional account of their origin is that one of the chief architects at the building of the abbacy of Dunferm-line obtained from King Malcolm Canmore the lands of Masterton in Fifeshire from which he and his posterity assumed their sirname. They were long designed Masterton of that ilk etc."

To which Mr. Stodart in his *Scottish Arms* in effect replies :— " Dunfermline Abbey was not built by Malcolm and Margaret, but by their son David." He further goes on to describe as

" a statement which seems to be quite groundless " that William Masteron of that ilk made in 1442 a donation to the Abbey of Dunfermline out of his lands of Masterton " pro salute animae suae."

To which Mr. A. V. Noel Paton, Editor of the Masterton Papers (*Misc. of S.H.S.* i.) replies :—" Douglas is responsible for this statement, and, except that the donation is of the whole lands of Masterton, . . . the statement is correct." The charter, he goes on, does not appear in the *Registrum*, but Douglas was not quoting from the *Registrum* but from a notarially certified extract of the charter which was taken in 1544 in the chapterhouse of the Monastery of Dunfermline, where the charter in question then was.

As for the suggestion that the lands could not have given their name to the family because they were not then known by that name, he says that the *Registrum* (39, p. 23) leaves no room for doubt that the names Ledmacduuegil and Masterton were applicable to the same lands, the one being the old name, and the other the new.

Now, all this sparring of protagonists may not be without its interest, but it throws little light on the so-called legend that the lands of Masterton were given to the architect of Dunfermline Abbey.

The only incidental reference to that question is Mr. Stodart's suggestion that the sole ground for the fable is to be found in the reference in the charters to the previous holder of the lands as a mason. That, however, is treating the reference much too lightly. It deserves, and should receive, much more serious consideration than that.

In the Confirmation Charter of Malcolm IV the previous owner is described as " Magister Aelricus cementarius " (mason).

The title " magister," especially in the earlier Middle Ages, is of somewhat wide application. Later, it is true, it came to be confined mainly to graduates, but it is doubtful if, in the days of Malcolm and Margaret, there was a University in existence, even on the Continent, and, without a University, there could be no graduates.

Prior to that time, however, references to masters of works and masters of ships are current medieval usage. Reference is also to be found to " magister coquus " (master-cook) and " magister camerarius " (master-chamberlain). From which it would not seem unreasonable to infer that the combination of *magister* and *cementarius* signified master-mason.

The name Aelric, too, deserves a little closer study. It sounds Saxon and bears at least a superficial resemblance to such names as Aelred and Alret, which appear in Domesday Book in 1086.

It is generally recognised that, about this time, there was a considerable infiltration of Saxons into southern Scotland, mostly as fugitives, like the Queen herself, before the advancing tide of Norman invaders, and the possibility cannot be excluded that the master-mason may have been one of them. If that is so, then we are confronted with the remarkable combination of a Saxon Queen looking around for a mason for the church she had set her heart on building, and a Saxon master-mason sitting, so to speak, on her own door-step—a combination that would very naturally give rise to the idea that in all probability he was the builder of that church. One is perfectly safe in saying that it would have been extremely difficult for her to have found another master-mason in Scotland at the time.

On the other hand, there is always the possibility that, finding it hopeless to secure an expert mason in Scotland, she appealed to her friends, or to the Church, in England, to procure one for her—in which case the building of the church by him and the gift of lands to him for his services would be the natural outcome of her appeal.

As for the change of name from Ledmacduuegil to Masterton, does it seem unreasonable to suggest that in time the place came to be known as that where the master-mason dwelt ?

Mr. M'Innes, of the Historical Department, Records Office, offers the following as a feasible explanation of the charters concerned. " Malcolm IV confirmed a grant of the superiority of the lands of Ledmacduuegil, which grant had been given to the Abbey of Dunfermline by his grandfather Malcolm Canmore —the lands being described as ' within the boundaries by which Aelric the mason held them,'—the said Aelric being evidently proprietor.

" In 1422 William of Masterton, Laird of Dalis (Dales), quite possibly a descendant of the mason, resigned all his lands of Masterton into the hands of William, Abbot of Dunfermline, and dedicates to God, and bestows on the monks of the Holy Trinity there, all the said lands for the salvation of his own soul and the souls of his predecessors and successors. The Church already possessing the superiority, the rights of superior and owner once again merged in the same hands—not now the king's, but those of the Church.''

Taking, then, a conjunct view of the facts that can more or less be relied upon, viz. :—that, in the time of Malcolm IV, it was known and accepted that the lands of Ledmacduuegil, in the immediate neighbourhood of Dunfermline, had been held by a master-mason of the name of Aelric ; that these lands afterwards came to be known as Masterton ; and that there is a definite tradition of long standing that they were given to Aelric by the king in recognition of his services as master-mason in connection with ecclesiastical buildings at Dunfermline—the conclusion becomes almost irresistible that the story told by Douglas is no mere baseless legend, but a genuine tradition to be seriously reckoned with.

Following the erection of Queen Margaret's Church, there was an almost continuous succession of building operations at Dunfermline—the first Abbot House, the temporary church for the monks to worship in while the Nave was in course of construction, the Conventual Church, and the whole range of monastic buildings. But, while the possibility cannot be excluded that Aelric's descendants and successors at Masterton may have had something to do with the later operations, one has to reckon with the fact that the further the probability is extended the more tenuous do the threads of the story become.

To return to the story of the buildings as a whole. We dropped it when we came to the third visit of Edward I and its sequel. Following that, we come upon a brighter patch.

'' In 1317 the troops of Edward's son and successor swept down upon the district, landing, according to some writers, at Donibristle, and, according to others, in the area west of Inverkeithing, with Dunfermline, apparently, as the objective.'' (*Stephen, Story of Invkg. & Rosyth*, 61.)

The rest of the story, as told by Bower, is more or less as follows. Five hundred cavalry under the sheriff had already been put to disgraceful flight when William Sinclair, Bishop of Dunkeld, who was then residing at Auchtertool, put himself at the head of sixty of his servants and others and rallied the fugitives.

Turning first to the sheriff, he declared:—" The King would do well, Sir, to hack your spurs from your feet." " Turn," he said to the others, seizing a spear from a soldier, " turn for shame, and let all who love Scotland follow me." So effectual were his words and actions that the English were driven back to their ships with the loss of five hundred men.

Bruce, on learning of the feat, declared that Sinclair should be his own bishop, and as the King's Bishop he was henceforth known, though popularly he was equally well known as " the fechtin bishop."

In 1385 the English were back, under Richard II, and again the great monastery, so recently restored, was given to the flames.

Dunfermline, however, was fortunate in one respect. It escaped the terrible invasions of the sixteenth century. More than once the English were almost within sight of it, but for one reason or another turned aside.

In 1544 the Earl of Hertford arrived in the Forth on 3rd May, with instructions from Henry VIII to burn and destroy wherever he went, putting man, woman and child to the sword, without exception, where he met with any resistance.

" Hertford did his best—or his worst—to carry out these merciless instructions, and, though he could not accomplish them all, he did an enormous amount of damage, as his despatches to his royal master show. He tells how Leith was seized, and Edinburgh stormed, and the neighbouring country devastated to within six miles of Stirling. The Castle of Edinburgh he could not take, but having made what he calls ' a jolye fyre,' the town and also the Abbey of Holyrood were ' yn maner holly brent and desolate.' Kinghorn and other villages in Fife were likewise burned." (H. Fleming, Reform. in Scot. 331.)

In 1547 he was back again, as Lord Protector Somerset. After the Battle of Pinkie (10th September) he seized Inchcolm, but his fame had preceded him—" the mounks wear gone."

The only comfort they could get from the Privy Council in their plight was a recommendation to raise a sum of £500 from the readiest of their resources to " fie wageouris and men of weir " for recovery of said place, and, in the meantime, to seek refuge as displaced persons in Dunfermline and other monasteries. (*Reg. P.C.* 80.)

Note.—One of the reasons assigned for the appointment of James Stewart, a lad of 13, and thus considerably under canonical age, as Abbot of Inchcolm was that " the monastery . . . cannot be properly preserved and maintained in its buildings and other rights unless it is defended from the attacks of the English and others by the might (potentia) of neighbouring magnates and noblemen, and considering that the relations and kin of James Stewart have aided the monastery and held themselves ready and prepared to defend, repair and preserve it, Richard appoints procurators. . . . " (*Charters of Inchcolm,* xxxvii.)

In this case " the relations and kin of James Stewart " seem to have proved a broken reed.

And so it went on from one generation to another.

It might be Englishmen who burned what would burn, or Scotsmen, like Angus, who, passing through Dunfermline with his men after the " affair " at Avonbridge, 4th September, 1526, " spoilzit " (pillaged) the Abbey.

Never for very long was it free from molestation.

Then came the great upheaval of the Reformation, and, in some ways, the damage consequent on it was the most regrettable of all. What Englishmen, in their invasions, did to our churches, our men were doing in their forays into England. There was not much to choose between them.

But for Scotsmen to burn and destroy their own churches and monasteries is an entirely different story.

It would be a thankless task to go back on the long, sad story of corruption that characterised the sway of the Roman Church in Scotland for long before the Reformation. Suffice it to say that nobody can read it without coming to the conclusion that it could not have ended otherwise than in disaster.

Whether the blame for that disaster lies mostly with those who were responsible for the corruption, or with those who dealt so drastically with the consequences of it, is a matter of opinion.

But one thing is now clear. The material damage done at the time of the Reformation was not nearly so great as was at one time thought.

A good deal of what is popularly attributed to the Reformation was really due to the earlier English invasions, and much more than is generally thought was the result of gross neglect and avarice on the part of the pre-Reformation church authorities themselves.

See, for example, what happened at Coupar Angus !

" There is no record of an attack on this monastery by Reformers ; but the account given in by the chamberlain of the abbey in 1563 suggests that the fabric had suffered considerable destruction, since provision is made for preserving the ' tymmer ' of the church and steeple and for gathering the slates in the cloister for safe keeping. . . . The fact that it was found necessary to provide for the erection of a new church at Coupar in 1618 seems to imply that the abbey church was regarded as beyond repair." (*Charters, Coupar Angus*, i. lxvii-lxviii.)

What happened at Dunfermline is set forth in the following bald statement :—

" Vpon the 28 March (1560) the wholl lordis and barnis that ware on thys syde of Forth pased to Stirling and, be the way, kest doun the abbey of Dunfermling."

That statement, brief as it is, is quite clearly an over-statement. The whole Abbey was not " kest doun."

The monastic buildings, it is true, were destroyed as completely as the means at their disposal would permit. But for that the Reformers would have offered no apology. The whole system was corrupt to a degree and the sooner it was ended the better for all concerned. With regard to the two portions of the Abbey Church, there is quite clearly observable a material difference in attitude. The nave—the Parochial Kirk, as it is generally called—they never meant to injure, just as there was never any thought or intention of destroying parish kirks. From the first the nave had been earmarked as the future place of worship. But it had to be purged of its idolatrous images and altars—they were quite definite about that—and, if needful, they would have been ready to quote various passages from the Old Testament in support of this contention.

The choir—the Conventual Kirk—was in quite another category. It had little or no association with the worship of the people and was so bound up with all that they had come to regard as sheer idolatry that the fate of the monastic buildings overtook it too.

This must not, however, be regarded as implying that they were completely rased to the ground. Walls so substantial were not so easily disposed of in these days. Considerable portions of the walls of the Conventual Kirk stood for a hundred years after the Reformation; the huge tower between it and the Parochial Kirk remained erect for two hundred years; and even the monastic buildings, against which the efforts of the Reformers were mainly directed, were not so completely destroyed but that some of the monks continued to find shelter in them.

Till 1818, Dr. Chalmers says, there were still standing four very tall and beautiful Gothic windows which were removed at the commencement of the building of the new church in that year. (i. 123.)

What gave the monastery in time such an air of complete devastation was the ever-recurring use of the site as a quarry for building purposes. (*Annals*, 465.)

It is much more difficult, one admits, to defend these later outbursts of destruction than the earlier ones.

The assaults in 1559 on the monasteries of Perth and Scone were committed in hot blood, the deep and bitter hatred of the townsfolk against the iniquities of the Roman system suddenly leaping into uncontrolled expression under the fiery eloquence of Knox. But the destructions of 1560 were premeditated and deliberate, the work of leaders who in cold blood had planned them in detail. The fact that they were carried out in the name of the law, as contrasted with the lawless outbursts of the year before, only serves to deepen the sense of difference.

One cannot help wondering whether or not it ever occurred to these " lordis, barnis, and uther kirkmen " when planning their campaign of destruction that they might so easily destroy a good deal more than they intended. Doctrinally they might be perfectly satisfied that they had a right to destroy images and altars with all pertaining to them. But monasteries, for the most part, had been a long time in existence and had naturally accumulated many things of value, not necessarily associated with idolatry.

Printing was of too recent introduction to fill the shelves of the monastic libraries, but there must have been a wealth of priceless manuscripts. An excited mob, urged on to the work of destruction by representatives of authority, was not likely to pick and choose when offered such fodder for the flames.

No doubt, in some cases, the monks themselves, foreseeing what was coming, would take time by the forelock and secure what they could of their treasures before the day of reckoning came. But that could have been done only on a very limited scale.

Abbot Durie, for instance, is said to have carried away the relics of St. Margaret for transportation to the continent, but, apart from that, there is no record of anything having escaped the conflagration save one solitary book. It was a book, however, that was well worth preserving—a beautifully written and illuminated copy (in MS. of course) of Jerome's Latin Bible. This Bible is still in existence. It is written on vellum, is quite entire, legible and clean, except at some parts where it is a little soiled with grease spots. Like the relics of St. Margaret, the book is said to have been carried away by Abbot Durie to France. Afterwards it came into the possession of a M. Foucalt, as appears from his arms upon it. At his sale it was bought by a Scotsman who brought it back to this country and deposited it in the Advocates' Library, Edinburgh, which regards it as one of its choicest treasures. (*Annals*, 41.)

The card accompanying it bears the following inscription :—
" Latin Bible of St. Jerome.
MS. of 13th century.
The initial L contains a Tree of Jesse, bearing the figures of David, the Virgin, and Christ.
The MS. was so much admired by Ruskin that he presented the show-case.''

The description of it as a thirteenth century MS. makes Dr. Henderson's suggestion that Abbot Gaufrid brought it with him from Canterbury in 1124 sound somewhat improbable.

Another priceless MS. of unusual historic interest, particularly for Dunfermline, is St. Margaret's copy of the Gospels, or, rather, such portions of them as were used in the service of the Mass at different times of the year—more prized by her than any other of her books. The story of its recovery runs as follows :—

" Six years ago (1887) a little octavo volume in worn brown binding stood on the shelves of a small parish library in Suffolk, but was turned out and offered at the end of a sale at Sotheby's, presumably as being unreadable to country folk, and capable of being turned into hard cash wherewith a few works of fiction might be purchased.

" The contempt for it thus displayed was apparently shared by the cataloguer, who described it as ' Latin Gospels of the Fourteenth Century, with English Illuminations.'

" For the sum of £6 it passed into the hands of the Bodleian Library, and came to be catalogued as an ordinary accession.

" It was noticed that the writing was of the eleventh century, and that the illuminations were valuable specimens of old English work of the same century, comprising figures of the four evangelists of the Byzantine type, which was common in the West of Europe; the drapery, however, colouring and accessories were purely English.

" The book itself was seen to be not the complete Gospels, but such portions as were used in the service of the Mass at different times of the year. Further, it was observed that a poem in Latin hexameters had been written, apparently before the end of the same century, on a fly-leaf of the volume, which began by thanking Christ for ' displaying miracles to us in our own days,' and went on to describe how this very volume had been carried in the folds of a priest's robe to a trysting-place, in order that a binding oath might be taken on it; but that unfortunately it had been dropped, without the priest observing it, into a stream, and given up for lost.

" But a soldier of the party at last discovered it, plunged head first into the river, and brought it up.

" To everyone's intense surprise, the beautiful volume was entirely uninjured, ' except two leaves, which you see at each end, in which a slight contraction appears from the effect of the water, which testify the work of Christ in protecting the sacred volume.

" ' That this work might appear to us still more miraculous, the wave washed from the middle of the book a leaf of silk.

" ' May the King and pious Queen be saved for ever, whose book was but now saved from the waters.'

" The silk was, no doubt, pieces placed loosely in the book

West end of North Aisle showing junction of Abbot de Bothwell's Scheme with original
Norman work.

to preserve the illuminations from contact with the page opposite; and sure enough, a leaf at each end of the book showed
unmistakeable crinkling from immersion in water.

" But who were the King and Queen ?

" By a curious accident connected with the name of Margaret,
a lady to whom this story was told remembered a similar
incident in Forbes-Leith's *Life of St. Margaret of Scotland*, and
the mystery was solved.

" There in the Life is a passage in prose, beginning : ' She
had a book of the Gospels beautifully adorned with gold and
precious stones, and ornamented with the figures of the four
evangelists, painted and gilt. . . . She had always felt a particular attachment for this book, more so than for any of the others
which she usually read.'

" Then follows a story almost identical with the one given
above, with some variant but not discrepant details.

" It, too, mentions the pieces of silk and the contraction on
certain leaves, and adds that it was found lying open at the
bottom of the river.

" If anything could add to the interest of the volume, it is
that in the same Life we read of the King, that ' although he
could not read, he would turn over and examine books which
the Queen used either for her devotion or her study; and
whenever he heard her express especial liking for a particular
book, he also would look at it with special interest, kissing it,
and often taking it into his hands.' " (*Books in Manuscript*,
Falconer Madan, p. 107.)

In 1896 a facsimile reproduction of this book was published,
edited by W. Forbes-Leith, S.J., F.S.A., Scot.—the impression
consisting of twenty copies on large paper, and ninety copies on
small paper. Two of the ninety are in Dunfermline Public Library.
Notes :—

" The discovery of this manuscript adds one more to the
very limited list of extant pre-Reformation Scottish Service-
books, increasing their number from twelve to thirteen. None
of these . . . except the Book of Deer and the Evangelistarium
of St. Margaret, are earlier than the 13th century." (*Facsimile*,
page 10.)

" It may be that King Malcolm could neither read nor write,
but he spoke English, French and Irish with equal ease, and

frequently acted as interpreter at his Consort's conferences with the Scottish clergy." (*Statuta Eccl. Scot.* i. xxiv.)

By 1563 the townsfolk and other parishioners had had time to think, and even, perhaps, to question the wisdom of much that had been done. Their immediate concern, however, was with the nave—the parish kirk, as it now came to be called. From the first they had looked upon it as their future place of worship, and they had been, and were, using it. But it was in a miserable if not dangerous condition, they had no clear title to it and no funds to fall back upon for its repair. What were they to do ? The only possibility that they could think of lay in an approach to the Privy Council.

The substance of their case was that, beyond the memory of man, the abbot had been in the habit of maintaining the walls and roof of the parochial kirk, and the sacristan, as vicar, the glass windows; while the township of Dunfermline had been responsible for the " reparaling " (repair) of the interior. The township was still prepared to do its part, but the commendator and sacristan denied liability. As things stood, they went on to represent :—

" The wallis in sindrie parts ar revin, and the volt thairthrow partit, near hand the ane side from the uther, and the glassin windois of the samyn decayit, and nane now being thairin; quhairthrow it is greit danger and perrell to the saidis compleneris of thair lyvis to enter, remane, or bide within the said kirk, owther in tyme of prayers, teching, or preching of the Word of God, or ony uther besines neidfull to be done thairin, without haistie remeid be providit in all things necessar." (*Reg. P.C.* 13 *Sept.,* 1563.)

The question naturally arises as to who was responsible for this lamentable state of affairs. Attention has already been drawn to the fact that neither the Reformers nor the townsfolk had any desire to destroy the nave. One could even go further, with confidence, and say that, almost certainly, they would take what precautions they could to safeguard it.

That does not necessarily mean that it would issue from the ordeal quite unscathed. But, in view of the fact that the great tower between it and the Conventual Church stood the test of other 200 winters without, one may safely say, any repairs worth

15A

speaking of being executed on it, it must be apparent that the damage cannot have been very serious. The removal of images and idols would undoubtedly cause a certain amount of disturbance, but was not in any way likely to affect the stability of the building.

On the other hand, everyone at all familiar with the story of the Medieval Church knows that the care and maintenance of these huge monastic properties, to say nothing of the smaller parish churches, was a constant source of worry to the authorities.

As early as 1242 we find David de Bernham, Bishop of St. Andrews, issuing an ultimatum to the effect that :—

" The church be roofed, that the walls be unbroken and not ruinous, the windows of glass and unbroken—those round the chancel to be kept in repair by the rector, . . . and those round the church to be put in order by the parishioners, and that the clergy be compelled thereto by the suspension of their stipend until the necessary repairs have been made, the laity by the suspension of their church privileges." (*Hay Fleming, Reform. in Scotland*, 350.)

Right down to the very eve of the Reformation one finds echoes of the same complaint. In a letter to the Pope in 1556 Cardinal Sermoneta reports as follows :—

" Moreover it was declared how in the said kingdom very many churches and monasteries had been established of old in stately buildings, but within the last ten years or thereabouts had been reduced to ruins by hostile inroads, or through the avarice and neglect of those placed in charge were crumbling to decay ; and this with their revenues undiminished, nay in some cases even greater than at the time of their foundation, with no one to pity these widowed churches, or to take their healing in hand." (*Ibid*. 351.)

In the last provincial council held in pre-Reformation Scotland, Archbishop Hamilton ordained and decreed that :—

" All ruinous and dilapidated churches within the realm of Scotland shall be rebuilt and repaired in their walls, roofs, ornaments, and all necessaries wont to be repaired by rector and parishioners, and they shall be compelled hereto by the ordinaries by the sequestration of their rents." (*Ibid*. 352.)

It is a well-established fact, familiar to everybody with practical experience of buildings, that continued and persistent neglect may be as deadly as wilful damage; and, in the case of the nave of Dunfermline Abbey in particular, as reported to the Privy Council, one may well feel justified in concluding that the one cause was at least as accountable as the other.

The Council, having heard both sides, ordained the commendator to repair the roof and walls of the parish kirk so as to make sure that they were water-tight and safe, and the sacristan to attend to the windows, in both cases at the expense of the convent, as in all time past they had been in the habit of doing (*Apud Striviling* (Stirling), 13th September, 1563)— which would seem to suggest that the Privy Councillors were definitely of opinion that a good deal of the disorder was due to previous neglect.

That same day the Council, understanding that in many cases parish churches had become ruinous, some having actually fallen down, so that preaching of the Word of God, ministration of the sacraments and reading of the common prayers were no longer possible; with the result that the people were coming to be without knowledge or fear of God, ordained that the said churches be repaired and rebuilt, where necessary, " upoun the expenssis of the parochinars and Persone, in maner following: that is to say, the tua part of the expenssis thairof to be paid be the parochinars, and thrid part be the Persone."

Whether due to the decree of the Privy Council or not, it does seem as if, in 1564, some half-hearted attempt at patching and repairing the nave was set on foot. It certainly did not amount to more than that, and how the congregation fared in the meantime is not indicated.

In 1570 another attempt was made to deal with the problem of repair under the direction of Sir Robert Drummond of Carnock (Stirlingshire), master mason to the king; but, probably through lack of funds, very little was accomplished.

In 1587 all the properties and revenues of the monastery of Dunfermline were annexed to the Crown, and, in the year following, the General Assembly appealed to King James VI, soliciting his intervention to avert the ruin which threatened Glasgow, Dunfermline and Dunblane churches. This appeal corroborates and confirms the impression already formed that the repairs effected so far must have been superficial and unsatisfactory. But again comparatively little seems to have been accomplished.

There was little difficulty as a rule about finding good and sufficient reasons for these annexations, but the reason annexed in this case strikes one as somewhat quaint.

" BECAUSE it is understood that the pouertie of the Croun is the speciall caus of the pouertie of the realme and inhabitantis thairof, and that the patrimonie of the Croun being augmetit is the greit weill and profitte baith of the kingis grace and to his leigis, THAIRFOIR . . . "

It was not till 1594—thirty-four years, that is, after the Reformation—that a genuine scheme of repair was at long last set on foot, and, as it took five years to complete, one imagines that it must have been somewhat far-reaching.

The work was carried out under the direction of William Shaw, master of works—whose memorial, it may be noted, has been removed from its original site, a little to the west of Robert Pitcairn's stone, to the place it now occupies at the north-west end of the nave, with a view to getting better light in the pulpit. (*K.S. Records*, 3rd October, 1670.)

" In succession to Sir Robert Drummond, William Schaw, a man of wide culture, who played a prominent part in the development of Freemasonry, was appointed Master of Work to the Crown, apparently through the kindly influence of Queen Anne. . . .

" In the month of May, 1590, he was paid £400 ' by his Majesty's precept for reparation of the house at Dunfermling, befoir the Queene's Majesties passing thereto.'

" In the entry he is called Master of Work, and had evidently been employed to repair the jointure-house of the Queen of Scotland at Dunfermline, which in the year 1600 he rebuilt.

" This entire lordship formed a portion of the dowry of Anne of Denmark, and William Schaw became her Chamberlain, and a great favourite with this Danish Princess.

" He also did good work in regard to the restoration of the great Abbey, now falling into decay. To the nave, the aisles, the steeple and the north porch he gave special attention. . . .

" He also sent James Murray, the Master Wright, from Dunfermline to Edinburgh, and observes :—' I never allowit less wages this year to James Murray than 13s. 4d. each day ' . . .

" His employment, however, by both the King and the Queen was not of long duration. In the midst of his active and useful career, he was cut off by sudden death on 18 April, 1602, and a very elaborate monument was erected to his memory by direction of the Queen. In the rather lengthy inscription, his intellectual accomplishments, his extensive knowledge of foreign lands and his excellent skill in architecture are highly praised.

" A curious monogram, making up the letters of his name, was cut on a small piece of marble and inserted in the upper portion of the sepulchral edifice.

" A side light is thrown on his character by the fact that an old record states that on one occasion he was wounded in a duel by ' Buccleugh,' being second to Sir R. Ker.

" His name will always be remembered in connection with the Abbey of Dunfermline. If his work shows any signs of foreign influence, we must trace the source to Denmark, and not to France." (*The King's Master Masons*, Mylne, 61-62.)

(*Note.*—From K.S. Minute of 1st November, 1711, we learn that he had a seat in the church, near the present site of his memorial.)

It has always been recognised that Shaw was a leading figure in the repair of the nave after the Reformation. The trouble is that he has so often been credited with more than he did.

Dr. Henderson (*Annals* 245) says that he built the north porch, took down and rebuilt the upper part of the western gable and erected uncouth buttresses as supports to the north and south walls.

Not one of these statements is correct.

The work upon the west gable and the erection of the porch were due to Abbot Richard de Bothwell, *c.* 1450, and the buttresses were not erected till after Shaw was dead. One of the buttresses on the south side bears the date 1620; one on the north side 1625. Shaw died in 1602.

On the north side of one of the pillars included in Abbot Bothwell's scheme of renovation there is a crest bearing a bull's head, which, according to *Fairbairn's Crests*, is that of an Oxford family of the name of Bull.

Bull was not a name in common use locally, but early in the sixteenth century we find references in the Burgh Records to members of a family of that name—William Bull, who was alive in 1525, but dead before 1543 ; a daughter of his, Isabella, who was fined 2s. for her part in a brawl in the abbey bake-house on Trinity Eve, 1520 ; and a son, John Bull, who had some property in the Netherton, adjoining the lands of David Bothwell.

From the appearance of such a device on a crest associated with the abbot's coat of arms on the renovated portion of the nave, one is tempted to surmise that a member of the Bull family may have been the architect or mason responsible, under the abbot, for the work.

But it amounts to no more than a bare possibility.

It is only recently that Abbot Bothwell has begun to get credit for the good work he did in his day. We have already shown, in the light of the provisions of his will, that it was he who was responsible for the erection of a grammar school in Queen Anne Street for the instruction of non-monastic pupils. Recent research work amongst Vatican papers has also made it clear that he carried out an extensive scheme of repair work at the west end of the nave, and this is amply borne out by the following extract from the report of the officials of the Office of Works :—

" Towards the end of the same century (15th) or possibly somewhat later, the west gable was reconstructed from above the doorway.

" The subsequent rebuilding of the north-west tower, as well as of the two adjoining bays of the nave-arcade and of the vaults of the corresponding bays of the north aisle, and the addition of a porch in front of the Romanesque north door can all be ascribed with certainty to Richard de Bothwell, Abbot from 1445 to 1471, since the arms of Bothwell of Hallbank appear on one of the tower buttresses, on the north porch and on the vault of the aisle.

" The upper part of the tower, however, as it now exists, with its bartizan and spire appears to be the work of William Shaw." (*Roy. Comm. Fife*, 107.)

From the extract already quoted from Mylne's *Master Masons*, with its reference to £400 paid to Shaw in the month of May, 1590, " for reparation of the house at Dunfermline, befoir the Queene's Majesties passing thereto," one gets the impression that Shaw was also responsible for the conversion of the monastic guest-chambers into a royal palace.

Baptism, being the rite associated with entrance to the Christian Church, was invariably, in those days, administered at the door of the church, but after the porch was built, it would doubtless be administered in the porch—hence the name " Christening Porch."

An occasional reference to it as the " Marriage Porch " is to be explained on the ground that the first part of the marriage ceremony was performed there, and also on the ground that in certain cases the marriage could not be solemnised at the altar.

In spite, however, of all that Shaw did for the interior of the nave, it may be questioned whether it ever constituted a really attractive place of worship.

It would be seen at its best, no doubt, when there were no seats of any kind within it—nothing but the pulpit, probably a double-decker, one for the preacher and another for the pre-centor, attached to one of the pillars on the north side. The worshippers would either stand throughout, or kneel on the floor during the prayers. If, like Jenny Geddes, they had a stool, they would carry it away with them when the service ended.

But soon the desire developed for some greater degree of comfort, a desire that quickly grew in urgency as the length of services increased. A man would ask the Session for leave to make a seat for his wife, he himself to stand behind it. This heritor or that would want a whole seat for his family—Robert Pitcairn, the commendator, claiming a particularly " heighe " seat. Some were moveable, some were fixtures, some forms, with or without backs, others " cradles " (completely boxed in, the very height of exclusiveness)—the only available floor-space for which there was no competition being " the place of repentance " in the body of the kirk, in front of the pulpit.

Then began the race for the " lofts." The members of the various guilds would combine to secure for themselves a loft built sometimes one above another, round the columns on both sides of the church, each, as a rule, with a stair of its own—the town council being as forward in asserting their claims as any.

" 9 Aug., 1653—This day James reid, prsnt provest for him-self and his successrs and in name and behalf of the baillies and consall of this brut, present and to come, proponed to the

minister and session, Desyring of ym libertie for building a
loft about the pillar aboue pittencrieff seate, on the north syde
of the kirk for the said prouist, baillies, and consell to sit in.
qlk desyre the session thot reasonable,—no one contravening
or opposing the same." (K.S.R.)

"11 June, 1665—The same day the said Provost baillies and
counsall all in ane voice did conclude & agrie that the Counsall
seat in the Kirk of Dunfermline be recovered & laid over in the
foirpte yrof wt. green cloth wt. ane green silk sase about the
burders yrof and yt upon the gild brethren & craftsmen yr
charges equally and yt the Dean of Gild and decon convener doe
the same with all diligence." (B.R.)

"6 Septr., 1665—Which Day the sd. Provost baillies &
counsall being convined and considering that whairas they
consisting of merchands and craftismen have upon ther awin
proper charges viz:—of the sd. merchands & craftismen
equallie built ane seat in the church off Dunfermline upon the
pillar on the west syde of the pulpit for the use of the provost
baillies and counsall of the sd. burgh And to the effect that in
all tym coming all difference and controversie may be taken
away betwixt ym & yr successors anent ther places and ordour
of sitting in the sd. seat. The said merds and craftismen of the
sd. burt of quhom the sd. Councal doeth (con)sist for ym-
selffs & in name of the remanent merchands & craftismen of
the samen burt & takand burden for ym Have unanimouslie
concordit setled & agried and for them & yr. successors doe
unanimouslie concord setle and grie that in all tyme comming
thay and ther successors shall sitt and possese the sd. seat in
maner following, viz:—the present provest and his successors
provests being for the tym to have his place & seit in the foir
seat being raised above the rest and the sd. merchands to have
any Oyr seit on the south syd of the sd. provest's seat
qrin the old provost shall sitt being the provest's right hand.
And the rest of the foirseat on the north syd fra the provest's
seat to the north end of the seat to be possest be the sd. merchds
& qrin the two baillies dean of gild & thesaurer pnt & yr
successors shall sitt. And on the Oyr parte the said craftismen
shall have belonging to them & shall sit and possese the remanent
parte of the sd. foirseat on the south syd fra the entrie yrof
to the nixt south-east. And the bak seat & parte of the sd.

Counsall seat to be possest & takin up wt. the sd. merchds & craftismen togidder on taking up yr. place & roum as they hapen to com in."

The front of the magistrates' pew may now be seen, with extensions, above the north-transept entrance to the parish church.

The royal arms in the central panel would, however, suggest that the king's seat also must have been drawn upon.

It was no doubt an imposing erection, but by that time there was a good deal more dignity attaching to the office than under the old regime.

When James IV granted, 19th May, 1488, a charter to Paisley Abbey he provided that the Abbot of Paisley should have rights similar to those held by the Abbot of Dunfermline, including " the right and power of chusing annually the provost, bailies and other officers of said burgh, and of removing the same as need shall be, and of chusing others anew in their room."

The Hammermen had not only a loft but seats down below, and very precise and rigid they were in their application of the regulations concerning the use of them.

" 2 January, 1639—It is ordained by ye hail brethren of craft that ye foir seat of our craft sal be keepit for ye deacon and his conjuncts, and none other to enter. And if it happen that any other sall come to the foir seat, they sall pay the sum of six shillings and sixpence—*toties quoties.*

" And likewise thay maun obsearve that ye second seat sall be for the rest of ye freemen, under lyke pain ; and others, ye servants and prentices, to sit in the other two seats—ye servants (journey-men) who are not in the loft, if the backseats are filled to repair to ye second seat." (*Thomson, Dunf. Hammermen,* p. 67.)

The most unexpected regulation was that which excluded women from the benefit of this provision.

" Craftsmen and Guildsmen were the lords of creation and were quite content to see their womankind squatting on the floor while they occupied the ' foir seat, the back seats and the loft.' " (*Ibid. 70.*)

" 22 Feb., 1711—George Walls, Deacon of the Wrights, with several others of that Incorporation, compeared before the

Session and represented their design of building a Loft in the east end of the Kirk for their better accommodation in hearing the Word, their seat below being too little for containing their Corporation and desired the Session's liberty and allowance for building the said Loft. They were removed and the Session considering the affair granted their desire with this provision :—

(1mo.) That they sell their seat below in the Body of the Kirk to the Session.

(2do.) That they get the concurrence of the Heretors and Town Council.

(3tio.) That they give in somewhat to the poor.

" Being called in, this was intimat to them. All which they undertook to do." (*K.S.R.*)

In the north-east corner the Session itself built a loft with a view to increasing funds.

" The Communion was celebrated in the ' Communion yle,' which extended along the east of the church and was entered by two doors, one on the north and the other on the south. In 1648, when a new north entrance to the church was made, the ' little stane walls ' at the sides of these doors were taken down and timber erections substituted.

" A wall corresponding to these stretched along the front of the ' yle ' to separate it from ' the bodie of the kirk,' and of such a height as not to interfere with the congregation there seeing the Communion service. The ' yle ' was thus an enclosure of fenced space (hence ' fencing the tables '), from which, on Communion occasions, all who had not the Session's passport were strictly excluded. Over it was a wooden ' loft ' or gallery, the supports of which, along with the church pillars, provided corners where worshippers on ordinary Sundays, obscured from the officiating minister's view, were tempted to indulge in censurable liberties, such as ' common discourses and conferences, and taking their sneising tobatto.' " (*Stevenson, Comm. in Dunf.*, 5, 6.)

Entrance to the gallery above the " Communion yle " was by a staircase inside the Great Tower at the east end of the nave.

The only " seat " one has any real difficulty with is " *the musicians' seat*," in the south-east corner of the church—under the king's seat—which, on 10th June, 1656, was given up to Sir Henry Wardlaw of Pitreavie " an to his household yrin, to big ane comlie seat for yr ease an profitable hearing of the word of god in tyme of divine service."

The precentor had a seat of his own, and there were, in post-Reformation worship, no other "musicians," either vocal or instrumental, requiring a special seat to be provided for them.

Is it not just possible that this particular seat was a survival of pre-Reformation days which had escaped both the " purging " of 1560 and the " repairs " of 1594 ?

Until the heritors were at length compelled to introduce a uniform scheme of seating, even the glorious nave, " one of the finest surviving examples of Scoto-Norman monastic architecture " (Roy. Comm., Fife, 107), with all its attractiveness, can hardly have been a seemly spectacle, or one calculated to foster a spirit of devotion.

" About nine years ago (1850), the interior of the nave underwent an extensive repair and alteration by parliamentary votes of money, under the direction of Her Majesty's Commissioners of Woods and Forests, and superintendence of Mr. R Matheson, then styled clerk-assistant, now Surveyor of Her Majesty's Public Works in Scotland. Three of the south columns, which were out of the perpendicular, were entirely removed and replaced by others ; a very difficult but successful operation, performed by Mr. Andrew Balfour, builder, Dunfermline. The floor was lowered and entirely renewed ; and, instead of the old sloping ascent to the new eastern church, steps were added, corresponding with the ancient *graditorium* to the site of the high altar. The small arches and columns of two of the ancient little chapels or altars on the north wall have been renewed, and the others on both sides are to be so, according as parliamentary grants of money are made. The restoration of one or two more is expected to be immediately commenced.

" The high windows of the Clerestory galleries have been opened and glazed, as also those of the north side of the Triforium, which is a great improvement. A new ceiling, too, has been given to the nave, divided into oblong compartments." (Chalmers' Hist. ii. 135-6.)

The eastern part of the choir and the Lady Chapel are said to have been blown down in 1672. (Royal Comm. Fife, 107.)

LATER DEVELOPMENTS

Fall of the Great Tower (or *Lantern Tower*, as it was sometimes called).

On 22nd January, 1753, the attention of the heritors was drawn to the fact that the great steeple, rising above the crossing between the conventual and parochial churches, was in danger of falling, and it was resolved to dispose of the stones by public roup, intimation being given to all who had tombstones in the neighbourhood to remove them if they thought they were in danger.

A week later the tower fell. As it is said to have been 150 feet high, and about 50 feet square, it is fortunate that it fell to the east, otherwise the nave would have been utterly destroyed.

For a time there was talk of offering the stones to the town council for public use, the town council to carry out, by way of compensation, some repair work rendered necessary by the fall; but eventually it was agreed to revert to the idea of a public roup intimated from the lectern on Sunday first and by "touk of drum" throughout the town. By the articles of roup the purchaser was to remove the fallen stones as soon as possible, at the same time carrying out the repairs already referred to. The first bid was to be 10s. with an advance of one shilling for every subsequent bid, the highest bidder "at the outrunning of the time prefixt by the heritors and magistrates present to be preferred." The heritors would provide a cart-road through the churchyard "where most commodious and where it will occasion least lifting of gravestones," and the purchaser would carry off the rubbish and spread it equally upon the road between the porch and the pend.

The roup took place in the churchyard on 5th February, the heritors thinking it unwise to wait for better weather "because of the many new and fresh graves disturbed and thrown up by the fall."

Dr. Stenhouse offered forty shillings, Thomas Anderson, baxter, forty-one, and eventually Mr. Anderson's bid of three guineas was, in accordance with the articles of roup, accepted.

The Tower at the South End of the West Gable.

On 2nd July of that same year (1753) the attention of the heritors was drawn to the insecure condition of " the old steeple on the south-west end of the paroch kirk " and, after consideration, it was again resolved to dispose of the stones, etc., and to contract for the necessary repairs by means of a public roup duly advertised, the purchaser having liberty " to throw down, land and carry off the sd. stones where most convenient and where it will do least harm to the tenants of the Frater-green and Bailly and Constable's house, and, if he inclines, to fill the bottom of the said old steeple wt. the rubbish thereof "—the first bid to be one guinea and every subsequent bid one shilling more. On the day appointed, Arthur Miller, factor for Colonel Forbes of Pittencrieff, offered one guinea.

Patrick Turnbull, glassier, offered thirty shillings. Miller's bid of thirty-one shillings being the highest offer at the out-running of the time prefixt, he was preferred to the purchase, and John Adie, skinner in Dunfermline, became cautioner for his performance of the articles in the exact terms thereof.

There is nothing in the record to indicate what was the nature of the superstructure that was removed, but no room is left for doubt as to the fact that there was a superstructure, that its condition had become dangerous, and that the stones were disposed of by public roup and removed.

It is well to note this because when this same tower collapsed fifty years later a wrong impression is apt to be created.

What fell on the second occasion was the remainder of the tower from which the superstructure had been removed fifty years before.

The Parish Church.

At the beginning of the year in which the last-mentioned tower fell, 15th January, 1807, a special meeting of heritors was called to consider the state of the Parish Church and to take measures for having it repaired and fitted in a suitable manner.

The meeting unanimously adopted a resolution to the effect that the church is incommodious and in bad repair, and that it ought to be thoroughly repaired and fitted up in a proper manner. It was further resolved to advertise for plans and estimates, twenty guineas to be offered for the best plan submitted and five guineas for the two plans next in merit.

And that, as it proved, was the first move in a campaign that was to last ten years.

On 22nd June, the heritors unanimously adopted a plan submitted by Mr. Stark, a native of Dunfermline and an architect of some note, with the following alterations :—

" (1) That an additional gallery at the east end of the church is necessary, and that the pulpit be brought into a line betwixt the second columns from the east.

" (2) That the seats between the second and third columns from the east be made partly moveable so that they may be fitted up as Communion Tables running across the church there when necessary.

" (3) That wooden benches be placed in the windows in the other passages above and below in such manner as shall seem best."

While this plan, with its suggested alterations, was being considered, the south-west tower fell.

Next day the heritors visited the scene and agreed to defer coming to any resolution till Mr. Stark had an opportunity of viewing the ruin.

" But in regard an adjoining stable occupied by Lawrence Millar is demolished by the fall of the steeple and three horses killed, the meeting authorise him to remove such part of the stones or rubbish as may be necessary to enable him to get out his property lying under the same, at the expense of the heritors. Recommend to Provost Wilson to employ a man to watch near the ruins to prevent boys and others from going near it, or doing any injury to the building or exposing themselves to danger."

" 3 September, 1807—The meeting resolve unanimously to rebuild the old steeple forming the south-west angle of the church in the manner proposed in Mr. Stark's Report, and request Mr. Stark to make out a plan and a specification accordingly. . . .

" The meeting recommend to the committee appointed on 20 July to communicate with Mr. Stark on the idea of *a New Church*, and, if it shall appear expedient to the committee, authorise them to get a plan and specification of a new church upon *the area south from the present church*."

" 9 October, 1807—Mr. Stark, architect, attended the meeting and produced plans for a New Church. . . . He also presented a comparative estimate of the expense of repairing and improving the present church. . . and of building a new church according to the plan now given in—the former amounting to £3,310 3s. 10d. Stg., and the latter to £3,700 16s. 2d. Stg.

" The meeting, with the exception of Mr. Scotland (of Brieryhill), are of opinion that a New Church, according to the plan now given in by Mr. Stark, ought to be built upon the area of ground to which it refers."

" 3 June, 1808—This meeting was called ' in order to come to a determination respecting the repairs of the present church or erection of a new one.' Before the heritors proceeded to discuss this, however, The Rev. Mr. McLean, who was present, was requested to say whether or not he had any objection to give up the ground proposed for the site of the new church.

" Mr. McLean thereupon laid down the conditions upon which he was prepared ' to treat.' "

The meeting apparently was so discouraged by Mr. McLean that it made no further progress that day.

" 30 August, 1808—The meeting direct advertisements to be again inserted in the Edinburgh newspapers for contracts to rebuild the old Tower or Steeple at the south-west corner of the church according to Mr. Stark's plan for repairs upon the church."

" 17 November, 1808—The meeting having been called for the special purpose of determining whether the present church should be repaired or a new church erected, the question was put to the vote, when all the gentlemen present, excepting Bailie Anderson and Mr. Hunt of Logie, voted for the old church being repaired, and Bailie Anderson and Mr. Hunt voted for a new church, so that the meeting did by a considerable majority (9 to 2) resolve to repair the present church.

" The meeting then resolved unanimously that the repairs should be executed according to the plans given in by Mr. Stark."

" 7 December, 1808—A Sub-committee appointed to see the building through—the committee to meet on the first Monday of every month and at such other time as their convener shall think fit until the business entrusted to them is concluded."

" 13 February, 1809—Meeting of Sub-committee.

" The Rev. Alan McLean making trouble in regard to the adopted plans—the committee is in no doubt that Mr. McLean's application to the Presbytery is ' altogether unnecessary and vexatious.' "

" 14 July, 1809—Mr. Black reported that he had . . . advertised for distinct estimates for rebuilding the old tower and repairing the church, and laid before them one estimate by Messrs. Hutton and Morton, being the only one that had been lodged in consequence of the advertisement.

" The estimate for the old tower is £849 Stg. and for the church repairs £2,301.   Acceptance agreed upon subject to confirmation by Mr. Stark."

" 2 August, 1809—The committee reported to the heritors the result of their meeting with the Presbytery.   They had waited upon the Presbytery and had laid before them the plans and specifications for rebuilding the old tower and repairing the church, and they had requested the sanction of the Presbytery thereto—which the Presbytery had declined to grant, and returned their plans because, as they alleged, sufficient accommodation could not thereby be afforded to the parishioners.

" The committee further reported that the Presbytery had found that the Town and Heritors of Dunfermline should provide accommodation for 2,800 to 3,000 persons and appointed them to produce at the next meeting of the Presbytery in October plans for a church of the above size, and the building is to be completed before Martinmas 1810, and had discerned accordingly."

(The Heritors, somewhat staggered, discussed taking the opinion of Counsel.)

" 7 December, 1809—Meeting of Committee—Mr. Black laid before the committee a letter which he received yesterday from Mr. Stuart, their Agent in the Process of Avocation respecting the church, informing that, after a full pleading on Tuesday last, Lord Robertson, Ordinary, in the Court of Session, had pronounced a decision in favour of the Heritors, finding that they are only liable in repairs of the present church so as to accommodate eighteen hundred persons, and not to build a new church."

" 15 May, 1810—The meeting having examined the different

241

estimates for rebuilding the old tower preferred the estimate given in by Alexander Morton, Mason in Dunfermline, to perform the whole work agreeable to a plan and specification in every respect that concerns the said tower, made out by Mr. Stark, architect, and that for the sum of Five Hundred and Ninety Pounds Stg.''

" 16 June, 1810—Mr. Black informed the meeting that he had received advice from the Agent at Edinburgh that, in consequence of another representation by Mr. McLean, the Lord Ordinary had appointed the heritors to name one person and Mr. McLean another to inspect the present church and report whether or not the same can be fitted up so as to accommodate eighteen hundred sitters and in what manner; that, at desire of the committee, he had communicated the above Interlocutor to Mr. Stark and requested information from him upon the subject, but had not yet received an answer.''

Before the meeting dispersed, however, Mr. Stark's letter arrived.

" The same was read and directed to be sent to Mr. Stuart, and the meeting agree that Mr. Stark be named on their part to report in terms of the Lord Ordinary's Interlocutor.''

" 11 September, 1811—Having considered Mr. Stark's design for finishing the old tower, the meeting unanimously resolve that the work shall be executed agreeable to that design, with the exception of the minaret, which is to be left out, and Mr. Morton having given in an estimate for that part of the work amounting to £60, the meeting agree to accept the same.''

" 22 February, 1816—Meeting called to consider condition of the Church—There is an absolute necessity for some measures being taken to accommodate the Parish, the present church being quite unsuitable for the purpose, and it is the sense of this meeting that under all the circumstances it will be most advisable to build a new church upon a different site from the present one.''

" 15 March, 1816—Meeting having considered the recommendation of the last meeting respecting the propriety of building a new church, appoints a committee to consider the whole subject.''

" 6 April, 1816—Meeting of Committee.

(Reversion to the idea of repairing the old church rather than building a new one.)

242

" The meeting having considered the several plans and conversed with a tradesman upon the subject and having ascertained by measurement upon the plan that the present church repaired according to Mr. Stark's plan, but with an additional gallery, would contain more than the number specified in Lord Robertson's Interlocutor, are of the opinion that it is more advisable to repair the church in this manner than to build a new church. They are of the opinion, however, that it is unnecessary to erect a second gallery at present and that the plan with one gallery should be submitted to the Ministers and Presbytery."

" 6 May, 1816—Meeting of Committee—Mr. Fernie and Mr. McLean attended this meeting at which Mr. Fernie protests that if the heritors do not agree immediately to repair the church so as to contain eighteen hundred hearers, he and others concerned who may join with him will, in effect, raise Cain in the law courts."

" 31 May, 1816—Meeting of Committee—Convinced that something must be done and that it ought not to vary materially from Mr. Stark's plan, Mr. Stirling of Dunblane is asked to come here on the 13th or early on the 14th to inspect the church (Mr. Stark having died in 1813) and report his opinion of the manner in which the wishes of the heritors can be answered."

" 14 June, 1816—Meeting of Heritors—The heritors decide forthwith ' to instruct Mr. Stuart, their agent on the Church Process, to waken the same and obtain proper warrants for enabling the heritors to repair the church.' "

" 28 June, 1816—Meeting of Heritors—Letter from Rev. Alan McLean submitted, in which he says he is ' inclined to accept Lord Robertson's decision relative to the Church of Dunfermline.'

" As, however, Mr. Stark's plan did not accommodate 1,800 persons when laid before the Presbytery, a new Plan or Sketch should be produced that all concerned may be satisfied how the above numbers of persons are to be properly accommodated."

" 16 July, 1816—Meeting of Heritors—Mr. Stirling attended this meeting and submitted plans of the alterations he proposes to make on Mr. Stark's plans so that the accommodation will be for 1,800 persons. Mr. Stirling's plan approved and he is

asked to lay the same before the Presbytery ' to-morran '
accompanying a small delegation of the Heritors."

" 17 July, 1816—The Presbytery ' appointed ' the heritors to
produce specifications and one or more estimates."

" 10 April, 1817—Meeting of Committee.

(Meeting called to deal with a letter received from Mr.
Howieson " urging the completion of his agreement for repairing the old church.")

" Mr. Landale, appearing for Lord Elgin, stated that ' His
Lordship is anxious that the contract for repairing the old
church should not be proceeded in further until his Lordship
can have an opportunity of submitting to the consideration of the
heritors plans of a new church which have been lately prepared
by Mr. Burn, Architect, by his Lordship's desire, with a view to
obviate the inconveniencies and disadvantages which his Lordship conceives would still attend the old church.' "

" 5 May, 1817—Meeting of Committee—Dr. Robertson
Barclay (although he had been present at the Committee Meeting
on April 10th) ' moved that the contract for repairing the old
church entered into with Mr. Howieson be now completed.'
He was trying to rush matters and was seconded by Mr. Whyte.
Mr. Stewart, representing the Earl of Elgin, moved that the
meeting should now consider whether the old church should
be repaired or a new one built. Dr. Robertson Barclay objected
that this was not a meeting of Heritors but a meeting of Committee called for the purpose stated in his motion, and ' was not
competent to adopt any measures with respect to a New
Church.'

" Mr. Stewart persisted with his amendment. It was put to
the vote and carried.

" It transpired that Lord Elgin, on his own initiative, had
procured all the necessary information for the meeting and had
communicated it to the Heritors ten days ago, and that Mr.
Burn, Architect, was in attendance with the plans and specifications for a new church.

" Mr. Stewart produced to the meeting a letter from Mr.
Strachan Blackwood of Pitreavie bearing that if the parish
should not be involved in a law suit by agreeing to erect a new
church he should certainly vote for it, and the Rev. Mr. McLean,
Minister of the Parish, mentioned that he and every member

of the Presbytery whom he had seen preferred a new church to the repairing of the old one.

" Dr. Robertson Barclay ' protests against any proceedings tending to build a new church and especially any assessment upon them exceeding that which would attach to them by the repairs agreed upon.' He also objects for himself and Sir Charles Halkett and others against any change of new plans before a General Meeting of Heritors shall order such."

(Note.—That Lord Elgin was imbued with public spirit is emphasised by the fact that he was the principal heritor and was liable for a greater share of the cost than any other person.)

" ' MEMORANDUM submitted by the Earl for the consideration of the Heritors of the Parish of Dunfermline :—

" ' Lord Elgin, being inclined to think that the preservation of the venerable Fabric of the old Church depended in a great degree on its continuance as the Church of the Parish, and understanding that it was possible to make such repairs upon it as would afford sufficient accommodation for the parish, originally approved of the Plan for the Repairs, though without any minute examination of its details, but he has since learned that the Church, repaired in that way, must necessarily be a very inconvenient place of worship, a great part of the Congregation, probably above one third, being unable, from the size of the Pillars, to see the minister, and, from distance and other causes, to hear him. His Lordship is therefore desirous that the Heritors and the Revd. Presbytery should reconsider the resolution for repairing the present Church, being confident that they will best consult the interests of the Parish by the erection of a new church as near as possible to the present site.

" ' A Meeting of the Heritors being already fixed to be held upon the 5th of May, Lord Elgin in the meantime begs leave to communicate this Memorandum to them individually, and also to the Ministers of the Parish, and to the Revd. Presbytery, that the subject may be duly considered, and that the Heritors may learn the grounds upon which his opinion is founded, and may come to the meeting prepared to adopt a final determination upon the subject.

" ' The preservation of the present building is certainly a very desirable object, but the circumstance, though it weighed much with Lord Elgin when he originally approved of the plan for repairing it, has appeared to his Lordship ever since he knew the impracticability of fitting up the present church so as to accommodate the parish, to be entitled to no consideration. The Barons of Exchequer, too, it must be known to the heritors, are entitled to give sums of money for the expense of repairs, to prevent such buildings from falling into decay.

" ' Acting under this impression Lord Elgin had recourse to the advice of persons well qualified to give him information before his opinion was decidedly formed in favour of a New Church.

" ' Mr. Burn, an architect of eminence in Edinburgh, will be ready to attend the Heritors upon the 5th of May and to satisfy them of the inexpediency of repairing the old church. From the communications with that gentleman, and the inspection of his plan and estimates, Lord Elgin has reason to believe that the expense of a new church upon a similar plan to that proposed by Mr. Stark may not far exceed, perhaps not at all, the expense of repairing the old church. On the other hand, the new church will contain a far greater number of persons, all of whom will be comfortably accommodated and hear and see well, and what is of considerable consequence, there will be no interruption of the performance of divine service during the erection of the new church.

" ' The new church will necessarily last for a far longer period than the old one repaired, and will necessarily last longer without requiring fresh repairs. The old building, too, is in all respects inconveniently constructed for a Church, having been erected as the Nave of the Church entering to the Choir and never intended for a Place of Worship. (sic)

" ' Lord Elgin has reason to suppose that the present Contractor for the repairs of the old church will not at all object to give up his agreement, on obtaining the Contract for the New Church on fair terms, to be settled by Mr. Burn. Mr. Stirling has had a great deal of trouble respecting the projected repair on the old church, and due compensation ought certainly to be made to him.

" ' The ground on which the new church would fall to be built belongs to Mr. Sutherland who has expressed himself as approving of the church being erected on it.

" ' Lord Elgin is confident that his conduct in pressing his opinion upon the Heritors can be ascribed to no motive but his belief of the public advantage to be derived from adopting it, to his most unqualified conviction that the repairing of the old church would be a great injury to the Community, and essentially in the way of the usefulness of the Ministers of the Parish.

" ' Although he is confident that no more time is necessary to erect a new church than to repair the old one, he is most anxious that the Plan should now be fixed, and the building proceeded in, no one being more thoroughly convinced of the propriety of obtaining the necessary accommodation for the Congregation in the Parish Church without further delay.

" ' Mr. Burn's Plan and Estimate will be in the hands of the Clerk to the Heritors for the inspection of all concerned, from Monday, 28th inst., to the day of the Meeting of Heritors. 2 North Charlotte Street, Edinburgh, 24th April, 1817.'

" He therefore craved the Meeting to appoint a Committee to be authorised to erect the New Church, to contract for the same, and to concert with Mr. Sutherland and Mr. Howieson respecting the erection, and he mentioned that, the sooner the business could be matured, it would be so much the more agreeable to Lord Elgin who was most anxious that the necessary accommodation should be afforded to the Parish without further delay.

" Provost Wilson seconded Mr. Stewart's motion and produced the extract of a Minute of the Town Council of the Burgh of Dunfermline of 3rd inst. in these terms :—

" 'The Provost stated to the Council that he had called the Meeting for the purpose of reconsidering the question respecting the Parish Church and whether it will be more advisable to erect a New Church than to proceed with the repairs of the old.

" ' On this subject he submitted to the consideration of the Council a Communication he had received from James Stewart, Esq., Writer to the Signet, containing various observations by the Earl of Elgin and recommending the adoption of a New Church in preference to the projected repairs which was read.

" ' The Provost then stated that although the Magistrates, in conjunction with the Heritors of the Parish, had agreed to the repairs and on entering into a contract with a builder for that purpose, yet upon more minute and serious consideration of the subject they do not now hesitate to declare their full conviction that the benefit of the parish will be more effectually promoted by the erection of a new church than repairing the old.' ''

'' (1) The Minute then repeats the arguments used by Lord Elgin in regard to the practical disadvantages of the scheme for repairs—difficulties of hearing and seeing from certain positions.

'' (2) The Minute states that the projected Repair Scheme has been estimated to cost £4,000. This sum the Magistrates (optimistically) have reason to believe will erect a New Church amply sufficient to accommodate a greater auditory than the number proposed to be accommodated in the repaired church.

'' (3) The Minute then repeats a few more of Lord Elgin's arguments on comfort—' every individual in the auditory will participate,' ' building will last longer,' etc.

'' (4) That from another consideration, and a consideration of the first importance to the Town of Dunfermline, the erecting of a New Church is preferable to repairing the old, from the certain prospect it affords of complete indemnification for the expense that must necessarily be incurred. In either case this must be considerable, and even although the Town's proportion of the expense of a new erection should exceed the expense of Repairs by some Hundred Pounds, yet the probability is, nay, it almost amounts to a certainty, that the Town will be able to dispose of their Proportion of the area of a New Church to such advantage as to indemnify that expense.

'' Whereas, were the repairs gone into, the prospect of indemnification by such means to any advantage, appears less than problematical, and consequently the Town must lay their account with the outlay of a large sum of money, without any probability of reimbursement, and what is more, without attaining any of the objects that ought to be chiefly attended to, the accommodation of the Parish in their most essential interests ; taking these circumstances into consideration, the Provost moved that the Council do Resolve to unite with those heritors who shall prefer the erection of a new church, and that the Magistrates be instructed to support the adoption of a New Church in preference to going into the proposed repairs of the Old Church. . . . ''

Extracts from minute to be sent by the Clerk to the Moderator of the Presbytery :—

" And that the Presbytery may take the necessary steps, if they see cause, for carrying the resolutions of this meeting into effect, the Meeting request Provost Wilson, Mr. Hunt and Mr. Sutherland to lay before the Presbytery the plans, specifications and estimate procured from Mr. Burn.

" Mr. Howieson, who was present, agreed to depart from his Contract with the Heritors, on his obtaining the Contract for the New Church, at the sum estimated by Mr. Burn."

Meeting of Heritors' Committee, 14th May, 1817 :—

" There was produced to the Meeting the following offer by Mr. Sutherland, and acceptance thereof, of both which the tenor follows.

" ' Dunfermline, 6 May, 1817. Gentlemen, Understanding that the Town and Heritors of the Parish of Dunfermline wish to have that piece of ground, part of my property lying south of the present Church of Dunfermline, extending from the east of the Parapet Wall on the east end of the old Buildings called the Frater Hall in a direct line north to the Psalter Churchyard wall as marked off at your site this day for the purpose of erecting a New Church and entry or communication thereto, I hereby make offer to sell to the Town and Heritors the above piece of ground with the Buildings or erections thereon.' "

General Meeting of Heritors, 26th May, 1817 :—

" Consideration of New Church postponed until June 10th, to give time for ' more correct ' information to be obtained on the subject of cost, and that Mr. Burn may also learn ' on what terms Mr. Howieson would consent to give up the proposed agreement for the Repairs of the Old Church, and, if these terms be moderate, may immediately proceed to advertise for Estimates for a Church to be built *to the east end of the present Church*, if the expense of a Church in that situation do not exceed £6,000.'

" Mr. Howieson offers to give up his contract on payment of £150.

" Mr. Burn thinks he has been moderate in his claim because ' he wishes to stand well with so respectable a Body ' (as the heritors). For himself, he feels obliged to say that it is quite impossible for him even to prepare plans of this new church, much less to get estimates for it, before 10th June; (and rashly adds that) he has ' the fullest confidence in concluding that the estimate will not amount to the sum of Six Thousand Pounds, as stated in the minute of the 25th.' "

The estimate, when it was received, amounted to £8,300.

The outstanding interest of that minute of 26th May, 1817, lies not in the fact that at long last the erection of a new church was definitely on the horizon, but in the fact that it was to be built at *the east end of the present church.*

The first reference to the possibility of a new church being erected was at a meeting held on 3rd September, 1807, and in the minute of that meeting it is expressly stated that the new church was to be " on the area south from the present church." During the ten years of long-drawn-out controversy no other site seems ever to have been so much as contemplated.

Who suggested the change of site we have no means of knowing now. The first reference to it occurs in a minute of a General Meeting of Heritors, which gives the impression that the suggestion must have emanated from one of them. But no name is given.

The one thing quite clear is that to have built the new church between the nave and the fratery would, from every point of view, have been little short of a disaster, and that Dunfermline is under a deep debt of gratitude to the unknown benefactor who, even at the last moment, made so happy a suggestion.

Mr. Burn, at least, had no hesitation about expressing his feelings on the matter.

" I have particularly considered the nature of the situation and the facilities attending the junction of the two Buildings and have no hesitation in saying that the whole is admirably calculated to make a very excellent and handsome church, and will afford a more secure means of having the old building kept in a proper state of Repair, independent of its being again appropriated to the very purpose for which it was originally designed and formerly used."

ADDENDA

PRIORS OF DUNFERMLINE

PETER—1120—Sent by Alexander I, along with other ambassadors, to Radulph, Archbishop of Canterbury, to congratulate him on his return from Rome and beg of him Eadmerus, one of his monks, to be Bishop of St. Andrews. Said to have died c. 1133.

ROGER—1141 and 1147—(*Circa* 1141, *Lawrie, E.S.C.,* 371)—a frequent witness in Reg. Dunf., signing as Roger, Presbyter. (*Reg. Pr. of St. And.,* 182, 353).

RICHARD MONGAL—1148—(See page 66).

LAMBINUS (Lambertus)—1195—Previous to 1198, while Archibald was Abbot in the time of Earl Duncan, and reign of King William the Lion. (*Reg. Pr. of St. And.,* 353).

GAUFRID—1231 and 1238—Afterwards Abbot. (*Reg. de Dunf. xi,* 107).

JOHN—1252—Afterwards Abbot. (*Ibid. xiii*).

" 1252—John, Abb. of Dunf., & J., Prior of that place." (*Ross, Aberdour & Inchcolme,* 133).

RALPH DE GRENLAW—1275—Sub-Prior—afterwards Abbot. (*Reg. de Dunf. xiv*).

MALCOLM—1305—(*Ibid.* 225).

ARCHIBALD—1379—20th November, 1379. (*Burgh Records*).

ROBERT DE SCOTLAND—1419—(*Scott. Suppl.* 25/6).

ANDREW AUSTIN—1448—(*Reg.* 309).

RICHARD PRIOUR—1448—(Sub-Prior). (*Reg. de Dunf.,* No. 424, *p.* 309).

ADAM FORMAN—1507 and 1525—(*B. R.* 354, 358). (*H. & H. iii.* 167).

ROBERT FERGUSON—1530 and 1531—(*B. R.* 266, 267).

JOHN BAXTER—1555-1560—(*Laing's Charters,* 633).

SACRISTANS OF DUNFERMLINE

WILLIAM REDE—1398.

WILLIAM DE BEATON—1398—7th July, 1398. After the death of William Rede, the sacristy and vicarage of Dunfermline were given to William de Beaton, monk there. (*Vat. Reg.* 322, *fol.* 307 *v.*).

WILLIAM DE ROSTAN—1420—William de Rostan, monk and sacrist of Dunfermline, dilapidated the goods of the sacristy, disponed them unprofitably and shamefully consumed them. Richard de Bothwell, who has studied canon law for more than three years in universities, supplicates for inquiry and provision for himself. (*Scott. Suppl.* 198—22 *May,* 1420).

From the Calendar of Papal Registers (vii. 290), under date 2 Non. Jan., 1423, we gather that Bothwell was appointed, the office having become vacant through the death of de Rostan.

There is a real difficulty here.

According to the Apostolic Camera (316), Robert, Sacrist of Dunfermline, visited Rome as Procurator for Abbot Andrew, 24 Septr., 1434, and from the same source (33) we get the information that Bothwell was appointed 26 June, 1444.

Dr. Annie Cameron, author of both Scottish Supplications and Apostolic Camera, is inclined to think that Bothwell was Sacrist from 1423 and that Robert may have been an intruder.

RICHARD DE BOTHWELL—1423—Abbot of Paisley, 1444, with dispensation to hold simultaneously the sacristanship of Dunfermline. Obliged himself to pay annates (£50 Stg.). Office void by death of William de Rostan—26th June, 1444 (*Apos. Cam.* 33).

WILLIAM DE BOYIS—1445-1456—Licentiate by examination. Paid 18 florins as composition of the annates of the sacristanship of Dunfermline, 25th February, 1444/5, office void by provision of Richard (*Apos. Cam.*, 268) as Abbot.

Afterwards Prior of Pluscarden and Urquhart.

JOHN DE BENNALA—1456-1478—Formerly Prior of Pluscarden. Presented by King James II as sacrist in room of William de Boyis.

DAVID ROUCH (Ruch)—1478—Monk of Dunfermline. Pays for annates as sacristan £30 Stg.—void by death of John de Bennala, formerly sacrist— 7th April, 1483. (*Apos. Cam.*, 192).

ROBERT HARWARE—1483—Office void by devolution to Roman Court. Annates £20 Stg. Mandate of provision, with summons to a certain Thomas Monemele, intruder—14th April, 1483. (*Apos. Cam.*, 205).

ROBERT SWINTON—1502 and 1520—Founder of the Altar of St. Katherine and St. Margaret. (*B. R.* 291).

In office as Sacristan 14th November, 1502. (*Charters of Edinburgh*, 186).

WILLIAM LUMSDEN—In office at the Reformation. (See page 75).

List of Works Consulted (In Addition to those Mentioned in the List of Abbreviations)

Acts and Decreets.

A Genealogical Deduction of the Family of Rose of Kilravock, ed. by Cosmo Innes. (Spalding Club).

Anderson. Early Sources of Scottish History.

Archaeologia Scotica, or Transactions of the Society of Antiquaries of Scotland, Vol. II.

Bannatyne Club Miscellany, Vol. II.

Barrett (Michael). Scottish Monasteries.

Boswell (James). Life of Samuel Johnson.

Brydall (Robert). History of Art in Scotland.

Burgess Roll of Dundee.

Calderwood (David). History of the Kirk of Scotland.

Calendar of Papal Letters.

Capgrave's Chronicle of England.

Carlyle (Thomas). Past and Present.

Carlyle (Thomas). Reminiscences.

Carr (C. A.). History of Coldingham Priory.

Chalmers (Peter). Historical and Statistical Account of Dunfermline.

Charters of the Abbey of Inchcolm.

Charters of the Priory of Beauly, by Edmund Chisholm Batten.

Coulton (G. C.). Scottish Abbeys and Social Life.

Crossley (F. H.). The English Abbey.

Digest of Session Cases.

Dowden (John). Bishops of Scotland.

Dowden (John). Medieval Church.

Ferguson (David). Tracts.

Fernie (John). A History of the Town and Parish of Dunfermline.

Ferrerius (John). Ferrerii Historia Abbatum de Kynlos. (*Bannatyne Club*).

Fleming (David Hay). The Reformation in Scotland.

Forbes (Duncan). Ane Account of the Familie of Innes. (*Spalding Club*).

Forfar Inhibitions.

Formulare.

Fraser (Donald). Life and Diary of the Rev. Ralph Erskine.

Fraser (Sir William). Douglas Book.

Fraser (Sir William). Eglinton Book.

Grant (James). History of the Burgh Schools of Scotland.

Hailes. Ancient Scottish Poems.

Hailes. Annals.

Harvey (John). Gothic England.

Hay. Scotia Sacra.

Innes (Cosmo). Scotland in the Middle Ages.

Jessop. The Coming of the Friars.

Laing (David). Poems of Robert Henryson.

Lamont (John). Diary, 1649-1671.

Lawrie. Annals of the Reigns of Malcolm and William.

Lawrie. Early Scottish Charters.
Lees. (J. Cameron). St. Giles.
Lesley (John). History of Scotland.
Liber S. Marie de Calchou Registrum Cartarium Abbacie Tironensis de Kelso.
  (*Bannatyne Club*).
Lorimer (John G.). Eldership of the Church of Scotland.
Madan (Falconer). Books in Manuscript.
Maitland (Sir Richard). History of the House of Seytoun to the year MDLIX.
Melville (James). Diary.
Miscellany of the Spalding Club, Vol. V.
Monasticon.
Ms. fol. Advocates' Library, Edinburgh, 1574.
Mylne. The King's Master Masons.
M'Crie. Life of John Knox.
Mackenzie. Scots Writers.
MacMeekin (J. W.). History of the Scottish Metrical Psalms.
Macphail (S. R.). History of the Religious House of Pluscardyn.
Old Statistical Account, 1794.
Patrick (David), Editor. Statutes of the Scottish Church, 1225-1559.
Pitcairn. Criminal Trials.
Porter (A. K.). Medieval Architecture.
Prynne. Records of the Tower of London.
Registrum Assedationum, Dunfermline.
Rogers (Charles). The Book of Wallace.
Rogers (Charles). History of the Chapel Royal of Scotland.
Ross. Aberdour and Inchcolme.
Row (John). History of the Kirk of Scotland.
Rymer. Foedera.
Scotichronicon.
Scottish Historical Review, January 1904.
Skene (W. F.). Celtic Scotland.
Spalding Club, Miscellany of the Vol. V.
Spottiswoode (John). History of the Church of Scotland.
Stephen. The Story of Inverkeithing and Rosyth.
Stevenson (Robert). The Communion and some other matters in Scotland
  in the 17th Century.
Stewart. Story of Scottish Education.
Stirling Burgh Records.
Stodart. Scottish Arms.
Synod of Fife. Selections.
Terry (C. S.). A History of Scotland.
Theiner. Vetera Monumenta.
Thomson (D.). Dunfermline Hammermen.
Walcott (M. E. C.). Ancient Church of Scotland.
Wardlaws in Scotland.
Wedderburne (David). Compt Buik.
Wilkins (David). Concilia Magnae Britanniae et Hiberniae.
Yester Writs.

LIST OF ABBREVIATIONS

Acts. Parl.—Acts of Parliament of Scotland.
A.D.C.—Acts of the Lords of Council in Civil Causes (*Acta Dominorum Concilii*),
ed. by Thomas Thomson.
Annals.—Henderson (Ebenezer). Annals of Dunfermline and Vicinity.
Antiq. of Abdn. & Banff.—Illustrations of the Topography and Antiquities of the
Shires of Aberdeen and Banff. (*Spalding Club*).
Apos. Cam.—Apostolic Camera, ed. by Dr. Annie Cameron.
B.R.—Burgh Records of Dunfermline.
B.R. Invk.—Burgh Records of Inverkeithing.
Brady.—Brady. Episcopal Succession.
C.P.R.—Calendar of Papal Registers.
Cal. Scott. Papers.—Calendar of State Papers Relating to Scotland and Mary Queen
of Scots.
Caledonia.—Chalmers (George). Caledonia.
Churchyard Memorials of Crail.—Beveridge (Erskine).
Compot. Thesaur.—*Compota Thesaurariorum Regum Scotorum.* Accounts of the Lord
High Treasurer of Scotland.
Crawfurd.—Crawfurd. Officers of State.
Coupar.—Charters of the Abbey of Coupar Angus.
Cupar.—Rental Book of the Cistercian Abbey of Cupar-Angus, ed. by Charles
Rogers.
Dalyell's Antiq.—Dalyell (J. G.). A Tract relating chiefly to Monastic Antiquities.
Edin. B.R.—Extracts of the Records of the Burgh of Edinburgh.
Edin. Tests.—Edinburgh Testaments.
Edgar.—Edgar (John). History of Early Scottish Education.
Exch.—*Rotuli Scaccarii Regum Scotorum.* Exchequer Rolls of Scotland.
Fasti.—Scott (Hew). *Fasti Ecclesiae Scoticanae.*
H. & H.—Herkless (John), and Hannay (Robert Kerr). Archbishops of St. Andrews.
H.R.—Heritors' Records.
Hall.—Hall (P. T.). The Kirk of Cleish.
Hist. Doc. Scot.—Calendar of Documents relating to Scotland, ed. by Joseph Bain.
History of Carnock.—Webster (J. M.). History of Carnock.
Inchaffray.—Charters, Bulls and other Documents relating to the Abbey of Inchaffray.
K.S.R.—Kirk Session Records (Dunfermline).
Laing.—Laing. Early Scottish Charters.
Lesley.—Lesley (John). History of Scotland
Lindores.—Chartulary of the Abbey of Lindores, ed. by John Dowden.
Macewen.—Macewen (A. R.). History of the Church in Scotland, 397-1560.
Melr.—Chronicle of Melrose. (Facsimile Edition).
P. to B.—Presentations to Benefices.
Pby. Rec.—Presbytery Records.
Prior. St. A.—*Liber Cartarum Prioratus Sancti Andree in Scotia.*
R.M.S.—*Registrum Magni Sigili Regum Scotorum.*
Reg.—*Registrum de Dunfermelyn.*
Reg. K.S. St. And.—St. Andrews Kirk Session Register, ed. by David Hay Fleming.
Reg. of Crail.—Register of the Collegiate Church of Crail, ed. by Charles Rogers.
Reg. of Deeds.—Register of Deeds.
Reg. of Ministers.—Register of Ministers and Readers in the Kirk of Scotland.
Reg. P.C.—Register of the Privy Council of Scotland.
Reg. of Royal Letters.—The Earl of Stirling's Register of Royal Letters.
Reg. Vat.—Vatican Registers.
Roy. Comm., Fife.—Royal Commission on Ancient and Historical Monuments,
Counties of Fife, Kinross and Clackmannan.
Scott. Suppl.—Scottish Supplications to Rome. (Dr. Annie Cameron).
Stephen.—Stephen (W.). History of Inverkeithing and Rosyth.
Vat. Transc. Reg. Ho.—Vatican Transcripts in Register House, Edinburgh.

INDEX

256

257